teach® yourself

Buddhism
clive erricker

294.3

teach yourself
70
1938 2008
celebrate with us

Launched in 1938, the **teach yourself** series grew rapidly in response to the world's wartime needs. Loved and trusted by over 50 million readers, the series has continued to respond to society's changing interests and passions and now, 70 years on, includes over 500 titles, from Arabic and Beekeeping to Yoga and Zulu. What would you like to learn?

be   urself

For UK order enquiries: please contact Bookpoint Ltd, 130 Milton Park, Abingdon, Oxon OX14 4SB. Telephone: +44 (0) 1235 827720. Fax: +44 (0) 1235 400454. Lines are open 09.00–17.00, Monday to Saturday, with a 24-hour message answering service. Details about our titles and how to order are available at www.teachyourself.co.uk

For USA order enquiries: please contact McGraw-Hill Customer Services, PO Box 545, Blacklick, OH 43004-0545, USA. Telephone: 1-800-722-4726. Fax: 1-614-755-5645.

For Canada order enquiries: please contact McGraw-Hill Ryerson Ltd, 300 Water St, Whitby, Ontario L1N 9B6, Canada. Telephone: 905 430 5000. Fax: 905 430 5020.

Long renowned as the authoritative source for self-guided learning – with more than 50 million copies sold worldwide – the **teach yourself** series includes over 500 titles in the fields of languages, crafts, hobbies, business, computing and education.

British Library Cataloguing in Publication Data: a catalogue record for this title is available from the British Library.

Library of Congress Catalog Card Number: on file.

First published in UK 1995 by Hodder Education, part of Hachette Livre UK, 338 Euston Road, London, NW1 3BH.

First published in US 1995 by The McGraw-Hill Companies, Inc.

This edition published 2008.

The **teach yourself** name is a registered trade mark of Hodder Headline.

Typeset by Transet Limited, Coventry, England.
Printed in Great Britain for Hodder Education, an Hachette Livre UK Company, 338 Euston Road, London NW1 3BH, by CPI Cox and Wyman, Reading, Berkshire, RG1 8EX.

The publisher has used its best endeavours to ensure that the URLs for external websites referred to in this book are correct and active at the time of going to press. However, the publisher and the author have no responsibility for the websites and can make no guarantee that a site will remain live or that the content will remain relevant, decent or appropriate.

Hachette Livre UK's policy is to use papers that are natural, renewable and recyclable products and made from wood grown in sustainable forests. The logging and manufacturing processes are expected to conform to the environmental regulations of the country of origin.

Impression number   10 9 8 7 6 5 4 3 2 1
Year   2012 2011 2010 2009 2008

contents

acknowledgements

To Jane for encouragement and criticism, hard work on the word-processor and forgiveness.
To Katy, Sam and Polly for putting up with it all.
To Karin for generously making the offer.
To Karunavira and Peter Murdock for the interviews.

The publishers would like to thank the following for their permission to reproduce copyright photographs in this book: FWBO – p. 188; C Erricker – pp. 26, 32, 47, 61, 139, 142, 150, 154, 163, 170; Peter Iseli – p. 68 (left); Andy Weber – p.68 (right), p. 72 (left); P Gold, Wisdom Publications – pp. 102, 172.

Every effort has been made to trace and acknowledge ownership of copyright. The publishers will be glad to make suitable arrangements with any copyright holder whom it has not been possible to contact.

introduction

This book is about what Buddhists think, what they do, and how they live their lives. This varies according to the type of Buddhism that is practised and where each Buddhist lives; essentially, however, all Buddhists follow the teachings of the Buddha – the Fully Enlightened One – as they have been transmitted over the last 2,500 years, although interpreted in various ways and, in some cases, with additions and amendments. A variety of sources have been drawn on in order to evoke the spirit of Buddhism and allow Buddhists to speak for themselves.

Buddhism today is very diverse; this diversity contributes to its richness, and nowhere more so than in the West. Moreover, Buddhism offers teachings and practices that are open to anyone with a little intellectual curiosity and the willingness to accept that the modern world can benefit from ancient and timeless wisdom.

In addition to presenting the teachings of and variety within Buddhism, this book presents an understanding of Buddhism, its changes and new directions, in the context of the modern world. It considers Buddhism's impact upon and responses to world affairs and current concerns, both globally and in the West.

In my own view there is a very real challenge to those within the diverse Buddhist communities to respond to significant and rapid changes that have taken place as we move through the first years of the twenty-first century. This is not to presume that this hasn't been the case previously but, with the Buddhist emphasis on living in the present moment, I have fashioned the last chapter to highlight questions of values, necessarily important to Buddhists, that are of contemporary global and community importance rather than just relating to individuals. In doing so, I have posed further questions as to how Buddhist responses to these issues impact on understandings of Buddhism, interpretations of *dharma* (teachings), *sangha* (community) and tradition. These questions take account of inter-generational issues as Buddhists in the West consider how to educate their children from a Buddhist perspective.

This volume is an introduction to Buddhism for the general reader with an interest in the subject. It offers both a Buddhist perspective on the world and an understanding of the variety of Buddhist movements, both historically and contemporaneously. The intention is to provide an understanding of the Buddhist tradition and the ways in which it has, and continues to have, an impact upon different cultures and movements, and has, in turn, been influenced by those cultures with which it has interacted.

It is important, at the outset, to explain that Buddhism is a term given to that movement instigated by the historical Buddha, Sakyamuni, or, to give him his name prior to attaining Buddhahood, Siddharta Gautama. The term Buddhism, and its general recognition as being one of the world's great faiths, implies that Buddhism is a religion and that, in its diverse expressions, has a unified or essential teaching. While neither of these statements should be regarded as false, there is a certain economy with the truth in accepting them at face value. Classifications tend to have a habit of unravelling once one penetrates deeper into the object of study. Teachings tend to change once they encounter new ideas.

I will cite an anecdotal example that occurred at the wedding in Japan of my daughter to my son-in-law, Yoshi. This took place at a Shinto shrine where, during the ceremony, spirits were evoked to assure the auspiciousness of the union and its good fortune. My son-in-law, however, assured me this was not a religious ceremony. Shinto shrines in Japan involve ceremonies that have been significantly influenced by the penetration of Buddhism into that culture, although the Buddhist, or syncretistic, practices involved are some way distant from the teachings of the historical Buddha himself. Additionally, when we investigate the Buddhism that is most prevalent in Japan, it has a caste that we in the West would recognize as theistic, in accordance with ideas of salvation and prayer that can be paralleled in religions with which we are more familiar, such as Christianity. This can be seen as being in tension with the agnostic stance taken by the historical Buddha.

In all of this we are experiencing the sort of complexity that attends changes in a tradition over time and within its different branches. Nevertheless, we can still speak of a tradition we can call Buddhist and of teachings at its core which, if lost, would compromise it significantly, if not irrevocably.

A final point. While I wish to present Buddhism in an objective fashion I cannot deny that, in a troubled twenty-first century world, I think its teachings still have relevance in assisting us in dealing with the global, social and personal issues we face.

Note on terminology

Due to the difference in languages used by the Theravadin and Mahayanist branches of Buddhism (Pali and Sanskrit respectively), Buddhist terms can appear in two forms: for example, *dhamma* (Pali) and *dharma* (Sanskrit). The Buddha's name also varies accordingly: Siddhatta Gotama (Pali) and Siddhartha Gautama (Sanskrit). The glossary indicates the alternative renditions of terms used in this book.

01 Buddhists and Buddhism

In this chapter you will learn:
- the basic Buddhist teachings and what makes them distinctive
- about the Buddhist idea of community
- about the practical effects of the Buddhist teachings and idea of community, and how these are related to the way Buddhists try to live their lives and respond to the world around them.

Thus shall ye think of all this fleeting world:
A star at dawn, a bubble in a stream,
A flash of lightning in a summer cloud,
A flickering lamp, a phantom, and a dream.

(*The Diamond Sutra*, 868AD)

Who are Buddhists?

This is a question that many people in the West might well ask. The quotation above is from the Buddha himself, and one answer to our question is that Buddhists are those who understand the world in this way. But such a statement is easily misunderstood, so perhaps we should start by approaching our question in a less poetic fashion.

How would Buddhists today answer it? Some might reply that Buddhists are the followers of the Buddha and his teachings. While this is an accurate response, it is open to misunderstanding. For example, Buddhists do not follow the Buddha in the same way as Christians follow Christ. The reason for this is that the Buddha is not understood to be a god; nor did he teach his disciples a way to God. Indeed, he did not even claim that his teachings were a unique and original source of wisdom; but he did maintain that they had a very specific practical purpose and that they were meant to be useful.

> Buddha always said, 'Don't take what I'm saying, just try to analyse as far as possible and see whether what I'm saying makes sense or not. If it doesn't make sense, discard it. If it does make sense, then pick it up.'

(John Bowker, *Worlds of Faith*, BBC, 1983, p 134)

Another way of answering the question might be to say that Buddhists practise the *dhamma* (Pali) or *dharma* (Sanskrit). This word has a range of meanings that interconnect. Most importantly, dharma means truth, law or teaching. Thus, Buddhists are stressing that the Buddha's teaching pointed to the truth; and moreover, that they are practising what the Buddha preached, truthful living, which is open to everyone.

> The *Dhamma* can be practised by anybody. It can be practised by any man, woman, even by any child. It can be practised by someone in India, and it can be practised by someone in England. By someone in America, or someone in China. If there are people on the moon, it can be practised by those people on the moon. The *Dhamma* is universal… it's for everybody – for every human being.

Because every human being is the brother or sister of every other human being. The more we practise the *Dhamma*, the more we come together. It doesn't matter whether we are born in India or whether we are born in England. If we practise the *Dhamma*, we are one. If we practise the *Dhamma*, we are brothers and sisters.

(Ven. Sangharakshita, *Friends of the Western Buddhist Order*, Newsletter No.54, p 2)

A third answer to the question would be to say that Buddhists are those who belong to the *sangha*. Sangha means community. Often it denotes the monastic community, but in a broader sense it refers to Buddhists in general. It could be said that Buddhists are part of the sangha in the way that Christians belong to the Church. However, the distinction of belonging to the Buddhist community is a commitment to living a life that cultivates well-being and happiness through following particular teachings, rules and practices. Sometimes the members of the sangha are referred to as 'spiritual friends'.

> For twenty-five centuries the Community has held Buddhism together. It is a refuge for the weary and an ideal of renunciation, a source of leadership and a standard of permanence in times of cultural change. It is an institution, and thus always available to those who need it. The religious vocation is given a home, the seeker is given a path, and the life of brotherhood is established as a model for all mankind.
>
> (Stephan Beyer, *The Buddhist Experience*, Dickenson, 1974, p 65)

If we put all three answers together we arrive at a more complete understanding of what it means to be a Buddhist.

The Three Jewels

The Buddha, dhamma or dharma and sangha are known as the Three Jewels, the implication of this being that they are what Buddhists hold most dear in life. It is usual to make a commitment to them; this takes place in a formal ceremony which marks the intention to live a life that can be summarized in a verse found in the *Dhammapada*, a popular compilation of the Buddha's teaching:

> Not to do evil
> To cultivate good
> To purify one's mind.

The importance of this commitment is made clearer by contrasting these Three Jewels with what Buddhists understand to be the unhelpful influences in life, also termed the three poisons: greed or craving, which is sometimes also termed desire; hatred or aversion; and delusion or ignorance. The opposition of these triple formulations succinctly defines the Buddhist path. By inclining to the former, and seeking to avoid the influence of the latter, Buddhists understand the purpose of life.

The Three Refuges

The Buddha, dhamma (dharma) and sangha are also known as the Three Refuges. Refuge is not used in its negative sense of hiding away from something; rather, it means that which provides safety and the possibility of growth, that which you can put your trust in. For this reason, the formal recitation of the Three Jewels is described as 'going for refuge'. Although Buddhists of different persuasions would want to say a lot more about what this means and involves, we may begin here by saying that a Buddhist is one who has taken refuge in the Buddha, dhamma and sangha; from here, like the Buddha himself when he resolved to leave home in search of wisdom, he or she 'goes forth'.

Through the simple act of reciting this formula three times, one declares oneself a Buddhist:

I go for refuge to the Buddha
I go for refuge to the Dhamma
I go for refuge to the Sangha.

The implication of this act is to radically reassess personal priorities and goals, as this passage written by a Japanese Buddhist teacher describes:

Taking refuge is the first step on the Buddhist path to inner freedom, but it is not something new. We have been taking refuge all our lives, though mainly in external things, hoping to find security and happiness. Some of us take refuge in money, some in drugs. Some take refuge in food, in mountain-climbing or in sunny beaches. Most of us seek security and satisfaction in a relationship with a man or a woman. Throughout our lives we have drifted from one situation to the next, always in the expectation of final satisfaction. Our successive involvements may sometimes offer temporary relief but, in sober truth, seeking refuge in physical possessions and transient pleasures merely deepens our confusion rather than ending it.

(Shunryu Suzuki, Zen Mind, Beginner's Mind,
Weatherhill, 1982, p 7)

Buddhist practice

What does this Buddhist way of life involve? First and foremost it is a practical path through life.

It is only useful to you if it's practical. For me it is. I developed my meditation into an awareness and mindfulness and learned to do just what I was doing at any one time and nothing else. I find I pick up on things much quicker and am more open to other people. I have a better perspective on things and am more in touch with myself.

In a business context, I've begun to investigate my motives for doing the things I do in the business world. What do we really need? Food, shelter, clothes and medicine. That's about it. Of course I'm not perfect. I do lose it sometimes. I'm only human. But my practice decreases the percentage.

(Paul Queripel, in *Target Magazine*, April 1988, p 12)

The Buddha's message stresses that speculation about the way things are is of little value. He spoke of investigating the human situation as a doctor investigates an illness, needing both diagnosis and cure. His teaching is a prescription. Speculation and discussion that does not focus on this is of no help. In a well-known passage he says that, if someone were struck by an arrow, he would not refuse to have it taken out until he knew who shot the arrow, whether he were married or not, what he looked like and so on: he would simply concentrate on removing it. In this way he indicated that he was not concerned with discussing the questions often regarded as of religious importance; for example, who created the world? how did it come into being? and so forth. These were considered by the Buddha as questions not tending to edification: what essentially matters is the here and now. Treading the Buddhist path should lead to a transformation in the self: a continuous refining of both thought and action, of the way we relate to others and to the world we live in and finally of our self-understanding.

In the West, because of our lack of contact with traditionally Buddhist societies, erroneous views of Buddhism are prevalent. Buddhists are often thought to be other-worldly, concerned solely with a monastic life, retreating from society, looking inward and being unconcerned with everyday affairs. Buddhism is often believed to be a highly abstract philosophical system, academic and self-absorbing, of no value to the ordinary person. Such views would have bemused the Buddha, and possibly brought a wry smile to his face; however, they represent a barrier to understanding present-day Buddhists.

The Five Precepts (*Panca Sila*)

At the heart of Buddhist ethical practice are the Five Precepts. These are rules which identify the aspirations of a Buddhist. They are not commandments; rather, they are the minimum essential 'prescription' for treating the human condition, and an antidote to the three poisons: greed, aversion or hatred, and ignorance or delusion. They consist of the following undertakings:

1 I undertake to observe the precept to abstain from harming living beings.

2 I undertake to observe the precept to abstain from taking things not freely given.

3 I undertake to observe the precept to abstain from sexual misconduct.

4 I undertake to observe the precept to abstain from false speech.

5 I undertake to observe the precept to abstain from intoxicating drinks and drugs causing heedlessness.

(adapted from Niyamatolika, *The Word of the Buddha*, The Buddhist Publication Society, 1971, p xii)

Of course, if carrying out these undertakings were as simple as it might seem, things would soon be well and good. However, the purpose of this commitment is, at least in part, to investigate what is *really* involved in leading this virtuous way of life. Thus, the more diligently you attempt to put the undertakings into practice, the more aware you become of their significance. This accords with the Buddha's exhortation that one should find things out for oneself. The cure can be prescribed by the doctor – but the patient must administer it and see if it works.

Of whatever teachings you can assure yourself in this way, these teachings lead to calmness, not to neurotic passion, to mental freedom, not to bondage, to a decrease of worldly entanglements, not to an increase of them... of such teachings you may affirm with certainty, this is the Dhamma, this is the Ethical Life, this is the Master's Message.

(*Vinaya*, 11:10, quoted in F.L.Woodward, *Some Sayings of the Buddha*, The Buddhist Society, London, 1974)

The Buddhist way of life is meant to consist in carrying a minimum of baggage, both material and spiritual. For this reason the Buddha's pronouncements can appear terse and austere, and imply a separation from society and a consequent introversion. However, if we apply the precepts in the way the Buddha intended, their function becomes clear. Here is the way one British Buddhist understands them:

It's not a rule or a commandment. It's a promise I make to myself. One thing I do each morning when I get up is to recite the simple Five Precepts: each morning I say them to myself – a bit loudly, but to myself: I take the view that I will not do such a thing. And then if I broke the promise I made in the morning, I'd feel a bit guilty, that I couldn't keep that promise today. But if I kept it, I'm quite happy that I did it. And then at night, just before I go to sleep, I repeat a stanza, which means that I have done such a thing, and I thank the Buddha for this doctrine, which I have learnt, and I have kept that side of it today.

(John Bowker, *Worlds of Faith*, BBC, 1983, p 133)

The Ten Precepts (*Dasa Sila*) and the Eight Precepts (*Attanga Sila*)

The Buddha laid down the Ten Precepts for *samaneras* (those in training for the monastic life) and pious lay people unattached to families. They are the basis of the monastic code followed by *bhikkhus* (monks). The following are added to the basic Five Precepts:

6 I undertake to observe the precept to abstain from taking untimely meals.

7 I undertake to abstain from dancing, music, singing and watching grotesque mime.

8 I undertake to abstain from the use of garlands, perfumes and personal adornment.

9 I undertake to abstain from the use of high seats.

10 I undertake to abstain from accepting gold or silver.

(The Eight Precepts put numbers seven and eight together and omit the tenth.)

Lay Buddhists may undertake the Eight Precepts on festival days, but the Ten Precepts effectively determine the separation of monks from the rest of society as those who have taken up the mendicant life (relying on others for their physical and material needs), and become renunciants. The ideal behind the practice of the Ten Precepts is to be freed from all sensual entanglements. Thus the prohibitions involved prevent indulgence in food, entertainment, adornment, the seeking of status, personal importance and luxury, and the accumulation of wealth.

The significance of the precepts

It is worth investigating the significance of the precepts a little further. For example, taking the first precept, to abstain from harming any living being: this, at its most obvious level, would involve not killing another human being. In a more subtle way, it could involve making the effort to support, rather than ignore, another who is suffering or in distress. Deciding not to do something for another's benefit is to harm him or her as much as deciding to do something that will obviously injure or kill. This is a precept that we can immediately relate to humans; however, our awareness may not so readily extend to other creatures. It may more easily extend to animals we are fond of, or find useful, than to those we do not value, or who threaten us and our well-being. The Buddha did not intend to instigate a long and ultimately unprofitable debate on this subject by advancing this precept as a guiding principle. For Buddhists, it is a matter of keeping the precept in mind when carrying out their day-to-day activities, whether they be cooking, driving, teaching or making important political decisions.

Thinking about the second precept, that of abstaining from things not given, we may interpret this as not stealing – in which case, to take another's property and not return it would be an obvious example; but to take something without permission would be another. To address the precept on a more subtle level might involve not invading someone's privacy, or their time to think or be alone; for thoughts, reflections and feelings are as much what one owns as material possessions.

When we start to consider the precepts as a whole, further considerations apply. Heedless actions suggest a lack of awareness of the influence of our own actions or presence upon others; when we relate this principle to a Buddhist virtue such as generosity, we become aware of the pervasiveness of this basic code. While not infringing upon another's private life, it is important to be alert to ways in which our presence may be of value to them; this involves the dedication of time and effort, to the extent of relegating one's own concerns accordingly.

One British Buddhist puts it in this way:

It's quite possible to be British and Buddhist – though it's not easy, as Buddhist values are diametrically opposed to the 'me' and 'must get more' values apparently prevalent in today's society.

However, with awareness and care it is possible for Buddhist practice to flourish. For most of us mundane actions form the greater part of life – getting up in the morning, washing, dressing, going to work. These are the repeated experiences of my life and therefore offer a great opportunity for practice. Do I get up each morning bad-tempered? Do the soap I use, or the clothes I wear, exploit or abuse other living beings? Can the pollution created by my travelling to work be diminished? Constant awareness of how we use our bodies, speech and minds is Buddhist practice.

This practice develops compassion towards oneself and others. It brings joy as one sees its effects, and leads to peace as one minimises greed, hate and delusion.

(quoted in C. Erricker, *Buddhism, E G Religions Source Book*, The *Guardian*, 1993, p 19)

In order to emphasize their value, a positive formulation of the precepts is sometimes used, which is recited as follows:

With deeds of loving kindness, I purify my body.
With open-handed generosity, I purify my body.
With stillness, simplicity and contentment, I purify my body.
With truthful communication, I purify my speech.
With mindfulness, clear and radiant, I purify my mind.

(*The FWBO Puja Book*, Windhorse Publications, 1984, p 18)

Mindfulness

Understanding the Buddhist view in the way described above leads us to consider how to achieve this refinement of attitude (or equanimity, to use a Buddhist term), while involved in the activity of our daily lives.

> There is a story about a group of learned Buddhist monks who spent all their time in scholastic debate. As part of their banter they would often wonder, half-joking, half-seriously, which one of them would get enlightened first. Whenever this topic came up, the only thing they could all agree on was that it would not be Stupid, the illiterate monk who was capable only of sweeping the monastery floor and whom nobody has any time for. Of course, it was Stupid who got enlightened first. The jealous monks went to the Abbot. How come Stupid had got enlightened? Had he been overhearing their intellectual conversations? 'Not at all,' replied the Abbot, 'It's just that while he was sweeping the corners of the monastery he made sure he was also sweeping the corners of his mind.'
>
> (Adrian Abbotts, in C. Erricker and V. Barnett (eds), *World Religions in Education*, The Shap Working Party, 1989, p 11)

Remaining positive in outlook depends on not reacting negatively to events. However, the watchfulness and discipline required are obviously difficult to attain. The Buddha's teaching stressed as a supreme quality the cultivation of mindfulness; this involves an ability to watch over our own state of mind at the same time as observing the emotional fluctuations that occur in those around us. We cannot give to others without taking account of, and dealing with, the volatility present in our own nature. In simple terms, anger provokes anger, meanness provokes meanness, heedlessness provokes heedlessness. A crucial implication of the Buddha's teaching is that no one is an island, but that by practising the dhamma it is possible to influence the attitudes of those around us and of society at large. Indeed, the substance of this message goes still further. Not only human existence, but the destiny of the world, depend upon this taking place. It involves being in harmony with nature, and respect for all living things. Returning to the Indian context in which this teaching was first formulated, it goes beyond the span of our lives from birth to death, and determines our future rebirth. Buddhists consider that the capacity to progress to a more elevated spiritual and moral state has a fundamental effect on the evolution of the world. Adhering to the dhamma will make the world a more harmonious place; the opposite will be true if the dhamma is ignored. Equally, the individual will find the dhamma easier or harder to follow as a consequence. Thus the microcosmic and macrocosmic understanding of individual action and cosmic evolution are intimately related. The capacity to be virtuous and to exhibit such qualities as generosity and loving kindness are steps on the path to becoming truly compassionate, which is one of the two supreme Buddhist attributes. The Buddha expressed this in one of his sermons to his first disciples:

> Go forth on your journey, for the profit of the many, out of compassion for the world, for the welfare, the profit, the bliss of *devas* (gods) and mankind.

> (*Vinaya* 1:21, quoted in F.L. Woodward, *Some Sayings of the Buddha*, The Buddhist Society, London, 1974)

Western Buddhist in meditation

Wisdom and compassion

Compassion (*karuna*) must be complemented by wisdom (*prajna*). The two are inseparable; they co-exist, and without the other neither is possible. The development of wisdom depends upon a more formal practice which, in Western terms, is understood as meditation. In its earlier Indian context, it was a form of yoga. Yoga means to yoke or bind oneself, and here the notion of commitment is present once again. Without the discipline of a formal practice that allows understanding of the way in which one's own mind works, and development of the capacity for insight, the cultivation of compassion is inevitably diminished. One word for meditation that identifies its instrumental role is *bhavana* (mental or spiritual development); bhavana presumes that the latent capacity we have needs to be cultivated, in order for our full potential to be achieved. The purpose of this activity has been beautifully described by an influential twentieth-century meditation teacher in this way:

> Try to be mindful and let things take their natural course. Then your mind will become still in any surroundings, like a clear forest pool. All kinds of wonderful, rare animals will come to drink at the pool, and you will clearly see the nature of all things. You will see many strange and wonderful things come and go, but you will be still. This is the happiness of the Buddha.

(Ajahn Chah, *A Still Forest Pool*, Kornfield and Breitner (eds), Quest Books, 1975)

This passage outlines succinctly the purpose of Buddhist meditation. Be calm (*samatha*) and you will become mindful. In this observant and detached state you will recognize what is actually happening and gain insight (*vipasanna*) into the way things truly are. From this arises a peace or happiness that allows a positive and virtuous response to others, regardless of the way in which you are treated. The result is attainment of both wisdom and compassion.

Another example can be found in the teaching of the Buddha, and his response to a situation that was far from the environment of academic debate and spiritual retreat. It emphasizes the Buddhist concern to treat the root of the problem of human suffering, while not admitting that the events that cause such suffering are immediately avoidable.

Here the Buddha is helping the distressed mother of a dead child:

The story of Kisagotami

Kisagotami was born into a very poor family, and had the reputation of being frail and tiring easily. When she was old enough to be married she went to live with her husband's family. Because she had come from a poor home, they treated her without much respect until she gave birth to a son. Then their attitude was quite different, and she was treated with both kindness and honour. Her situation was now a happy one, but this did not last for long. When her son was old enough to run about and play he became ill and died. Kisagotami was desolate. She had not only lost the child she loved, but also her respected position in her home. In her grief she picked up the body of her child and wandered from one house to another, asking for medicine for her son. The people who met her laughed and sneered. 'Whoever heard of medicine for the dead?' they said.

By now Kisagotami was almost driven out of her mind by her sorrow. A wise man saw her wandering about and realized how much she needed help. He had heard some of the teaching of Gotama Buddha, and thought that he might be able to help her come to terms with her grief. He approached Kisagotami gently and told her that the Buddha was staying nearby and that he might have medicine for her son. 'Go and ask him,' he said.

Kisagotami went to find the Buddha and stood on the edge of the crowd, listening to him. When she had the chance, she called out to him, 'O, Exalted One, give me medicine for my son.'

Part of the Buddha's greatness lay in his skill in knowing how to help other people. He told her kindly to go to the city nearby and visit every house. 'Bring me some grains of mustard seed from every household in which no-one has ever died.'

Kisagotami was delighted. Here was someone who took her seriously. She went to the city, knocked on the first house and asked for some grains of mustard seed from the householder, if no one had ever died there. The householder told her with great sadness that he had recently lost his wife. Kisagotami listened to his story with growing sympathy, understanding his grief from her own. She eventually moved on, but found that in every house there was a story of sickness, old age and death. Her own grief seemed different now that she shared that of others, and she realized that the Buddha had known when he sent her out that she would find that her predicament was the common experience of human beings. Death is the law common to all that lives. She now took the body of her dear little son to the cremation ground and let it be cremated, fully realising that all is impermanent.

Kisagotami then returned to Gotama Buddha. He asked her whether she had brought him the grains of mustard seed. She told him what had happened, and what she had realized. She then asked him to accept her as his follower and to teach her more about the nature of reality and the path to understanding.

> (taken from Peggy Morgan, *Buddhist Stories*,
> private publication from the author at Westminster
> College, Oxford OX2 9AT, p 22)

Though wisdom and compassion are the quintessential aspirations of all Buddhists, they are equally aware that they are not immediately attainable, and may take many lifetimes to achieve; in fact they represent Buddhahood itself. Therefore it is important to focus on the task in hand, rather than continually to attempt to peer over the horizon. The Dalai Lama, a revered figure in the Buddhist world who attracts the devotion and respect of Tibetan and Western Buddhists alike, is very adept at expressing Buddhist concerns in a much more down-to-earth way:

> Simplicity is important for happiness. Having few desires, feeling satisfied with what you have is vital. Many are making a great effort to control external things – like arms control. But without being able to control inner things, how can you control external arms? Real arms control is to control anger.

> Now I am talking as a human being, not as a Buddhist. This I think is most important, because ideology and religion are for human beings, not the other way round. They are secondary. Emphasis should be on humanity.

> My religion is very simple – my religion is kindness.

> There is so much effort spent on external matters, like space travel. But there is still quite a big area of inner space left to explore. And it's not so expensive!

People think patience is weakness. But I think not. Anger comes from fear, and fear from weakness. So, if you have strength then you have more courage. This is where patience comes from.

Deep down we must have real affection for each other, a clear recognition of our shared humanity. At the same time, we must accept all ideologies and systems as a means of solving humanity's problems.

(*The Dalai Lama, Kindness: Clarity and Insight,* quoted in *Resurgence,* Issue 123, July/August 1987, p 23)

Skilfulness

We have noted that following the precepts, and developing insight through meditation, are two basic and interconnected practices of the Buddhist life, and that through these Buddhists seek to become wiser and more compassionate. There is a third element that plays a necessary part in this development. Skilfulness, or skill in means (*upaya*), was a supreme quality of the Buddha. As a teacher he was not giving information which, once received, could immediately be understood. In fact, one of the most crucial moments in the Buddha's life came when, after achieving enlightenment (*bhodi*) or awakening, he was daunted by the prospect of trying to convey what he now knew to anyone. He perceived that humans were too caught up in worldly attachments to hear and understand that happiness lay beyond worldly concerns, and that suffering was a result of living in ignorance of this knowledge. His resolve changed, and his teaching career began only when, in the mythological but highly poetic way in which this event is conveyed in the Buddhist scriptures, the god Brahma came to the Buddha and exhorted him, out of compassion for the world, to share his wisdom because, 'There are beings with a little dust in their eyes who, not hearing the Dharma, are decaying.'

For Buddhists, this event, along with the Buddha's first sermon in the Deer Park at Sarnath near Benares, is of seminal importance. This is the point at which the Buddhist tradition began, with the Buddha's resolve to teach the dhamma, and it illustrates why Buddhists often refer to themselves as 'followers of the dhamma' rather than as Buddhists or followers of the Buddha.

Only because the Buddha taught it did the dhamma appear in the world, and only because of the Buddha's supreme skilfulness in the way he taught – by word and deed – was it possible for others to understand and follow the dhamma themselves. This skilfulness is therefore also a quality to which Buddhists aspire, and which they value highly. Without it the dhamma would not be passed on.

We have already read one example of the Buddha's skilfulness in addressing the plight of Kisagotami. Another example of skilfulness is revealed in this Zen story, called *The Muddy Road*:

> Two monks were walking down a muddy road, and came across a young woman trying to cross it but unable to avoid a large pool of water. The first monk was inclined just to walk on. The second promptly helped the woman by lifting her up and carrying her across. Following this incident the two monks walked on, but there was obvious tension between them. After a while the first monk, unable to contain his anger any longer, remonstrated with the second, saying, 'You know it is against our vows to touch a woman, why did you lift her up and carry her?' The second monk replied 'I may have carried her back there but you are still carrying her and you haven't yet let her go.'

> (P. Reps, *Zen Flesh, Zen Bones*, Penguin, 1972, p 28)

This ability to let go is an example of skilfulness. The first monk still harboured his latent desire in his mind. The second was aware that eradicating such a desire was more important than just following the monks' rule of not touching women. The first monk had forgotten what the rule was there for. The story illustrates that skilfulness (or lack of it) relates to the motivation behind the act, whether or not it does harm to oneself or the world. The skilfulness required to let go of desire is described in a very practical fashion by this teacher:

> To be aware, we have to use skilful means ... The obsession of 'letting go' is a skilful one – as you repeat this over and over, whenever a thought arises, you are aware of its arising. You keep letting go of whatever moves – but if it doesn't go, don't try to force it. This 'letting go' practice is a way of clearing the mind of its obsessions and negativity; use it gently, but with resolution. Meditation is a skilful means of letting go, of deliberately emptying out the mind so we can see the purity of the mind – cleaning it out so we can put the right things in it.

You respect your mind, so you are more careful what you put in it. If you have a nice house, you don't go out and pick up all the filth from the street and bring it in; you bring in things that will enhance it and make it a refreshing and delightful place.

(Ajahn Sumedo, *Cittaviveka: Teachings from the Silent Mind*, Amaravati Publications, 1992, p 31)

This pinpoints what really matters to Buddhists: the purity of the mind uncluttered by greed and self-concern, which leads to compassionate activity in the world.

Awakening

The Buddha's great achievement was to attain enlightenment or *nirvana* (*nibbana*). He is said to have attained nirvana under a pipal tree in Bodh-Gaya, in north-east India. In Buddhist tradition, this tree is now named after his achievement and called a *Bodhi* (enlightenment) tree. This event provides the inspiration for all Buddhists. The term 'awakening' perhaps explains the significance of this event in a more accessible way. It is an awakening to the way things truly are, and an extinguishing of the ignorance that fetters us to continual rebirth in the realm of *samsara*, which we can translate as motivation by desire, ignorance and aversion. Nirvana literally means 'to extinguish'.

Nirvana is not a place, in geographical terms, other than where we are. It is not a heaven, in the other-worldly sense of the term. But it *is* a recognition that our potential is not fulfilled by our day-to-day concern for advancement or survival, nor is it denied by our ultimate fear of extinction or death. The Buddha's teaching is, as one Zen saying puts it, like a finger pointing at the moon. To mistake the teaching for the truth is to misunderstand the nature of the journey. The teaching is a vehicle, and the Buddha told a parable to this effect:

'Using the figure of a raft, brethren, will I teach you the Dhamma as something to leave behind, not to take with you. Do you listen to it. Apply your minds. I will speak.

'Just as a man, brethren, who has started on a long journey sees before him a great stretch of water, on this side full of doubts and fears, on the further side safe and free from fears ... Then he thinks thus: ... "How now if I were to gather together grass, sticks and branches, and leaves, bind them into a raft, and resting on that raft paddle with hands and feet and so come safe to the further shore?"

'Then brethren, that man gathers together sticks ... and comes to the further shore. When he has crossed over and come to the other side he thinks thus: "This raft has been of great use to me. Resting on this raft and paddling with hand and foot I have come to the further shore. Suppose now I were to set this raft on my head or lift it on to my shoulders and go my ways?"

'Now what think ye, brethren? Would that man in so doing have finished with that raft?'

'Surely not, Lord.'

'Doing what then, brethren, would that man have finished with that raft? Herein, brethren, that man who has crossed and gone to the further shore should think thus: "This raft has been of great use to me. Resting on it I have crossed to the further shore. Suppose now I haul it up on the shore or sink it in the water and go my ways!" By so doing, brethren, that man would have finished with that raft.'

'Figuratively, then, Nirvana is that 'further shore' of full realization.

'Even so, brethren, using the figure of a raft have I shown you the Dhamma, as something to leave behind, not to take with you. Thus, brethren, understanding the figure of the raft, ye must leave behind righteous ways, not to speak of unrighteous ways.'

(*Majjhima Nikaya*, Vol. I, 134, quoted in
F.L. Woodward, *Some Sayings of the Buddha*,
The Buddhist Society, London, 1974)

In conclusion

This chapter has provided a survey of the basic tenets of Buddhism and what constitutes being a Buddhist. Necessarily it has not introduced varieties of interpretations of these tenets, which will emerge in later chapters in this study. Nevertheless, it is worth noting certain issues at this stage:

- **The precepts** We have noted that the monastic sangha are required to follow ten precepts but lay Buddhists just five. The five precepts followed by all Buddhists give a code for ethical conduct. The further precepts followed by monastics are different; they mark out the renunciant from the householder. In turn, this established complementary but distinctive roles in society. These roles affected the paths and expectations of the two different groups. The laity supported the monks while the monks pursued the path towards enlightenment. The laity gain merit through *dana*, giving to the monastic order, and this will influence their karma and, subsequently, their rebirth. As Buddhism has developed in a variety of ways, so this strict differentiation in roles has been contested and subjected to new interpretations. This in turn has influenced interpretations of sangha.

- **Wisdom and compassion** We have also noted how wisdom and compassion are developed through the practice of mindfulness and meditation. Later we shall see how different branches of Buddhism developed specific understandings of wisdom and compassion and how these complementary qualities could be achieved according to different underlying philosophies and meditational techniques and systems.

02

the life of the Buddha

In this chapter you will learn:

- about the Buddha's life and his enlightenment, which is related to the world of his time
- about the monastic community he founded and the rules by which they live.

The Buddha's significance

The word 'Buddha' is a title given by his followers to the teacher Siddhartha Gautama (Siddhatta Gotama), who lived in India 2,500 years ago. We might well ask what relevance such a figure and his life can have for us today. Our pursuit of progress in the modern world suggests that we constantly gain more knowledge as time goes by. Yet we only have to reflect on the weight of human suffering that remains and re-emerges throughout human history (and was just as prevalent, if not more so, in the twentieth century) to realize there are certain problems that our accumulated knowledge simply cannot address. More sophisticated technology and scientific advances do not get to the root of the problem of human conflict and suffering. More efficient communication in a technological sense is not to be equated with better communication between human beings. Ultimately, some problems just will not go away, however hard we address them. Such problems can be understood as matters of the heart as well as of the mind. We cannot solve them with logic alone, by creating a more comfortable material life for ourselves, or even by furthering our medical knowledge and skill. When we understand that scientific and technological achievement is not a panacea for all ills, we can comprehend the persistence of ancient wisdoms in the context of searching for answers to apparently insoluble human dilemmas; we also see what it is about the Buddha that makes him as fascinating a figure in today's world as he was in the far-off Indian culture within which he lived. Here are two personal reflections that give us some clues to his importance:

> Among the ruins of Anuradhapura, the ancient capital of Sri Lanka, there rests alone on a pedestal above the grass a seated image of the Buddha in stone, slightly larger than life. The statue is conventional, probably more than a thousand years old, of a type found throughout Buddhist Asia. The legs are folded in meditation, the hands laid one upon the other in the lap. Buddhists hold that it was in this posture, seated beneath a tree more than 2500 years ago, that the Buddha was awakened, attaining decisive knowledge of the human condition and the unshakeable certainty that he was released from its suffering.

> In its excellence, however, the Anuradhapura image is far from conventional. The back and head are disciplined and upright; but the arms are relaxed and the face reposes in tranquillity. The figure seems intelligent and serene, wed

perfectly to the unmoving granite. Standing before it an elderly English socialist told me that in the whole mess of human history this at least – the statue and all it stands for – was something of which we could be proud. He said that he had no use for religion, but that he felt he had unknowingly been a follower of the Buddha all along.

(M. Carrithers, *The Buddha*, Oxford
University Press, 1983, p 1)

Additionally, Carrithers quotes the anthropologist Claude Levi-Strauss as saying:

What have I learnt from the masters I have listened to, the philosophers I have read, the societies I have investigated, and that very science in which the West takes such pride? Simply a fragmentary lesson or two which, if laid end to end, would add up to the meditations of the Sage at the foot of his tree.

(Claude Levi-Strauss in ibid., pp 1–2)

Buddhists, of course, are much more precise about his relevance and the way in which his life unfolded. This is illustrated, as follows, according to Buddhist tradition.

The Four Sights

Siddhartha was born into comparative privilege, the son of a chief (king or raja) of the Sakya people of north-eastern India (in present-day Nepal). His early life equipped him for government and the inheritance of his father's position. However, his education and social standing also allowed him a degree of choice as to his future; and, so the narrative tells, his father was well aware of this possibility. The traditional story describes how Queen Mahamaya, the wife of King Suddhodama and Siddhartha's mother, was troubled by a dream which was interpreted to mean that she was to have a son who would one day become either a king or a *sadhu* (a holy man who has renounced worldly things). When Siddhartha was born, and throughout his childhood and adolescence, the king was anxious that he should choose the former vocation, and so organized his life to ensure, as far as possible, that this would occur. He was surrounded by beautiful things and kept within the palace grounds. He was married to the beautiful Princess Yasodhara, who then gave birth to their son. The combination of a pleasant, fulfilling life, with the responsibility of a family, was thought to prepare the young prince for his inheritance – socially and psychologically – and his education also reflected this. The king's hope was shattered by what, in Buddhist tradition, is called the Four Sights. Siddhartha grew restless of his palace life, and sought to know of the world outside. He directed his charioteer to take him out into the world beyond the confines of the palace, and encountered experiences that had an abiding effect and shaped his future life. The first time he ventured beyond the palace precincts he saw an old man, and questioned his companion as to why he was so bent and frail. Siddhartha was struck by the answer he was given: that this was the eventual lot of all human beings, including himself. It was a natural and unavoidable event. His response was, 'What is the use of this youth, vitality and strength, if it all ends in this?'

The second sight, on his next excursion beyond the palace, was of a sick person. Again, he was struck by the fact that disease and malady afflict even the strongest and healthiest of individuals and, more importantly, that there is no way of anyone preventing it.

The third sight was of a corpse being carried to the cremation ground on a stretcher. This was, and still is, a common sight in India, where the dead are not hidden from the public eye by coffins or hearses, and where the burning of the dead is open to public view, most conspicuously on the *ghats* beside rivers, for example at Varanasi beside the Ganges. Again, what the charioteer understood to be an everyday event and a typical aspect of life stunned Siddhartha. What struck him most forcibly was the lack of control and direction people ultimately have over their own life and destiny. You don't want to grow old but you can't help it. You don't want to fall sick but you can't ensure against it. Death is unavoidable and yet it makes a nonsense of living. Where is the meaning and purpose in all this? The agonized questioning of Siddhartha is contrasted, in the story, with the unquestioning acceptance of this state of affairs betrayed by Khanna, his charioteer. Siddhartha awoke to the true nature of being in this world, to the state of samsara, characterized by old age, sickness, death and continual becoming. It was pointless nonsense to live with the acceptance that there is nothing humans can do to alter this state of affairs, whatever other knowledge and sophistication they may achieve. For him, perhaps the most striking discovery of these ventures into the outside world was that humans accept this as their lot, as natural.

Siddhartha's reaction to the first three sights exemplifies the Buddhist starting point: seeing to the heart of the matter. What happens after that, in terms of the decisions one makes and the life one leads, is rooted in the understanding that this is the fundamental problem that must be addressed. Similarly, therefore, we can appreciate that to see that life is characterized by suffering, but not to act upon that awareness, is a wholly 'un-Buddhist' attitude. Such pessimism, or fatalism, is completely contrary to Buddhist understanding. Once the problem has been identified, one is immediately committed to doing something about it. The retrospective telling of the Buddha's journey to enlightenment reveals that, behind the serene smile and composed form of later Buddha images, lies a story of inner struggle revealed in the narratives of the Buddha's life. The story of the Four Sights indicates the resolve of a restless heart to pursue resolutely an uncompromised goal. What is told as four brief excursions into a matter-of-fact and everyday world highlights the significance, for Buddhists, of waking up to the reality that the world we take as given and ordinary is really a fantastic state of affairs. It is only by dwelling on this, and by resolving to transform our own understanding of what it means to take full advantage of a human life, that we can fulfill our human potential.

For Siddhartha, the fourth sight was the inspiration to this end. This fourth sight was of a sadhu, or holy man, walking the streets with his alms bowl. This is a relatively common sight in Indian life. It was, and is, the alternative way of life to that of the householder, the one who has fulfilled his duty of bringing up a family and following a traditional occupation. Such a person was understood as a mendicant, one who has given up wealth and material gain by virtue of relying on others for his basic sustenance, shelter and livelihood. In contrast to the householder, the sadhu is a 'wandering one' (*anagarika*) who has acknowledged that this ordinary world of change and suffering (called the realm of samsara) is one in which no home, in the spiritual sense, can be found. To put it bluntly, the riddle of existence and human destiny cannot be resolved simply by pursuing one's social duties.

This was the dilemma that confronted Siddhartha. To pursue the life of the sadhu, everything had to be given up: his expected future career, his marriage and family, his security in the life of the palace and his fulfilment of parental expectations. We have no knowledge of how he came to resolve this dilemma, but he did; without that Buddhism would not have come into being.

Going forth

The stories tell how, on the night of a full moon, Siddhartha bade farewell to his sleeping wife and child. He rode to the edge of the Sakya kingdom, divested himself of his clothes, long hair and beard, and resolved to go forth as a wandering one. This event is understood in Buddhist terms as Siddhartha's 'going forth': the moment of commitment to a renunciant's life and the beginning of his search, his new career. It was not an interim rite of passage between an adolescent life and adulthood responsibilities that could be shelved for a while. Nor was it the irresponsibly conceived act of an impetuous young man. It was a resolute change of direction that established a tradition whose impact would last for millennia. Should we wish to criticize such an act we should also have to take into account its positive consequences. This is why, for Buddhists everywhere, commitment is fundamental.

However, this is not to say that it necessarily entails the same social consequences as it did for Siddhartha. In the history of Buddhist tradition it is true that joining the sangha has often entailed leaving behind family life for a monastic one. For this reason, monks and monastic life have always been at the centre of traditional Buddhist societies. Taking up the monastic life is seen as imitating the commitment of Siddhartha in his going forth to a mendicant's existence. Becoming a monk is to become a mendicant. However, Buddhism has also always taken into account the need to adapt its form to different cultural and social circumstances. It has been able to do this because the idea of commitment is not fundamentally a matter of changing one's status in society, but of adapting one's outlook and goals.

Buddhist understanding of the distinction between the outer form and inner resolution has been highlighted (especially in the West today), such that there are Buddhist groups which understand renunciation and commitment to the Buddhist tradition to be a way of living within conventional society with different codes and aspirations, rather than an opting out of the given social order. This amounts in part to an understanding of the difference between the Indian society of the Buddha's day and our own. Monasticism was an obvious route for the development of the Buddhist ideal of community, given the options open to spiritual searchers in the Buddha's time. Today it represents something different. The question of adaptation versus the appropriate vehicle for the life lived in pursuit of the truth (dharma) has always been a live issue, but no more so than now. What has always been important is the Buddhist notion of a spiritual community, and this is what the term sangha denotes.

However, this takes us beyond the point which Siddartha had reached in his own journey. After leaving home, he was confronted with the alternatives available to him in Indian society. Foremost among these were the ascetic practices of yogis who, through austerity and denial of physical nourishment, sought to realize their spiritual aspirations. Subjugation of the flesh was for them a necessary prerequisite to spiritual advancement. (This is not just a matter of historical interest since, in India at least, it is still practised.) Unlike in the West, where the notion of austerity belongs more to the past, as redundant as the monastic life, in India the large number of sadhus who devote themselves to this cause can be witnessed readily at dawn on the banks of the Ganges, and at the great pilgrimage festivals, such as Kumbh Mela in Allahabad, which they attend.

Self-mortification

Siddhartha pursued the path of self-mortification for six years, limiting his food and sleep, not washing and living naked, or in the sky-clad state, as it was known. He gained a reputation amongst fellow ascetics, gathering disciples and companions. His fame, it is said, spread like the sound of a great gong in the canopy of the sky. Though he achieved states of higher consciousness and greater awareness, he finally gave up these practices because he came to the conclusion that they did not lead to the realization of the truth (the cessation of suffering). He started eating again, and his followers and companions deserted him. He continued to travel alone, seeking out other teachers, but finally became disillusioned by all their practices. He eventually reached a spot where he resolved to remain until he achieved enlightenment. This is now a well-known moment, both in Buddhist tradition and in world history. Beneath the shade of a great pipal tree, later named after this event as a Bodhi (enlightenment) tree, beside a river, he resolved, 'I will not rise from this spot until I am enlightened. Flesh may wither away, blood may dry up, but until I gain enlightenment I shall not move from this seat.'

the Buddha in meditation

The enlightenment

It is not easy to imagine what occurred in the mind of one sitting
so motionless. It seems ironic that such a great event – the
rediscovery of truth – should outwardly be so uneventful. But it
is indicative of the character of Buddhism that it should be so:
truth is found in silence and stillness rather than activity. He sat
there in a meditative state, gaining greater concentration and
control of his mind. This state of purification was not achieved
instantly, but was the result of all the training he had
undertaken since leaving home. It involved overcoming the
mental hindrances that disrupt and unbalance the mind.

These are graphically described in Buddhist writings as the
attacks of Mara, the Lord of Death, who recognized the
significance of the Buddha's quest and opposed it with all his
power. We can be sure that this was not a serene and easily
accomplished endeavour, but called on all the Buddha's resolve
and skill. All doubt, indecision and compromise had to be
exposed, rather like a tortuous inner struggle in which this was
the final battle. We are told that on the night of the full moon
of Wesak (the month of May in the western calendar), the
Buddha fixed his mind on the morning star as it was rising, and
the moment of full enlightenment occurred.

Essentially, Siddhartha became the Buddha at this point when he eradicated all ignorance, and saw things for exactly what they were with crystal clarity. If we try to imagine what this could be like, we might think of times when, in trying to understand apparently complex, insoluble problems, we have hit on an instant when answers revealed themselves so obviously that it was as though we had previously missed what was right before our eyes; moments when we have said, 'Of course, how could I have been so blind!' This helps us to understand why the event is referred to as 'The Great Awakening', and why the term 'letting go' is so often used by Buddhists to indicate the nature of such wisdom.

The idea of striving for the truth does not really communicate the whole nature of Siddhartha's achievement. It is as though the truth has been there all the time, but we have not had the capacity to realize it. It was this capacity that Siddhartha developed and finally fulfilled. This was the end of Siddhartha's original search but, like all ends, it created a new beginning. As the Buddha, the fully enlightened one, Siddhartha was not the same person he had previously understood himself to be. The wisdom and compassion conferred on him by this event also registered new responsibilities. He who knows is the only one who can make the truth known to others.

The practical significance of truth is what constitutes its ultimate value. It is conquest over death. The individual is freed from the fetters of this life. No longer is he or she condemned to constant rebirth and the dis-ease that results from this. From a Buddhist point of view, this does not mean that we are changed into other beings, gods or angels; rather, we have realized our true nature, our complete potential. (Were this not the case, the Buddha's achievement would amount to a comfort or solace, a way of living well within the prison-house of existence – but nothing more). In this respect, the Buddha becomes a unique historical figure, because his achievement is to present a spiritual goal achievable without the aid of a god. This is not to say that Buddha or Buddhists are necessarily antagonistic towards theistic belief, but that it is not seen as either skilful or helpful to look to a god to solve the riddle of human existence.

Turning the wheel of the dharma

The difficulty of disclosing this truth to others was something that did not immediately resolve itself for the Buddha. As we have seen, he was initially unsure that it could be comprehended by anyone, but the Buddha's teaching career began with his sermon at Sarnath, where he encountered his former companions and preached the dharma for the first time. The distance from Bodh Gaya, the place of his enlightenment, to Sarnath, is one hundred miles, and we can only speculate on what went through his mind while he made the journey. However, when he met his first audience, they were struck by his overall disposition, which radiated those virtues held in high esteem by Buddhists. The confidence and equanimity with which he encountered them were a prelude to the acceptance of his teaching, and drew to him the community that was to grow up around him.

It was not just what the Buddha had to say, but the confidence he inspired in those whom he addressed, that won over his audience. At first, his five former companions greeted him with scepticism, for he was that same Gotama who had given up the path of ascetic practice. However, struck by his authority, they received him back into their company and subsequently became his followers. One writer relates the event as follows:

Upon this the Buddha told them of his experience and claimed recognition of his enlightenment. The monks were once more sceptical. They failed to use the new and higher title of Tathagatha (one who has gone beyond), which implies the status of Buddhahood, and which the narrative makes the Buddha claim for himself. After all, they argued, Gotama had not arrived at this exalted knowledge when he had practised austerities, so why should they believe that he had done so when he reverted to ordinary ways of living? The Buddha retorted that a Tathagatha was not one who had reverted to a life of abundance, giving up the quest for self-mastery. And he repeated his claim to have reached perfect enlightenment and to have found 'the deathless'. The other monks should hear his teaching, and they too would arrive at the goal which they sought when they first left home. Still the monks demurred, and as the narrative gives human truth in story form, the argument is repeated three times. Finally the Buddha makes them admit that he had never talked in such a way before, and that he therefore really did have something to say. So they decided to hear him out. Although by this time he had already trodden quite a few miles and spoken not a few thoughts, we now come to what is usually known as the Buddha's first teaching, or more picturesquely, the first rolling of the wheel of the Dhamma.

(M. Pye, *The Buddha*, Duckworth, 1979, p 41)

Such stories as these also remind us that the Buddha's teaching career was not just a matter of preaching to a willing audience, but that the complex quality of skilfulness (*upaya*) was an essential ingredient for winning over committed individuals (often of great integrity), to an acknowledgement of his claims, which are presented in the formulation of his teachings. There is no doubt that the Buddha was a charismatic figure, but his charisma was understood as radiating not from cleverness or intellectual status (which would have attracted only those with an inclination towards such attributes), but from a deep knowledge that went beyond aspects of his personality.

The mission

The Buddha practised the life of an itinerant preacher, roaming across north-eastern India for the remainder of his life, from his enlightenment at the age of thirty-five. Following climatic conditions, the pattern he established was to wander from place to place for nine months of the year, and take shelter during the three-month monsoon period; these three months became established as a time of retreat and remain so for some monastic Buddhist communities today.

Taking one meal a day, whenever he came to a village, he established the practice of standing at the villagers' doors silently with his alms bowl; once he had collected sufficient food, he would retire to a mango grove on the outskirts of a village to eat. After his meal, villagers would gather round to hear him teach. In this way his following increased, drawn from different strata in the caste-orientated Indian society. From these occasions are drawn various conversations which have entered into the Buddhist scriptures. The story of Kisagotami is one such, but there are others, which reflect the character of the Buddha's teaching, the people whom he met, and their response to him. Some of these accounts may well have been elevated to mythology, but they provide us with some valuable information. One of the first of the Buddha's village meetings is related in this story:

Dona and the Buddha

Journeying along the high road, the Buddha met a man called Dona. Dona was a brahmin, and skilled in the science of bodily signs. Seeing on the Buddha's footprints the mark of a thousand-spoked wheel, he followed in his track along the road until he eventually caught up with the Buddha, who was sitting beneath a tree. As the Buddha was fresh from his Enlightenment, there was a radiance about his whole being. We are told it was as though a light shone from his face – he was happy, serene, joyful. Dona was very impressed by his appearance, and he seems to have felt that this wasn't an ordinary human being, perhaps not a human being at all. Drawing nearer, he came straight to the point, as the custom is in India where religious matters are concerned. He said, 'Who are you?'

Now the ancient Indians believed that the universe is stratified into various levels of existence, that there are not just human beings and animals, as we believe, but gods, and ghosts, and yaksas, and gandharvas, and all sorts of other mythological beings, inhabiting a multi-storey universe, the human plane being just one storey out of many. So Dona asked 'Are you a yaksa?' (a yaksa being a rather terrifying sublime spirit living in the forest). But the Buddha said 'No'. Just 'No'. So Dona tries again. 'Are you a gandharva?' (a sort of celestial musician, a beautiful singing angel-like figure). Once again the Buddha said 'No', and again Dona asked 'Well, then, are you a deva?' (a god, a divine being, a sort of archangel). 'No'. Upon this Dona thought, 'That's strange, he must be a human being after all!' And he asked him that too, but yet again the Buddha said 'No'. By this time Dona was thoroughly perplexed, so he demanded 'If you are not any of these things, then who are you?' The Buddha replied, 'Those mental conditionings on account of which I might have been described as a yaksa or a gandharva, as a deva or a human being, all those conditionings have been destroyed by me. Therefore I am a Buddha.'

(Ven. Sangharakshita, *A Guide to the Buddhist Path*, Windhorse Publications, 1990, pp 36–7)

What is evident from this story is that the Buddha's knowledge and experience challenged the world view of his own culture, and of succeeding cultures up to the present day. It was not that he offered an understanding of the world and our experience within it, for that complemented what we already know. Rather he turned our understanding upside down, such that it had to be fundamentally changed to accommodate his teaching. As with all the great religious teachers, a new way of looking at the world and reflecting on the human condition was being offered. If this hadn't been the case, the Buddhist tradition would never have developed in its own unique and independent way.

The story also suggests that it is not enough to know about the Buddha and his teachings because his claims, as with all great religious teachers, confront our own self-awareness. What is being questioned is not whether we need to know more, but whether our understanding is fundamentally ignorant – without real knowledge. This amounts to a confrontation of view, without which the Buddha would not have gained so many followers, nor established a lasting tradition. It is a matter of commitment that involves the whole person, rather than simply adding to individual personal philosophy. For this reason it is not appropriate to regard the Buddha simply as an ancient philosopher, in the manner of Plato or Aristotle. One could investigate the Buddha's teaching as a philosophy, but that would not amount to knowledge in the Buddhist sense because it does not confer what Buddhists call 'right view'. Only by applying his teachings in practice does realization arise; then the truth is confirmed and self-transformation occurs.

The Buddha was by no means uniformly successful in his encounters. Another early meeting was with the wandering ascetic Upaka, described as an *ajiveka* (who are sometimes known as naked ascetics, renowned for their austerity):

Upaka and the Buddha

Upaka met the Buddha on the road near Bodh Gaya and noticed that he seemed particularly clear of complexion. He greeted him respectfully and asked him, in the way such travellers did, who his teacher was or what his Dhamma was. The Buddha replied in words of incomparable self-assurance that he was victorious, omniscient, teacher-less and unequalled among gods and men. He alone was completely enlightened. He had attained nirvana. Upaka replied, perhaps ironically, that he certainly sounded as if he had conquered 'the unending'; with which the Buddha did not hesitate to agree. Upaka was unconvinced. 'That may be so', he said, and off he went down another road, shaking his head.

(Michael Pye, *The Buddha*, Duckworth, 1979, p 40)

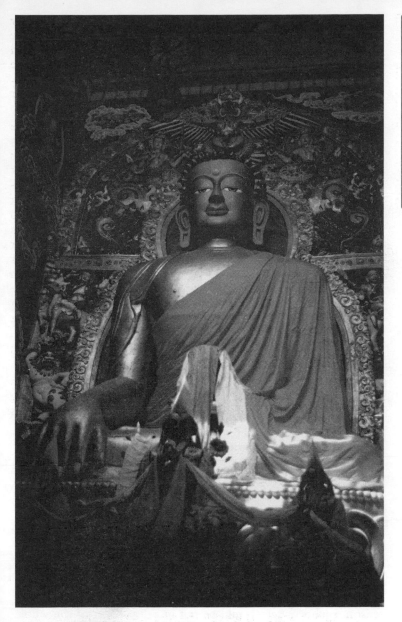

statue of the Buddha (at the Buddhist temple in Sarnath)

This helps us to understand that in the world of his time there were others who belonged to already established spiritual traditions sharing the same aspirations as the Buddha had done. It was by no means easy to convince such determined searchers that he had already achieved what they were still looking for. Indeed it is apparent that today also such scepticism acts as an important antidote to naïve commitment or 'blind faith'. It was an important aspect of the Buddha's teachings that you had to commit yourself to the practice, as was mentioned in Chapter 1. It was this recognition in fact that determined the way in which the Buddha formulated his discourses; on the basis that unless they addressed the fundamental message he had to convey – the overcoming of suffering – and unless their truth was discernible through application, they were of no recognizable value.

The growth of the sangha

Starting with the five former companions, the Buddha's followers grew into an Order of Monks (the *Bhikkhu Sangha*) which drew in lay people to the mendicant life. As the missionary preaching of the order spread, so lay people 'went for refuge' to the Buddha, without renouncing their status as householders, and the lay community developed. This balance between monastic and lay life in the Sangha was one of the main features of the Buddha's mission during his teaching career, which spanned forty years. It was the blueprint for harmony and balance in the social order that transformed the movement, from its initial character as a mendicant group, into an influential Indian tradition that, centuries later, was to convert the Emperor Ashoka, who sought to rule the sub-continent according to Buddhist principles.

Women had been ordained as members of the Order, though the Buddha's attitude had been ambiguous; he accepted them with some reluctance and warned monks of the need to be vigilant in their presence. In answer to his disciple Ananda's question, asking how monks should behave in the presence of women, he is recorded as saying, 'No talking' and, 'Keep wide awake.' This may be ascribed to his belief that attachment to women was a major obstacle in the attainment of nirvana; whatever the reason, such sayings should be put in the context of the whole code of monastic discipline (*vinaya*) that the Buddha laid down.

Paranirvana

The Buddha's death, in his old age, was said to be by food poisoning, from having inadvertently eaten unwholesome mushrooms, truffles or pork, which had been offered to him. It is said that he passed away in a state of meditation, reclining on his right side, his head supported by his hand. This posture has been recorded in Buddhist iconography, and is understood as the Buddha's passing into *paranirvana* – nirvana without remainder; a state in which he was no longer subject to rebirth. This occurred in the woodlands outside the town of Kusinara. He appointed no successor and, it seems, he wished the Sangha to remain a relatively non-hierarchical organization. Among his last words were these to Ananda, who, aware of the imminent death of the Buddha, was leaning against the doorframe weeping. The Buddha called Ananda to him, saying, 'Do not mourn, do not weep. Haven't I told you that we are separated, parted, cut off from everything dear and beloved? ... You have served me long with love, helpfully, gladly, sincerely and without reserve, in body, word and thought. You have done well by yourself, Ananda. Keep trying and you will soon be liberated.'

In conclusion

In this chapter we have focused upon the life of the historical Buddha, Siddhartha Gautama, who became known to his followers as Sakyamuni (the sage of the Sakyas) upon achieving liberation. While all Buddhists acknowledge the enlightenment of the historical Buddha, what Buddhahood entailed is interpreted differently in the diverse branches of Buddhism:

- While the story of the enlightenment of the historical Buddha exemplifies the importance of individual effort, self-reliance and determination, later we shall see how different interpretations of Buddhahood, within different schools of Buddhism, argue that support for the individual is there in the form of former Buddhas and Buddhas to come.

- While Sakyamuni Buddha is the exemplar for some Buddhists, other schools of thought argue that it is possible to attain enlightenment by different means, for example through faith and devotion to Amithaba, the Buddha of the Pure Land, or Maitreya, the Buddha to come.

- We shall see that different understandings of Buddhahood will also influence other ideas, for example with regard to sangha and devotion as a path to enlightenment.

03

the Buddha's teaching

In this chapter you will learn:
- the Buddha's teaching on the nature of life
- about the Buddha's teaching on the 'self'
- about the Buddha's teaching on liberation, or the end of suffering.

Thus have I heard. The Blessed One was once living in the Deer Park at Isipatana (the Resort of Seers) near Varanasi (Benares). There he addressed the group of five bhikkhus.

This is the beginning of what is referred to as the first discourse (*darsana*) of the Buddha, as it appears in the collected writings of the Buddhist canon, the *suttas* (*sutras*). Sutta means thread, and this term is used to express the connected ideas that constitute a discourse of the Buddha. In this case we are listening to the way in which the Buddha formulated his basic understanding of the human condition, and expounded it to those who first listened, his original companions, who were to become his *bhikkhus* (monks or followers).

This teaching addresses the Four Noble Truths and the Middle Way – the crux of the Buddha's teaching pared down to the single concept of *dukkha* (suffering or 'unsatisfactoriness'), why it is the fundamental aspect of the human condition, and how it can be overcome. It relates to the Buddha's own life and experiences:

> Bhikkhus, these two extremes ought not to be practised by one who has gone forth from the household life. What are the two? There is devotion to the indulgence of sense-pleasures, which is low, common, the way of ordinary people, unworthy and unprofitable; and there is devotion to self-mortification, which is painful, unworthy and unprofitable.
>
> (W. Rahula, *What the Buddha Taught*, Gordon Fraser, 1982, p 92)

The Buddha knew about indulgence in sensual pleasures from his life in the palace, and about self-mortification from his early renunciant experiences; and by reflecting on these he developed the teaching of the Middle Way, which leads to 'vision, knowledge, calm, insight, enlightenment, Nibbana'.

The Middle Way is also the fourth of the Noble Truths that the Buddha expounded. To understand this we must first look at the three propositions that lead up to it, which resulted in his exposition of the Buddhist path, and which, together with the fourth, the Middle Way, constitute the Four Noble Truths:

1 *Dukkha*, disease or suffering
2 *Samudaya*, the arising or origin of dukkha
3 *Nirodha*, the cessation of dukkha
4 *Magga*, the way leading to the cessation of dukkha

The first Noble Truth: all is suffering (*dukkha*)

It is very difficult to translate the term dukkha accurately. One word, such as suffering, is insufficient and misleading. It is not a purely philosophical term, and it would be wrong to treat it in that way. Suffering is one meaning ascribed to it, but this suggests a pessimistic view, somehow stressing the bad things and ignoring the good that happens in the course of human experience. It is necessary to understand that *experience* is the key word here. What the Buddha is pointing to is the weight of understanding brought about by reflecting on the totality of a life lived, not simply by weighing its pros and cons. Other words that help to elucidate its meaning are dis-ease, imperfection and inadequacy. It is not that life does not have its happy moments as well as the unhappy ones, but that the sum total of human experience is inadequate or imperfect. It is not all one might hope for or expect. Such expectation or hope is not a matter of false optimism or fantasy, rather it is a recognition that what is achieved in life is ultimately insubstantial, fleeting and unfulfilling. The term, *sukkha*, the opposite of dukkha, denotes happiness, comfort and ease. The Buddha's insight is only fully understood by looking at the first three Noble Truths together as a complete analysis of the human situation; but it is already clear from analysing the first Noble Truth that what we wish to achieve lies beyond our reach; not that the goal we seek at any moment is inaccessible, but that the achievement of this goal does not confer the happiness we sought through it. Professional ambition, fame, material wealth, financial security, physical and mental health, romance, admiration and friendship are all understandable goals, but the nature of life is such that we are not fulfilled in our achievements. Whatever we gain in any of these spheres is not enough to satisfy us. Dukkha is a deep-seated internal condition brought about through our relationship with a world which cannot satisfy that which we crave.

However, we cannot fulfill ourselves by changing that world, rather we have to look for a cure for this condition within ourselves. The fundamental reason for this is that the world – in the Buddhist sense of the samsaric realm which we experience – is subject to impermanence. All is impermanent (*anicca*) and subject to change. This is the second aspect of dukkha, in the Buddha's analysis. It is this fact that causes dukkha. We constantly seek to create permanence, to hold on to things, but our aspirations slip through our grasp. This is the important point about the Buddha's description of life being dukkha. Nothing abides: no moment, no feeling, no thought, no person. (This is self-evidently true, at least in the long term, since everybody dies.) However, there are little deaths and new beginnings throughout life – at every moment, in fact. Change is inevitable and necessary; change is the condition of impermanence; impermanence prevents the possibility of anything abiding. This description is neither happy nor sad, optimistic nor pessimistic; from a Buddhist viewpoint, it is a true analysis, the analysis of the one who has an enlightened view and sees clearly. However, if we bring any sense of sadness or revulsion to this understanding, then this too is understandable from a Buddhist position, because it points to the next proposition.

The second Noble Truth: the origin of suffering (*samudaya*)

The second Noble Truth recognizes that dukkha goes deeper still, and has even more radical implications.

We are used to thinking about there being *a world I live in* and *I, who live in the world*. In other words, we distinguish quite clearly between ourselves as individuals and the world outside us, which is made up of things, events and people. While this way of understanding ourselves is conventionally and practically useful, it proves dangerous when it becomes rooted too deeply.

Objectively speaking, it would seem highly foolish to suggest that the world – that which is not me – is impermanent, but that *I*, however, *am* permanent. Nevertheless, we often live and think as though that were true. It is as if I am standing alone on a station platform, watching a train go by, and I am aware of the movement of the train; that the people in it are travelling from one place to another; that their lives are changing as they travel along the track between departure and destination; but I am standing still, watching, unmoving, and fully aware of what is happening in front of my eyes.

However, on the train, a person looks out of the window, and as the train passes the station, he sees me standing there alone – in one moment in his present, then just a past image and memory. For me, the passenger moves in time and does not abide; for the passenger I do the same – but the realities perceived are contradictory. In truth, says the Buddha, neither abides. What moves is neither the train nor the person, but the greater, all-embracing, unseen vehicle that passes through train and station alike: time.

Another way of perceiving this view is to imagine standing and staring up at the stars in the night sky, and being aware that what you are seeing is light years away from you and therefore at a considerable distance in *time* from you as well as in *space* (due to the time it takes for their light to reach you). It seems that you are the central fixed point in the universe. Yet now imagine yourself on one of those stars viewing the earth at that same moment. You would not see yourself: you would not yet be there.

Just as Copernicus revolutionized our understanding of the universe, so the Buddha's teaching completely changes the way we understand ourselves. We are also a part of the universe's ceaseless *becoming*; there is no abiding self, but merely a constantly changing and impermanent aspect of that becoming. This Buddhist doctrine of *anatta* (no self) is the third aspect of dukkha; together dukkha, anicca and anatta are known as the three marks, or the fundamental characteristics of being.

This analysis immediately begs the question, 'If there is no self in this sense, what do we consist of? What constitutes an individual?' The Buddha's answer was that we are a combination of ever-changing forces or energies which can be divided into five groups (aggregates or *skandhas*), which themselves are dukkha. They are dukkha because they cause attachment; in fact, they are the basis of attachment.

The five aggregates

The aggregate of matter
This includes our five material sense organs – eyes, ears, nose, tongue and 'body and mind' objects – thoughts, ideas and conceptions.

The aggregate of sensations
This includes all sensations: pleasant, unpleasant and neutral. Sensations are experienced through the contact of physical and mental organs with the world and include the creation of visual form, sounds, smells, taste, touch and thoughts or ideas. (Note that, unlike in the Western view, mind is understood to be a sixth sense organ or faculty, because its operation is intrinsic to this activity of contact with, and response to, the world.)

The aggregate of perceptions

Perception involves recognition, and arises from sensation in relation to matter. Perceptions are produced through the contact of our six faculties with the external world.

The aggregate of mental formations

By this the Buddha meant volitions, mental acts of will which include intuition, determination, heedlessness and the idea of self. They also include what we previously referred to as the three poisons: desire or craving, ignorance and aversion. The important thing about mental formations is that they are the basis of *karma* (to which we shall return later), because they are the basis on which we act. The relationship between mental formations and actions is so close that they cannot be separated. As the first two verses of the *Dhammapada* explain:

> What we are today comes from our thoughts of yesterday, and our present thoughts build our life of tomorrow: our life is the creation of our mind.
>
> If a man speaks or acts with an impure mind, suffering follows him as the wheel of the cart follows the beast that draws the cart.
>
> … If a man speaks or acts with a pure mind, joy follows him as his own shadow.
>
> (Translation by J. Mascaro, Penguin, 1973, p 35)

The aggregate of consciousness

In this context, consciousness does not contain the idea of recognition; rather, it denotes awareness in its most rudimentary form. Consciousness creates awareness of a sense object, so that visual consciousness arises when the eye comes into contact with a colour or form. It is perception that then identifies the colour as blue, or the form as round, for example. The same is true of the process occurring with each of the other sense organs.

The significant issue, from a Buddhist point of view, is that the five aggregates together identify the process of becoming as it takes place in each individual. When we draw this process together, into one illustration, its logic is clear in its application to the everyday working of things: I am hungry and I am presented with a plate of food. I *see* it, *smell* it and *anticipate* the taste. I am aware of what is in the dish. *Sensations* arise and *perceptions* follow, with the *recognition* of what it will be like to taste it. *Volition* is brought into play. I wish to eat. I pick up my knife and fork; all other concerns vanish from my mind as I indulge in the pleasure of eating. As my stomach becomes full, my desire decreases. My mind turns to other things. New sensations, perceptions and mental formulations arise. I am more interested in my partner's conversation. I dwell on the discomfort in my stomach. I wish to do other things. I suggest it is time to leave. I look forward to what happens next, or I view it with disappointment – the end of an enjoyable evening and a new working day. I am enveloped in the never-ending process of continual arising (or 'dependent origination'), a chain of cause and effect that never ceases.

A second tangible, but less pleasant, example can be as mundane as having toothache:

> Normally, one simply says 'I have a toothache'. But to Buddhist thinkers this appears as a very inconsistent way of speaking. Neither 'I', nor 'have', nor 'toothache' is counted among the ultimate facts of existence (dharmas). In Buddhist literature, personal expressions are replaced by impersonal ones. Impersonally, in terms of ultimate events, this experience is divided up into:
>
> 1 There is physical form – that is, the tooth as matter.
> 2 There is a painful feeling.
> 3 There is sight, touch, and pain-perception (ideation) of the tooth; perception can exist only as ideation.
> 4 There is, by way of volitional reactions, resentment of pain and desire for physical well-being, etc.
> 5 There is consciousness, an awareness of all of the above. The 'I' of common-sense talk has thus disappeared; it forms no part of this analysis. It is not the ultimate reality. Not even its components are reality. One might reply, of course, that an imagined 'I' is a part of the actual experience. In that case, it would be listed under consciousness, the last of the five above-mentioned categories. But this consciousness is not ultimate reality. In living human existence there is a continual succession of mental and physical phenomena. It is the union of these phenomena that makes the individual. Every person, or thing, is therefore a putting together, a compound of components which change. In each individual, without any exception, the relationship between its components is always changing, is

never the same for two consecutive moments. It
follows that no sooner has individuality begun than
its dissolution, disintegration, also begins.
(H. Dumoulin and J.C. Maraldo (eds), *Buddhism in the
Modern World*, Collier Macmillan, 1976, pp 9–10)

The Buddha's teaching emphasizes the fact that life does not have
to be like this, moving constantly between desire and aversion;
changing states of mind and circumstance within which I identify
myself. Desire inevitably leads to aversion, and worldly
happiness can never be more than a passing sensation. The only
way out of this ceaseless circle is to understand that the 'I' who
craves for happiness and contentment is the very obstacle that
prevents it. It is born of the ignorance of attachment. Self is
dukkha, but letting go of self is true happiness.

The analogy of the chariot

The Buddhist monk Nagasena expressed this understanding in
another more concrete and witty way with the analogy of the
chariot. Nagasena is in conversation with King Milinda, who
had continually harassed the local Buddhist monks with his
questions and arguments:

Thereupon the Venerable Nagasena said to King Milinda:
'As a king you have been brought up in great refinement
and you avoid roughness of any kind. If you would walk
at midday on this hot, burning and sandy ground, then
your feet would have to tread on the rough and gritty
gravel and pebbles, and they would hurt you; your body
would get tired, your mind impaired, and your awareness
of your body would be associated with pain. How then
did you come – on foot, or on a mount?'
'I did not come, Sir, on foot, but on a chariot.' – 'If you
have come on a chariot, then please explain to me what a
chariot is. Is the pole the chariot?' – 'No, reverend Sir!' –
'Is then the axle the chariot?' – 'No, reverend Sir!' – 'Is it
then the wheels, or the framework, or the flagstaff, or the
yoke, or the reins, or the goad-stick?' – 'No, reverend Sir!'
– 'Then is it the combination of pole, axle, wheels,
framework, flagstaff, yoke, reins and goad which is the
"chariot"?' – 'No, reverend Sir!' – 'Then is this "chariot"
outside the combination of pole, axle, wheels, framework,
flagstaff, yoke, reins and goad?' – 'No, reverend Sir!' –
'Then ask as I may, I can discover no chariot at all. Just a
mere sound is this "chariot". But what is the real chariot?'

'Where all constituent parts are present,
The word "a chariot" is applied.
So likewise where the skandhas are,
The term "a being" commonly is used.'

> (E. Conze (trans), *Buddhist Scriptures*,
> Penguin Classics, 1959, pp 148–9)

It is important to be aware that this teaching was not meant to suggest that the absence of selfhood meant annihilation, nor to suggest a consequent lack of meaning or purpose in human life. Were this the case, it would not matter how one behaved, since there would be no person to be blamed. Instinctive desires, whims and wishes could be fulfilled to the full. Hedonism would be the order of the day, for there would be nothing to lose. On the contrary, to see things in this fashion and behave in this way is to bring about the worst of conditions; the way in which this is experienced is through the law of karma. Karma also ensures that this sort of analysis of the human situation is not just an academic exercise, a way of cleverly justifying whatever view one finds appealing or conducive to one's own proclivities.

Karmic conditioning

For Westerners, the Indian term karma is most often taken to refer to a determinist and fatalist view of human life. Equated with the notion of destiny (but in a pejorative way), it suggests that what happens to an individual is the outcome of unchangeable events, and the best one can do is to suffer the inevitable outcomes in life. This does not accord with the rich interpretation of karma in Indian thought. Karma was a pivotal concept in Indian thinking, around which turned the whole question of why life is as it is. It offered the possibility of different causal explanations for events. The word karma means 'action'. As a result, the relationship between what you do and what happens to you is open to different sorts of explanation. At one end of the scale, it can act as an explanation of why misfortune happens when it is not recognizably the result of particular actions. Common Western explanations of this would be 'luck', 'fate' or 'chance'. In other words, where no obvious historical causal connection can be found, the cause must lie elsewhere. In Indian terms, this would relate back to a previous life and its bad karma, which needs to be worked out in this one. Notice, however, the crucial distinction between the Western and Indian notions. It is not that what happens is inexplicable or random, but that the explanation lies beyond our everyday cognition or observations. Initial reflection may lead to a form of fatalism ('how can I ever know?'), but this is not necessarily the case.

The reason why karma became a central theme in the Buddha's teaching was because he was concerned with liberating individuals from a state of ignorance and suffering. To see the Buddha's teaching as pessimistic and fatalistic, as some do, is to caricature it in a similar sense as to understand Christianity to be all about sin rather than salvation.

The importance of karma is that it demonstrates the practicality of Buddhist teachings. Ethical considerations become paramount, because liberating oneself from the dis-ease of samsaric existence is a karmic matter, embedded in our everyday activities and behaviour.

Let us take the earlier illustration of reacting to one's desires while eating a meal. In this situation, our happiness is always transitory and provisional, because we understand the satisfaction of our desires to be paramount. Such attachment can never remain fulfilling. However, our ignorance prevents us from envisaging any other way of pursuing life. For a Buddhist, the result of this is more calamitous than we might imagine: the effect is cumulative. By not recognizing the cumulative effect of our karmic habits, we cannot conceive of their result. Just like a habit to which we are addicted, so our karmic conditioning determines our thoughts and deeds. The Buddha saw this state of being as one of ignorance and craving, over which we exercise no control. It is strong and blind, and he compared it to thirst (*tanha*). When we are thirsty, we cannot help desiring water. It becomes so necessary that we are overwhelmed by it and cannot think about anything else. Such is the nature of our craving – and yet, in ignorance, we are oblivious to its effect upon us.

Rebirth

For Westerners, even the admission of this unsatisfactoriness would not equal the importance that the Buddha placed on it. If we only have one life anyway, we might still affirm the importance of seeking happiness, through the achievement of our mundane goals. After all (we might argue), that is all there is; and to have a life of warmth, food and shelter is infinitely preferable to one in which we lack these fundamental things.

The Buddha's view rooted karma in the process of rebirth, or *re-becoming*. In India this was a generally recognized idea: that we live through succeeding rebirths which are determined by our karmic habits. When our actions bring about bad effects we shall reap their consequences in a later life. Equally, good acts will produce a better rebirth. In this way a rigid distinction between human and other life forms is not made. We may be reborn in a higher or lower human situation, and subject to greater or lesser hardship; but we may also be born in a different form – as an animal, for example, and therefore subject to even greater ignorance.

In the *Jataka Tales* (popular Buddhist fables), the previous rebirths of the Buddha as various animals are recounted: he is reborn as a bird, a monkey, a buffalo and an elephant amongst others.

It is when the consequences of our ignorance and craving are recognized in this way, and when the state of affairs is understood as endless, that the purchase of the Buddha's teaching is registered more emphatically. The value of a present, relatively comfortable existence is rendered negligible in the light of future striving. Imprisoned in samsara for life sentence after life sentence, it matters little whether your present cell offers comparative ease or luxury, since it cannot last.

If we regard karma and rebirth as speculative theories or ideas, it is unlikely that the Buddha's teaching will hit home. We may regard it as a noble and improving guide to living, but not as a salvific message. For Buddhists, rebirth is axiomatic, because it is the teaching of an enlightened mind; a mind which, in the last stages of achieving that enlightened status, actually witnessed its experience of former lives. Western Buddhists often embark on the path without fully accepting this understanding, but the important point is to trust in the Buddha's teaching – even though it may not be fully comprehensible.

One Western monk, reticent to undertake ordination, remarked to his teacher that he could not affirm the idea of rebirth. His teacher's reply was that it was not necessary to do so, but that *not* to go for refuge, on the basis that he could not yet affirm it, was tantamount to committing himself to ignorance because he was not already enlightened. It was the practice itself that confirmed the truth or otherwise of the Buddha's teaching. A summary of the Buddhist teaching on samsaric existence, concentrated in the first two Noble Truths, is depicted in the *Wheel of Becoming*.

The Wheel of Becoming

At the centre of the wheel (its hub) are the three driving forces: ignorance, desire or greed, and aversion, represented by a pig, a cockerel and a snake. These three are linked together, with each biting the others' tail. Surrounding the hub is a circle divided into two, a black and a white half. In the white half the figures are ascending. In the black half they are moving down. This depicts the karmic movement of figures absorbed in rising to a higher state and those, in horror, sinking to a lower existence.

The six realms

The spokes of the wheel separate it into six samsaric realms. At the top are the *devas*, or gods, in their heaven; a place of luxury, pleasure and ease. To their right are the *asuras*, jealous gods, driven by their desire to achieve the top realm and, in so doing, warring with armies. Notice how the tree, rooted in their realm, gives its fruit to the gods above. Their state of mind is epitomized by the figure at the base of the tree seeking to chop it down, in order to achieve the wish fulfilment (symbolized by the fruit).

Below them is the animal realm, where consciousness is duller and ignorance greater. The animals' constant activity is to find food, by preying on other animals or other life forms.

In the bottom realm are beings in a tormented state, their consciousness filled with pain and fear as they burn, freeze and undergo horrific deaths. This is the opposite of the gods' realm: hell as opposed to heaven.

The next realm upwards is that of the hungry ghosts, or *pretas*. They are in a state of constant hunger or thirst which can never be sated. Their enormous, swollen bellies can never be satisfied by the amount of food they can take in through their thin necks and tiny mouths. The little fruits of the stunted trees are protected by protruding thorns and sharp branches. Whatever they touch turns to fire or filth.

The final realm is that of humans. They go about their daily lives, eating and drinking, giving birth, being treated for sickness, becoming old and frail, being attacked and dying, and carrying on with their work. There is also a figure meditating and reflecting on the sum total of what he sees. Here is depicted the suffering that the Buddha witnessed, and the higher possibility of a precious human birth to reflect on and escape from it.

the Tibetan Wheel of Becoming

These six realms represent the inevitability of past and future rebirths in different states, since we travel through them and never abide in any particular realm for ever – not even as gods. They also represent the states of mind which determine our continual revolutions.

To Buddhists we are part of the ceaseless rhythm of nature, which flows through us as through everything. In fact, to speak of ourselves is only to speak of this rhythm. The constant motion of every moment in the rising and falling of the sea; the movement of the river and the air and our own breathing; thoughts, growth and decay are all one process at work, becoming and returning in endless cycles. Resisting this is our attachment to the fiction that we are each abiding entities, and the frustration this fiction entails is the dukkha that is founded on a compounded ignorance. Letting go of this, by seeing through such delusion, is the path to liberation. Beyond this *maya* (the repeated movement of creativity and destruction) lie peace and happiness, untouched by death and rebirth (which are simply moments of momentous change in the samsaric cycle, equivalent to the submersion of continents and the arising of new species). The fact that we cannot see what lies beyond is attributable only to our own ignorance and lack of sight or wisdom, which cling to the self as though it were an immutable object. Ignorance is part of that self, its creator in fact. Over time, it can endure no more than a rock in a stream, a leaf in the wind, a pebble on the beach or a cloud in the sky. Our myopic vision, extending from birth to death, is incapable of conceiving this, and so invents the concept of the soul to ensure our eternity. But such an invention merely seals our fate. And far beyond this lies the happiness of the Buddha.

For the gods, pride will eventually cause their downfall. For the asuras, jealousy is their undoing. The animals are conditioned by their instinctive behaviour. The figures in the hell realm cannot escape fear and pain filling their minds. The hungry ghosts are completely absorbed in the need to satisfy their hunger. The humans (although this realm offers the possibility of release) are too absorbed in their own karmic desires and conditioning, their everyday activities, hopes and fears.

We may ourselves identify our own consciousness travelling through these realms at different times, as we experience temporary pleasure and fulfilment, anger and jealousy, instinctive drives, pain and torment (from toothache to heartache), lack of fulfilment and overarching ambition. In the human realm, it is possible to be aware of all these phenomena as they affect us and others, and to observe dispassionately.

In each realm is an encircled Buddha figure, whose teaching is skilfully adapted to those who inhabit it, and is depicted by what he holds in his hands. Everywhere in samsara the truth is available, but it is more accessible to some than to others.

Dependent origination

The rim of the wheel is divided into twelve segments and scenes. These show how beings pass from one realm to another, and are called the *nidanas*. They are

1 a blind man with a stick
2 a potter with a wheel and pots
3 a monkey climbing a flowering tree
4 a boat with four passengers, one of whom is steering
5 an empty house
6 a man and a woman embracing
7 a man with an arrow in his eye
8 a woman offering a drink to a seated man
9 a man gathering fruit from a tree
10 a pregnant woman
11 a woman giving birth to a child
12 a man carrying a corpse to the cremation ground

These scenes depict Buddhist teaching on *dependent origination*: the causal chain which ensures that the Wheel of Samsara keeps revolving. Relating to the figures shown, dependent origination states:

1 Because of ignorance, we suffer.
2 Because of ignorance, there arises Will-to-Action.
3 Because of Will-to-Action, Consciousness.
4 Because of Consciousness, Psychophysical Existence.
5 Because of Psychophysical Existence, the Six Organs of Sense (eye, ear, nose, tongue, body [the sense of touch], and mind).
6 Because of the Six Organs of Sense, Contact.
7 Because of Contact, Sensation (or Feeling).
8 Because of Sensation, Craving.
9 Because of Craving, Attachment (or Grasping).
10 Because of Attachment, Becoming (or Worldly Existence).
11 Because of Becoming, Birth.
12 Because of Birth, decay, grief, lamentation, (physical) suffering, dejection, and despair. (All of these constitute suffering in general.)

The Wheel is held by a fearful master with three eyes, fangs and a crown of skulls. He is Yama, the Lord of Death, who has ultimate control over the fate of those who live in samsara, conditioned through their ignorance to see it as reality – as their natural state.

The Wheel can also be understood as a mirror. Yama holds it up to each one of us, and in it we recognize what we understand to be our own reflection – this is what we are. Only through understanding the truth communicated by the Buddha (as when he gave his first darsana – teaching – in the Deer Park at Benares, and turned the wheel of the dharma) can we transform our delusion into knowledge.

The third and fourth Noble Truths explain how this can be done.

The third Noble Truth: the cessation of suffering (*nirodha*)

Nirodha means to control. Control of the craving or thirst of attachment is the third teaching. If we accepted only the first two Noble Truths and eschewed the last two, we would have a teaching about the way things are, but no remedy for this depressing state of affairs. The first two truths diagnose the condition, but the great achievement of the Buddha was to offer a cure; therefore, as far as Buddhists are concerned, he is the physician *par excellence*.

Nirodha is the extinguishing of thirst or craving, to be achieved by rooting out attachment. It results in a state called nirvana (nibbana) in which the fires of craving have ceased to burn and there is no more suffering.

One of the problems we have in understanding nirvana is that this word is used for a state in which something has happened, without describing what that state is actually like. Buddhists maintain that it would be erroneous to speculate about what nirvana is like, because it would achieve nothing: the important thing is to treat the condition. If we were to ask someone with an apparently incurable disease whether they wished for a newly available cure, they would not stop to speculate about what it would be like once they were cured. If it cured them, they would know they were well, because they would no longer be suffering from their illness. Thus nirvana may be likened to setting down a heavy load after a long journey, to being released from a worrying debt or being set free from prison. In other words, it is described in terms of a cessation of those things which cause suffering.

As with all illness, of course, the proposed cure is of no value unless you accept the diagnosis, so this third truth is to be understood in the light of the first two. The possibility of nirvana cannot be realized unless our present existence is understood as dukkha.

Buddhist scriptures use many metaphors to contrast dukkha and nirvana. One of the starkest is that used in the *Fire Sermon*:

> **The Fire Sermon**
> Bhikkhus, all is burning. And what is the all that is burning? Bhikkhus, the eye is burning, visible forms are burning, visual consciousness is burning, visual impression is burning, also whatever sensation, pleasant or painful or neither-pleasant-nor-painful, arises on account of the visual impression, that too is burning. Burning with what? Burning with the fire of lust, with the fire of hate, with the fire of delusion; I say it is burning with birth, ageing and death, with sorrows, with lamentations, with pains, with grief, with despairs.
>
> (W. Rahula, *What the Buddha Taught*,
> Gordon Fraser, 1982, p 95)

The Buddha recounts the same experience for all the senses, the body and the mind; he explains that one who knows this becomes dispassionate, and:

> Being dispassionate, he becomes detached, through detachment he is liberated. When liberated there is knowledge that he is liberated. And he knows: Birth is exhausted, the holy life has been lived, what has to be done is done, there is no more left to be done on this account.
>
> (W. Rahula, *What the Buddha Taught*,
> Gordon Fraser, 1982, pp 96–7)

Nirvana

In another darsana he speaks of nirvana as 'getting rid of all cares and troubles' (*Sabbasava sutta*). Other poetic terms which he uses include: the harbour of refuge; the cool cave; the home of ease; the place of bliss.

Perhaps the greatest difficulty for non-Buddhists is that we want to understand nirvana through ideas and language with which we are already familiar. Thus, we might equate 'nirvana' with 'heaven', and expect to find luxuriant and elaborate descriptions of how life there will be immeasurably better than in the here and now. This conception is fraught with problems, because nirvana is part of a world view constructed in quite a different way. There is a continuing selfhood in heaven which nirvana denies; there is a tendency to understand heaven as a future state, following on from earthly life, that nirvana is not; there is a belief that heaven is, at least to some degree, understandable in earthly terms, whereas nirvana is not even the opposite of samsaric existence. Nirvana entails the cessation of everything.

The problem we then have is that nirvana sounds dreadfully negative, as though everything precious to us is denied and destroyed. The Buddhist response to this is that speculation of this kind is simply unhelpful. Nirvana is realized in the midst of our everyday existence:

> He who has realized the Truth, Nirvana, is the happiest being in the world. He is free from all 'complexes' and obsessions, the worries and troubles that torment others. His mental health is perfect. He does not repent the past, nor does he brood over the future. He lives fully in the present. Therefore he appreciates and enjoys things in the purest sense without self-projections. He is joyful, exultant, enjoying the pure life, his faculties pleased, free from anxiety, serene and peaceful. As he is free from selfish desire, hatred, ignorance, conceit, pride and all such 'defilements', he is pure and gentle, full of universal love, compassion, kindness, sympathy, understanding and tolerance. His service to others is of the purest, for he has no thought of self. He gains nothing, accumulates nothing, not even anything spiritual, because he is free from the illusion of Self, and the 'thirst' for becoming.
>
> (W. Rahula, *What the Buddha Taught*,
> Gordon Fraser, 1982, p 43)

So, rather than speculate, we must discern this way of being in the examples of others and cultivate it in ourselves. The Buddhist teacher, Nagasena, was once asked:

> 'Venerable Nagasena, does he who has not received Nirvana know how happy a state Nirvana is?'
>
> 'Yes, he knows it.'
>
> 'But how can he know that without his receiving Nirvana?'

'Now what do you think...? Do those whose hands and feet have not been cut off know how sad a thing it is to have them cut off?'

'Yes, Sir, that they know!'

'But how do they know it?'

'Well, by hearing the sound of the lamentation of those whose hands and feet have been cut off, they know it.'

'Just so ... it is by hearing the glad words of those who have seen Nirvana that they who have not received it know how happy a state it is.'

(E. Conze (trans), *Buddhist Scriptures*, Penguin Classics, 1959, p 156)

Here we are confronted with an apparent paradox in Buddhist thinking. If our aim is to cultivate peace, ease, bliss and well-being in ourselves, does this not make nirvana or enlightenment a selfish goal? How can it equate with the Buddha's emphasis on the extinction of self (anatta)? The Buddhist answers that this is a misunderstanding of why these goals are sought. The self is composed of self-centredness, which arises from attachment or craving. It constantly needs to be re-affirmed – and yet such re-affirmation is ultimately unattainable, because this self is a fiction. Throughout our everyday lives we look for this affirmation from those around us. When someone praises me I feel confident and happy. When I am blamed or deprecated I feel anxious, even angry. When someone else is praised I feel jealous; I experience envy. These negative states of mind are a result of attachment to my own self-centredness; even my positive states of mind depend on the same thing. In this condition I cannot freely give and be altruistic. When we speak of cultivating nirvana it is not dependent on my self-centredness, my ego, being affirmed. It is a release from that need. In this release it is possible to give without receiving, to offer loving kindness without first being its recipient. Freed from this flux of emotions and mental instability, I can now act freely and give when needed. I am also able to direct my attention to others' needs, rather than being preoccupied by my own. An enlightened state of mind is one in which this creative giving occurs spontaneously and without hindrance. Were the qualities inherent in an enlightened mind to be cultivated for the ego's own sake, i.e. if that were the motivation, then they could not be achieved.

In Camus' novel *The Fall*, we encounter a character who sees through such self-deceit, and opts out from the status and respect he is accorded because of his mistrust of his own motives. Similarly, from a Buddhist point of view, the self-delusion this character formerly suffered from could not result in the ease, equanimity and contentment that is conferred by the extinguishing of craving. For this reason, the path to nirvana involves overcoming specific obstacles in oneself. This is expressed in the Five Hindrances (*Nivarana*): attachment to sensuality; ill-will; torpor of mind or body; worry; and wavering doubt. Reflecting on these purifies understanding and counteracts such self-deceit. By reflecting on and learning from them a greater awareness occurs. One teacher puts it as follows:

> All these feelings of hunger or thirst or restlessness or jealousy or fear, of lust and greed and sleepiness – all these we can regard as teachers. Rather than resenting them, saying: 'What did I do to deserve this?' you should say: 'Thank you very much. I'll have to learn this lesson some day, I might as well do it now, rather than put it off.'
>
> (Ven. Ajahn Sumedho, *Cittaviveka: Teachings from the Silent Mind*, Amaravati Publications, 1992, p 68)

The fourth Noble Truth: the path to the cessation of suffering (*magga*)

This is known as the 'Middle Way', and avoids the two extremes of indulgence in sensual pleasures and self-mortification. It is also known as the 'Noble Eightfold Path', because it outlines eight categories through which purity of mind, calm and insight can be achieved.

These eight divisions are grouped into three aspects of Buddhist practice: Ethical Conduct (*Sila*); Mental Discipline (*Samadhi*); Wisdom (*Panna* or *Prajna*).

The Eightfold Path

1	Right Understanding (*Samma ditthi*)	
2	Right Intention or Orientation (*Samma sankappa*)	} Wisdom
3	Right Speech (*Samma vaca*)	
4	Right Action (*Samma kammanta*)	} Ethical Conduct
5	Right Livelihood (*Samma ajiva*)	
6	Right Effort (*Samma vayama*)	
7	Right Mindfulness (*Samma sati*)	} Mental Discipline
8	Right Concentration (*Samma samadhi*)	

As with all things in Buddhism, it is important to understand the interrelationships of these categories. The Eightfold Path is sometimes likened to a ladder with eight rungs, as though one might develop by practising each discipline in turn. This is a misleading idea, because the Buddha stressed that progress is made by the practice of each aspect of the path in concert with the others.

For example, it is important to recognize that Ethical Conduct is absolutely necessary in order to achieve Wisdom, and that without Mental Discipline we lack the capacity for Ethical Conduct. Similarly, therefore, the achievement of Compassion and Wisdom, which are the characteristics of an Enlightened One, cannot be gained separately and are not distinct. Everything goes hand in hand. The wise person is the one who acts compassionately, the compassionate person is the one who acts wisely.

One who treads the Eightfold Path is, therefore, doing something quite different from one who 'wanders' on the Wheel of Becoming. He or she recognizes the possibility of improvement and eventual emancipation and, acting on that possibility – with the Buddha's teaching and his or her own practice as the guide, alongside others who are treading the path – works creatively toward a more refined awareness of how to live well. The Eightfold Path is like a map which charts this journey; its practice is like the raft to the other shore.

Ethical Conduct

The Buddha said his teachings were 'for the good of the many, for the happiness of the many, out of compassion for the world'. If Ethical Conduct does not arise through following the teachings, then they are of no use whatsoever. The quality of compassion is the pinnacle of Buddhist achievement, and Ethical Conduct therefore is not an end in itself but a means to develop compassion. It is the cultivation of loving kindness, generosity and forgiveness. These qualities will manifest themselves in our activity in the world, in that which we give out in Right Speech, Right Action and Right Livelihood. To the extent that these are practised, so we will decrease the suffering of others and ourselves. We shall also purify ourselves. Understanding and practising these three aspects of the path should not be seen simply as a matter of duty and discipline. Certainly it is that, but it is more. Ultimately, such actions should become effortless and spontaneous, rather than a matter of grim resolution.

Right Speech means abstaining from telling lies, slandering and promoting division and enmity, using abusive language, and indulging in careless gossip. In some cases, if one cannot say something helpful, it is better to keep a noble silence.

Right Action promotes peaceful and harmonious conduct. It has exactly the same aims as Right Speech, but a different form of expression. Doing that which causes harm to others is its exact opposite, whether this be through taking life, stealing or taking advantage of someone sexually.

Right Livelihood determines that one should abstain from making a living through causing harm, whether by trading in arms or intoxicating drinks, killing animals or cheating.

All these abstentions are indications of what does not improve the lives of others or ourselves; but we need to analyse the reasons why this is so important. On one level it is clear that the quality of life is dependent on our conduct. When someone does an injustice to me, in word or deed, I immediately feel aggrieved. Anger arises, and I want to hit back in some way. My state of mind is imbalanced, and I am tempted to act hastily and without due thought for the consequences. Multiply this by the number of acts of this kind committed, and we move from individual antagonism to social unrest – and ultimately to war. Look around the world and you will see that the effect of this is endemic. It is not that this happens sporadically, but that there is a perpetual chain of events caused by the continual cycle of such activities. They have a momentum evoked through the mind and hearts of individuals and groups which engulfs us at work, in the home and even between friends. This momentum has a history in individual lives and within nations that is hard to rectify. Its result is a lack of trust and willingness to put things right. For Buddhists, this is part and parcel of karmic conditioning; the law of cause and effect that ensures samsaric existence continues to flourish. The only way to reverse this process is to take responsibility for it individually, and determine not to contribute to it. Unless individuals alone decide that in the context of their own lives and sphere of influence they are going to behave differently, there can be no diminishing of this state of affairs. This is dukkha in action, and there is no other agency to which we can appeal for help but ourselves. *Sila* is the only antidote to dukkha; there is no other palliative and no other way of aspiring to true happiness. However, the point about Sila being an aspect of the Eightfold Path is that Ethical Conduct is not attainable without Mental Discipline and Wisdom.

Mental Discipline

The Buddha addressed his brethren thus: 'It is through not understanding and not grasping the Four Noble Truths, O brethren, that we have had to run for so long, to wander for so long in this weary path of transmigration, both you and I.'

The power of the Noble Truths lies in this aspect of Mental Discipline: Right Effort, Right Mindfulness and Right Concentration. Without these nothing is attainable. Right Effort involves preventing evil and unwholesome states of mind from arising; ridding oneself of such unwholesome states of mind that have already arisen; producing, or causing to arise, good and wholesome states of mind and bringing them to perfection. This necessitates generating the will for this to happen, and a single-minded application to the task. Without effort, which is itself an act of will, doubt, anxiety and other hindrances will distract the mind from its task. We are reminded here of numerous crucial events in the Buddha's life which could have been resolved quite differently: the episode of going forth and leaving his loved ones; the exertion of denying Mara's temptations; heeding Brahma's exhortations to preach the dharma. Without Right Effort and its motivation of the will, it is difficult not to be sidetracked into admitting the possibility of a different way of dealing with things, and of thinking of one's goal as being over-ambitious, idealistic or extreme.

Right Mindfulness provides the context for Right Effort. It relates it to the here and now. It is concerned with immediate states of consciousness, not speculative possibilities. It involves diligent awareness of the activities of the body, sensations and feelings; the activities of the mind, and ideas, thoughts and conceptions. In other words, it monitors what is actually going on. Without mindfulness effort would be blind, random and ineffectual. Without effort mindfulness would be barren and unproductive. Without both, morality, or ethical conduct, would be no more than just a duty.

Right Concentration underpins Right Mindfulness. Without concentration mindfulness, let alone Ethical Conduct, is impossible. Concentration is a fundamental skill, in that is develops attentiveness. In the various schools of Buddhism it is practised in different ways, but all concentrate on attention to detail, bringing the capacity of the mind to a full awareness of every thought, action and sensation. One of the basic practices is concentration on breathing (*anapanasati*). If Right Mindfulness is a matter of awareness, Right Concentration is the basis upon which that awareness is attained. Being able to be aware of the process of breathing – a fundamental physiological function – enables us to discern what is actually happening. When this concentration is applied to sensations and feelings; the activities of the mind; the ideas, thoughts and conceptions that arise and fall away in our mental habits; then a true understanding of the way things are is arrived at. It is all too easy to rationalize what is going on in ourselves as individuals, such that we affirm our desires and longings, but the antidote to this is to present ourselves with evidence for things being otherwise.

The purpose of Right Concentration is to attain a focus of mind that cannot be knocked off balance by inclinations that arise as a result of desire or craving. For example, in an attitude of meditation, or within our daily life, we may suffer from boredom and seek to relieve it by pursuing a different goal that will produce immediate pleasure or interest. Immediately, our efforts are put into achieving this aim. We are no longer mindful of the overall context in which we live, nor the wish to follow the dharma, and we pursue short-term pleasure and happiness. Our concentration is then not connected to what is happening in our bodies and minds, but to how we might achieve what we momentarily crave. We are no longer in control of what is going on, we simply serve the interests of that desire which has arisen. Right Effort, Right Mindfulness and Right Concentration are the safeguards against such forgetfulness and the foundation of sila.

Wisdom

Wisdom consists in Right Intention or Orientation and Right Understanding. They are dependent on Right Mindfulness, since Right Thought constitutes selfless renunciation or detachment (as opposed to *attachment*, outlined previously) and Right Understanding is the realization of things as they are (as opposed to suffering the delusion that arises from pursuing desires).

Wisdom is not the result of cleverness or intellectual capacity, which are as much prey to karmic inclinations as any other capacity of mind. This is a common misreading of the Buddha's teaching, since it is presumed that following the logic of such an analytical summary of human experience necessitates great intellectual acumen. But cleverness can be as much an obstacle as it can be an aid to wisdom. It can be a tool used to proliferate self-deceit, as well as being used to cut through it. Wisdom is the summation of what has already been practised, but Right Intention or Orientation and Right Understanding are also the basis of the practice itself, since they are the motivation for Right Effort and the further aspects of the path. Clearly, therefore, wisdom can be seen as the final factor of enlightenment, but it is also cumulative; a refinement that grows as thought and understanding become progressively freed from ignorance. This unfettering is gained by practising the path as a whole. The term that sums up this process is *bhavana*, or mental development. It involves a devotional aspect, in that it is a wholehearted commitment to self-transformation. It also has a reflective aspect, in that it demands an awareness of what is happening in the here and now. It involves a highly practical aspect, in that it has a necessary purchase on the way we act in every situation. Different Buddhist movements address these forms of practice in their own particular ways, but all concur on the need to address all three.

The result of this path, pursued to its conclusion, has been preserved in the words of the Buddha, addressing his disciple Ananda, concerning the question of the mystery of death, when close to his own eventual passing:

> Those who have died after the complete destruction of the three bonds of lust, of covetousness, and of the egotistical cleaving to existence, need not fear the state after death. They will not be in a state of suffering; their minds will not continue as a Karma of evil deeds or sin, but are assured of final deliverance. When they die, nothing will remain of them but their good thoughts, their righteous acts, and the bliss that proceeds from truth and righteousness. As rivers must at last reach the distant main, so their minds will be reborn in higher states of existence and continue to press on to their ultimate goal, which is the ocean of truth, the eternal peace of Nirvana.

> Men are anxious about death and their fate after death; but there is nothing strange in this, that a human being must die. However, that you should inquire about them, and having heard the truth still be anxious about the dead, this is wearisome to the Blessed One ...

> Hell is destroyed for me, and rebirth as an animal, or a spirit, or in any place of woe. I am converted; I am no longer liable to be reborn in a state of suffering, and am assured of final deliverance.

> (H. Dumoulin and J.C. Maraldo (eds), *Buddhism in the Modern World*, Collier Macmillan, 1976, p 21)

In conclusion

In this chapter we have studied the core teachings expounded by the historical Buddha, which have been accepted as axiomatic by all his followers. However, different types of Buddhism have built on these in differing ways, which will be more fully presented later. For example:

- Further teachings were attributed to the Buddha by certain schools in the Mahayana tradition (see Chapter 4), which contextualized the teachings in this chapter within a larger cosmological canvas and thus expanded upon them.

- The further teachings presented also changed the orientation of Buddhahood. Nirvana was not an end in itself but rather the beginning of a new quest to save others from the sufferings endured in samsara.

- A new metaphysical dimension was introduced to the Buddhist view of reality. It was no longer just about individual liberation but about how all beings could be saved from suffering by different means according to their capacities and dispositions. This was to radically revise the relationship between the monastic sangha and the laity.

04

Buddhist scriptures and schools

In this chapter you will learn:
- about the main Buddhist scriptures and schools
- about the differences in their teachings and doctrines
- about how Buddhism changed as it entered new cultures.

Like other religious traditions, Buddhism has divided into various branches over its history, and its scriptures reflect this diversity.

After teaching for forty-five years, the Buddha died at the age of eighty. This is called his paranirvana, and is seen as a final release from the round of rebirth. His teachings were memorized by his followers and passed on by oral tradition. By 480 BCE a council was called to ratify the Buddha's teachings. The aim of this council, held in Rajgir, was to agree a definitive version of the Buddha's message.

By 380 BCE, a second council was called at Vesali to ensure that the *Vinaya* – the code of discipline – was adhered to by all Buddhist monks. At this gathering, differences of opinion arose as to what the Buddha actually taught. At this point the first division in the Buddha's followers arose. This division increased until, eventually, two main schools in Buddhism emerged. One became known as the *Mahayana*, meaning 'Great Vehicle', and the other comprised a number of more conservative groups, of which the surviving example was the *Theravada*, meaning 'Way of the Elders'. The Mahayana spread north-west from India into present-day Nepal, China, Tibet, Japan, Korea and Vietnam. Theravada Buddhism spread southwards into Sri Lanka, Burma, Thailand, Cambodia and Laos.

leaf from the Bodhi tree with Buddha image

The Theravada Scriptures

It is said that the first Buddhist scriptures were written down by Theravada monks at the fourth council in Sri Lanka, during the first century BCE. They used the ancient colloquial Indian language of Pali, spoken by the Buddha. The scriptures were written on palm leaves and became known as the *Pali Canon* or *Tipitaka*. The term tipitaka means 'three baskets', which refers to the threefold division of the scriptures, known as *Vinaya Pitaka*, *Sutta Pitaka* and *Abhidhamma Pitaka*.

The *Tipitaka*

The *Vinaya* is the book of discipline for monks containing the 227 rules by which they must live. The *Sutta Pitaka* contains the teachings of the Buddha on the Four Noble Truths, Eightfold Path and the popular Buddhist literature that constitutes the *Dhammapada* and the *Jataka Tales*. *Sutta* means 'thread', and indicates the connection seen to exist between the different teachings of the Buddha that constitutes the overall world view of the tradition. *Dhammapada* means 'Path of Truth'. It consists of an anthology of the Buddha's sayings, collected between 563 and 483 BCE. They act as a source of guidance for Buddhists everywhere but especially for those in the Theravada tradition. The *Jataka Tales* are a collection of stories of the Buddha's previous lives. They focus on the Ten Perfections which lead to perfect Buddhahood: generosity, virtue, renunciation, wisdom, energy, patience, truthfulness, resolution, loving kindness and an even temper. The *Abhidhamma Pitaka* contains the more philosophical teachings which underpin the Buddhist understanding of life. They were intended as a basis of the Buddhist outlook which opposed other Indian conceptions of reality. They are essentially philosophical and psychological, arguing the Buddhist perspective against other prevailing philosophical positions in the Indian sub-continent, and are the source of its doctrinal formulations.

The *Dhammapada*

The *Dhammapada*, however, remains the most common source of inspiration to which lay Buddhists refer. Its teachings and value can perhaps best be indicated by quoting from the text itself.

The verses below refer to controlling the mind:

> The mind is wavering and restless, difficult to guard and restrain: let the wise man straighten his mind as a maker of arrows makes his arrows straight ...

> The mind is fickle and flighty, it flies after fancies wherever it likes: it is difficult indeed to restrain. But it is a great good to control the mind; a mind self-controlled is a source of great joy ...

> An enemy can hurt an enemy, and a man who hates can hurt another man; but a man's own mind, if wrongly directed, can do him a far greater harm.

> A father or a mother, or a relative, can indeed do good to a man; but his own right-directed mind can do to him a far greater good.

> (Translation J. Mascaro, Penguin, 1973, p 40)

The *Jatakas*

Equally, the example of the Buddha on his route to enlightenment through previous lives, is exemplified in the following story from the *Jatakas*:

The Bodhisattva and the Hungry Tigress

The Buddha told the following story to Ananda: Once upon a time, in the remote past, there lived a king, Maharatha by name. He was rich in gold, grain and chariots, and his power, strength, and courage were irresistible. He had three sons who were like young gods to look at. They were named Mahapranada, Mahadeva and Mahasattva.

One day the king went for relaxation into a park. The princes, delighted with the beauties of the park and the flowers which could be seen everywhere, walked about here and there until they came to a large thicket of bamboos. There they dismissed their servants, in order to rest for a while. But Mahapranada said to his two brothers: 'I feel rather afraid here. There might easily be some wild beasts about, and they might do us harm.' Mahadeva replied: 'I also feel ill at ease. Though it is not my body I fear for. It is the thought of separation from those I love which terrifies me.'

As the princes strolled about in the solitary thicket they saw a tigress, surrounded by five cubs, seven days old.

Hunger and thirst had exhausted the tigress, and her body was quite weak. On seeing her, Mahapranada called out: 'The poor animal suffers from having given birth to the five cubs only a week ago! If she finds nothing to eat, she will either eat her own young or die from hunger!' Mahasattva replied: 'How can this poor exhausted creature find food?' Mahapranada said: 'Tigers live on fresh meat and warm blood.' Mahadeva said: 'She is quite exhausted, overcome by hunger and thirst, scarcely alive and very weak. In this state she cannot possibly catch any prey. And who would sacrifice himself to preserve her life?' Mahapranada said: 'Yes, self-sacrifice is so difficult!'

Greatly agitated, the three brothers carefully watched the tigress for some time, and then went towards her. But Mahasattva thought to himself: 'Now the time has come for me to sacrifice myself! For a long time I have served this putrid body and given it beds and clothes, food and drink, and conveyances of all kinds. Yet it is doomed to perish and fall down, and in the end it will break up and be destroyed. How much better to leave this ungrateful body of one's own accord in good time! It cannot subsist for ever, because it is like urine which must come out.

'Today I will use it for a sublime deed.'

'For the weal of the world I wish to win enlightenment, incomparably wonderful. From deep compassion I now give away my body, so hard to quit, unshaken in my mind.'

The friendly prince then threw himself down in front of the tigress. But she did nothing to him. The Bodhisattva noticed that she was too weak to move. As a merciful man he had taken no sword with him. He therefore cut his throat with a sharp piece of bamboo, and fell down near the tigress. She noticed the Bodhisattva's body all covered with blood, and in no time ate up all the flesh and blood, leaving only the bones.

'It was I, Ananda, who at that time and on that occasion was that prince Mahasattva.'

(E. Conze (trans), *Buddhist Scriptures*,
Penguin Classics, 1959, pp 24–6)

The significance of this story is, of course, not that we should look for opportunities to sacrifice ourselves, but that we should recognize the need to act compassionately. Not an easy task in the course of life, but a signal that our own value lies beyond our usual preoccupations.

The arahant

The highest aspiration in Theravada Buddhism is to become an *arahant* (*arhat*), or one who has passed beyond the fetters of samsaric existence.

> Ah happy indeed the Arahants! In them is no craving found. The 'I am' conceit is rooted out; confusion's net is burst, lust free they have attained; translucent is the mind of them.
>
> (*Samyutta Nikaya* III:83)

The arahant is the ideal of the Theravadin school. The word refers to those saints or sages who, having followed the Buddha's teachings, upon death, will enter into nibbana (nirvana). They are fully emancipated.

The scriptures describe an arahant by a standard formula, as one in whom the 'outflows' (sense desire, becoming, ignorance, wrong views) have 'dried up'; one who has 'done what has to be done'. However, the question remained (and later exercised Buddhist thinkers) as to the distinction between an arahant and a buddha. It was this distinction that the Mahayana school exploited, indicating that the ideal of arahantship and the goal of nibbana were inferior to the larger aspiration of buddhahood and the bodhisattva path (described later), which accentuated the virtues of compassion, and of gaining emancipation for the sake of others rather than for one's own entry into nirvana.

The Mahayana Scriptures

The spread of Buddhism in different directions resulted in a diversity of doctrines and scriptures. For the Theravadins, the authenticity of the scriptures was determined by which texts, historically, actually came from the Buddha himself. But in opposition to this, Mahayana Buddhists asserted that certain other scriptures were just as authoritative, even though they could not be traced back to the Buddha in a historical way. They claimed authority more by mythological connection than historical. For example, the *Prajna Paramita Sutras* (the teachings on Perfect Wisdom), which are scriptures of great significance in the Mahayana tradition, are said to have been revealed by the Buddha himself, but were too difficult to be understood by his contemporaries. Because of this they were stored in the palace of the *nagas* (serpents) in the Nether World. When the time was right to reveal them the great Buddhist thinker, Nagarjuna, brought them back into the human realm.

The Mahayana scriptures are written in the ancient, classical Indian language of Sanskrit. Mahayana texts vary in form and introduce both mythological and philosophical features not found in the *Theravada*. Siddhartha, the historical Buddha, often takes on a more mystical and poetic character. An important development was the Mahayana emphasis on the accessibility of other Buddhas, that he was not the only Buddha: there were others before him and others yet to come. While the Theravadins did not deny this, they didn't regard these various Buddhas as accessible in the present time. Visiting a Tibetan shrine room, one is struck by the plethora of forms of enlightened beings. These represent particular qualities or energies, and appear not in strictly naturalistic form, but expressing their symbolic significance. Thus, for example, Avalokiteshvara represents the quality of compassion, Manjushri represents the quality of wisdom.

Avalokiteshvara   Manjushri

Most significantly, in one of these representations Avalokiteshvara has one thousand hands, each containing an eye. This indicates his ability to see all and extend his service to the suffering of all living beings. Manjushri wields a sword which represents the capacity of wisdom to cut through all ignorance.

Behind these representations is the development of doctrine, which serves to explain them.

The bodhisattva

The *bodhisattva*, literally *bodhi* (enlightened) and *sattva* (essence), is a being who delays his entry into nirvana in order to help all sentient beings. Out of compassion, he or she returns to the samsaric realm to help others along the path.

The *Diamond Sutra* says: 'A bodhisattva is not attached to anything when he gives, like a person in the daylight who can see things as they really are.' For this reason Mahayana Buddhists take what is called the Bodhisattva vow, which states:

> The deluding passions are inexhaustible.
> I vow to extinguish them all.
> Sentient beings are numberless.
> I vow to save them all.
> The truth is impossible to expound.
> I vow to expound it.
> The way of the Buddha is unattainable.
> I vow to attain it.

Such an exercise in idealism has to have a rationale. This is located in the Mahayana emphasis on no-self, which denies individualism or 'self-ness' in all its forms. The *Diamond Sutra* explains this in the following way:

> If a bodhisattva has any notion of a being, a person, or a self, he could not be called a bodhisattva. A bodhisattva should not give a gift while basing himself on the notion of form, sound, smell, taste, touch, or while basing himself on any thought. He should give without the notion of a giver or a gift. That great being who gives without basing himself on any notion, his merit is not easy to measure.
>
> (*Diamond Sutra* 3)

This idea is based on the teachings of the *Prajna Paramita*. The wisdom of a bodhisattva is perfect, and goes beyond the wisdom of the world. It fully understands the absence of abiding entities, such as selfhood. It is based on the notion of *sunyata*, meaning emptiness or void.

Sunyata

The *Heart Sutra* states:

> In emptiness there is no form, nor feeling, nor perception,
> nor impulse, nor consciousness; no eye, ear, nose, tongue,
> body, mind; no forms, sounds, smells, tastes, touchables
> or objects of mind; no sight-organ elements, and so forth
> until we come to no mind-consciousness element.
>
> (*Heart Sutra* 5)

Sunyata, according to the Madhyamika school of thought,
central to Mahahyana Buddhism, rests on the logic of giving up
all views. Views and perceptions of reality are ultimately false
because they rely on conceptual constructs. Conceptual
constructs rely on dualistic thinking (i.e. every construct evokes
its opposite, from hot–cold to real–unreal, absolute–relative).
Since this is the case, no conceptual construct can be a reflection
of reality. All conceptual constructs are the creation of the
samsaric mind and thus delusory. Once this is understood, the
emptying of the mind of these constructs is the equivalence of
what is called nirvana. *Sunyata* (emptiness) is the term given to
this. It is not nihilation since that would presume the positive
value of the constructs that have been negated. Rather it is the
negation of the negative. From the negative (samsaric) point of
view, emptiness is a lack; nirvanically, it is the apotheosis. Thus
it can also be equated with what, samsarically, we lack: bliss
(the contrary of dis-ease or suffering). However, having moved
beyond conceptual constructs in this realization we have moved
beyond their expression, in language. Therefore, what is being
pointed to is beyond our capability to communicate
linguistically. As a correlate to this understanding comes the
recognition that awareness of our Buddha-nature, that synthesis
of wisdom and compassion, is not developed by intellectual
means alone even though the logic of the intellect has been used
to expose the falsity of our conceptual constructs of the world.

Here we have arrived at a highly abstruse philosophical position
which, nevertheless, has important practical consequences. In
order to live well in this world, attain our inherent buddha-
nature, and avoid rebirth, selflessness has to be realized through
developing wisdom and compassion. So, in the *Mahayana*,
cultivating insight and devotion go hand in hand. This creative
process neither ignores the intellect nor renders it supreme. As a
consequence, the relationship between the monastic sangha and

lay life becomes closer. The way to buddhahood becomes broader, without lessening the qualities aspired to. The bodhisattva path is rooted in the practice of the six perfections: patience, giving, morality, vigour, meditation and wisdom. The difficulties encountered in this are poetically described in the career of Avalokiteshvara.

Avalokiteshvara

It is said that Avalokiteshvara was entrusted with the task of rescuing all living beings from samsara. In attempting to accomplish this he grew exhausted and despaired. At this moment he gave vent to tears that fell to the ground and grew as lotuses (illustrating the creative power of his compassion). From these lotus flowers were born the Bodhisattvas Green and White Tara. Their destiny was to assist him in his task. As an indication of this, Green Tara is always depicted with one foot released from the meditation posture towards the ground, illustrating her readiness to come to the aid of suffering beings. There is also a story that removes Tara from the mythological realm, indicating not only the practicality of the doctrine of compassion, but also the ignorance of thinking that form is the means of detecting the presence of a compassionate being. This story goes as follows:

> In lifetime after lifetime Tara has manifested in female form, demonstrating that enlightenment is attainable by all – men and women alike.

> Once there was a lone traveller making his perilous way across the forbidding plateau of Tibet. Exhausted and without food he was in immediate danger of losing his life when he came across a young girl tending a herd of yaks. She took the weary man into her tent, nursed him back to health and fed him until his strength returned. As the man was recovering he observed that the young girl was alone. Single-handedly she was doing the work that even a number of strong men would have found difficult. Eventually he was fit to travel again and the girl sent him on his way with a bag of provisions. Although it was a long journey, the man discovered that the food she had given him never ran out until he was back in his own valley again. Marvelling at all that had happened he thought, 'Perhaps that girl was actually Tara!' When he went to his lama and told him the story, the lama upbraided him saying 'Of course she was Tara, you blockhead! How stupid of you not to recognize her. You

must have a strong connection with her, but if you ever want to see her again you had better purify your delusions and practise harder.'

(J. Landaw, *Tara's Colouring Book*, Wisdom Publications, 1979)

Green Tara

White Tara

The Three Body Doctrine

Clearly, this development of the idea of buddhahood to include the historical Buddha, buddhas of other ages, and the principle of sunyata, or voidness, needed to be systematically expounded; we find this in the Three Body (Trikaya) Doctrine.

The historical Buddha (Siddhartha Gautama) was identified as the *nirmanakaya* (form body), a particular expression in one place and time of the eternal truths of the dharma. The *dharmakaya* was identified as the eternal principle of Truth, which transcended space and time. Through meditation and devotion Buddhists came to describe images of buddhas which are not historical but which are archetypal. These are identified as *sambhogakaya* (bliss bodies). Each of these different images represents a particular aspect of the enlightenment experience. They are a more refined understanding of the nature of enlightenment than the Buddha as an historical figure, pointing to the more abstract awareness of the idea of the ultimate truth expressed in the idea of dharmakaya.

The *Lotus Sutra*

The *Lotus Sutra*, or *Lotus of the True Law* (*Saddharma Pundarika*), is often referred to by some Mahayana Buddhists as the final teaching of the Buddha, and thus has a venerated place in the *Mahayana Canon*. One emphasis for which it is acclaimed is its teaching on 'upaya' or 'skill in means'. We have already referred to skilfulness but it is expounded at great length in this particular text.

The *Lotus Sutra* explains that there are different teachings used by the Buddha to encourage the faithful to perfect buddhahood, according to their individual propensities and capacities. All the same, though there may be said to be many paths to the same goal, they all constitute aspects of one vehicle, that is, one overall path, that of the Bodhisattva Mahasattva or Great Being. However, the *Lotus Sutra* allows the Buddhist message to become available to all, relative to their particular capacities. It is an acknowledgement that people do not start in the same place with regard to their apprehension of the truth. In much the same way, to teach quantum physics to a child would be an unproductive way of furthering their development. This idea is explained in the *Parable of the Burning House*.

The Parable of the Burning House

A father owns an old house which, while he is out, catches on fire. He hears his own children still playing in the house, unaware that it is burning. Absorbed in their amusement, the children pay no attention to their father calling them out of the house. He then tells them he has special carts of different kinds for each of them to play with, and encourages the children to run out and find them. Once out of the house and free from danger, they find the carts are all the same – but better than any of them had expected.

The burning house is the samsaric world in which, foolishly, we are absorbed, like the children. The father is the Buddha who finds a way to deliver us from our predicament through his skill in means (upaya). Firstly, he offers gifts to get the children out of the house. Secondly, he offers them their favourite carts to encourage each of them.

From the perspective of the Lotus Sutra, the inferior carts represent the early teachings of the Hinayana (lesser vehicle) which, nevertheless, were a skilful means of getting the Buddha's followers to start on the path that leads to nirvana.

The final, best cart that the children find outside the house represents the higher ideal of perfect Buddhahood, as taught in this sutra.

Again, we see the emphasis on the practical significance of teaching in Buddhism. The *Lotus Sutra* acknowledges that it is not one's understanding at the beginning of the journey that matters, but whether the teacher can skilfully lead his or her pupils to the appropriate final understanding. Thus this teaching recognizes that the dharma is understood by various means and achieved by different strategies. It constitutes a pragmatic realism that is nevertheless not open ended, but carefully planned. It allows for a great diversity in the same way that the branches of Mahayana Buddhism developed without causing schism. This served the tradition well as it transplanted itself into the various cultures of China, Tibet and Japan.

The *Lotus Sutra* is not an easy text to read. It does not have the strict formulation of the Theravada Scriptures. Rather, it reads like a mystery play set in a super-mundane world, where the Lord Buddha reveals the immense span of his existences and the illusory way in which he appears to enter nirvana, but actually continues his bodhisattva career endlessly for the salvation of all beings. He appears in whatever guise is suitable for the furtherance of his subjects, and offers them teachings and practices suitable to their capacities. Gone is the austerity of Theravada practice as a single route to nirvana. The world is a phantasmagorical place quite beyond the ken of ordinary mortals.

Emphasis on faith in the Buddha's authority to release us from suffering is a key theme. The Buddha states:

> I reveal the law in its multifariousness with regard to the inclinations and dispositions of creatures.

> I use different means to raise each according to his own character. Such is the might of my knowledge.

> *(Lotus Sutra 2)*

> Hence we will raise many Bodhisattvas by the display of skilfulness and the encouraging of the wish of obtaining fruits.

> *(Lotus Sutra 2)*

In his omniscience the Buddha reveals that the destiny of all creatures is buddhahood – nothing less. The most important issue is erasing the self-imposed ignorance that blinds beings from seeing the truth. Even devout Buddhists suffer this continuing blindness. A constant theme of the *Sutra* is that Theravada Buddhists are blinded by their short-sighted conception of nirvana as the ultimate goal. Arhathood (the saintly aim of the Theravadins) and Pratyekabuddhahood (the aim of those who have become enlightened, but who have chosen not to preach the dharma to others) are indications of this limited awareness. What has now been revealed is far beyond their thinking. But the Buddha will, ultimately, lead them to this recognition.

The Parable of the Rain Cloud expresses this clearly:

> Like unto a great cloud the Tathagatha appears and sends forth his call to the whole world … lifts his voice and utters these words: 'I am the Tathagatha, O ye gods and men! The Arhat and the perfectly enlightened one; having reached the shore myself I carry others to the shore … By my perfect wisdom I know both this world and the next as they really are. I am all-knowing, all-seeing …
>
> 'I shall refresh all beings whose bodies are withered, who are clogged in the triple world.'
>
> 'I shall bring to felicity those that are pining away with toils, give them pleasures and final rest.'
>
> So, it is the very nature of the law to promote the everlasting weal of the world; by the law the whole world is recreated, and as the plants, when refreshed, expand their blossoms, the world does the same when refreshed.
>
> So then, Kasyapa, is the preaching of the law, like the water poured out by the cloud everywhere alike; by which plants and men thrive, endless and eternal blossoms are produced.
>
> (*Lotus Sutra* 5)

The power of this poetic vision of a boundless creative and benevolent energy, producing creativity and happiness as it overcomes samsaric conditions by moving the world towards its final destiny, contrasts with the emphasis of the Theravadin teachings. Its liberating salvific message became the foundation of popular Buddhism across Northern Asia.

Pure Land Buddhism

When Buddhism reached China and Japan many new schools of thought developed; two of these were particularly influential: the Pure Land School and the Ch'an (Chinese) or Zen (Japanese) School.

The two *Sukhavativyuha Sutras*, written in the second century CE, describe a Pure Land (*Sukhavati*) free from suffering. Sukhavati is a spiritual realm created by the Buddha, which is conducive to spiritual progress. It is a state of bliss (sukkha) and as such is the opposite of the samsaric realm we presently inhabit, which is marked by the pervasiveness of dukkha (unsatisfactoriness). The scriptures describe the Pure Land as 'a world called Sukhavati where there is neither bodily or mental pain for living beings. The sources of happiness are innumerable.'

The *Sukhavativyuha Sutras* gave rise to a Buddhism of faith during the fifth and sixth centuries CE in China. It revolved around the Pure Land of Amitabha (Amida in Japanese) who is the Buddha of infinite Light and Compassion. To be reborn into his Pure Land, one only has to call his name ten times at the point of death and he will appear and escort his devotee to Sukhavati. While in the present world gaining enlightenment is difficult, in death one will be helped on the path to that goal.

This is a Buddhism of Faith, in which the principal means of salvation is the invocation of the name of the Buddha, which will ensure attainment of a state from which there is no falling back. Its popularity was rooted in its ranking equally with more rigorous meditative practices and lifestyles through which wisdom was accomplished. For many lay Buddhists, especially those whose situations in life and possibilities of education were limited, this provided a suitable path. It also emphasized the Mahayanist teaching on the universality of salvation, because scholarly progress and monasticism were no longer required.

In the modern world, this form of Buddhist practice is particularly stressed by the followers of Nichiren Daishonin, a Japanese master of the thirteenth century, who established his own Nishiren school of Buddhism. He regarded the *Lotus Sutra* as the supreme teaching of the Buddha, and faith as the supreme attribute. Faith is increased by daily chanting of the *Gongyo*, the fruits of which are more positive energy and a deeper, more positive outlook as faith thereby increases. Chanting the mantra 'Nam–myoho– renge–kyo' assiduously and mindfully becomes a practice of purification, which will affect daily living and develop wisdom and compassion. In his teachings Nichiren Daishonin stated:

> The common mortal himself is the Buddha when he single-mindedly chants Nam-myoho-renge-kyo with strong faith. This is how he attains enlightenment naturally without discarding his life as a common mortal.
>
> (Honninnmyo Sho, quoted in J. Cowan (ed.),
> *The Buddhism of the Sun*, Nichiren Shoshu of the
> United Kingdom, 1982, p 78)

'Nam–myoho–renge–kyo' is rendered as 'devotion (*nam*) to the *Lotus Sutra*', the supreme law or all-embracing truth which, by implication, is buddhahood itself.

The Ch'an and Zen Schools

Ch'an (Chinese) and Zen (Japanese) are derived from the Indian word *dhyana*, which refers to meditation. As Buddhism extended into China, then Japan, so the meditation school developed from the teachings and practice of the sixth-century Indian monk, Bodhidharma. Ironically, Bodhidharma's message was that the tradition had become too attached to the scriptures, and that the Buddha's teaching was understood by simply watching the mind or looking into one's own heart (hence the emphasis on meditation, seen as a stripping away of external trappings). Such simplicity of expression was well-suited to a Chinese culture much influenced by Taoist philosophy, which also emphasised a one-pointedness of mind, a seeing to the heart of the matter within our everyday life but beyond our everyday understanding, as this verse illustrates:

> Thirty spokes share one hub.
> Adapt the nothing therein to the purpose in hand, and you will have the use of the cart.
> Knead clay in order to make a vessel.
> Adapt the nothing therein to the purpose in hand, and you will have the use of the vessel.
> Cut out doors and windows in order to make a room.
> Adapt the nothing therein to the purpose in hand, and you will have the use of the room.
> Thus what we gain is Something, yet it is by virtue of Nothing that this can be put to use.
>
> (Lao Tzu, *Tao Te Ching*, Penguin, 1968, p 67)

This represented a rigorous refusal to indulge in scriptural study or philosophical debate, in favour of a purely intuitive approach to enlightenment. Though the meditation school appeals to scripture to ground its practices in the authority of the Buddha, it does so only to support the efficacy of meditation as an end in itself, as the truth realized in action.

'Directly pointing to the mind' and 'becoming a Buddha just as you are' involves doing away with all thought, which is the means of attachment to the external world. The effect of this is to see into one's own Buddha-nature, which is obscured by defilements and attachments. Enlightenment may come suddenly or gradually. Either way, the intuiting of Truth involves the cultivation of the mind so that it is in sharp focus and constantly alert. Thus moments of pure awareness (*satori*) arise. As it developed, the meditation tradition identified patriarchs, enlightened teachers who developed their own techniques for training their pupils and became founders of branches of the tradition. These techniques were often novel and unorthodox. For example, the followers of Lin-Chi used the 'lightning' method of scolding and beating disciples. Ts'ao-tung masters preferred the question-and-answer method, whereby the disciple would be interviewed by his master to test his capacity to intuit the truth.

The story of the enlightenment of the sixth patriarch, Hui-Neng, illustrates the character of Ch'an teaching well:

Hui-Neng: The Sixth Patriarch
One day the Fifth Patriarch (Hung-Jen) suddenly called all his pupils to come to him. As they assembled, he said, 'Let me say this to you. Birth and death are serious matters. You people are engaged all day in making offerings (to the Buddha), going after blessings and rewards only, and you make no effort to achieve freedom from the bitter sea of life and death. Your self-nature seems to be obscured. How can blessings save you? Go to your rooms and examine yourselves. He who is enlightened use his perfect vision of self-nature and write me a verse. When I look at his verse, if it reveals deep understanding, I shall give him the robe and the Law and make him the Sixth Patriarch. Hurry, hurry!'

At midnight Shen-Hsui, holding a candle, wrote a verse on the wall of the south corridor, without anyone knowing about it, which said:

> Our body is the tree of Perfect Wisdom,
> And our mind is a bright mirror.
> At all times diligently wipe them,
> So that they will be free from dust.

The Fifth Patriarch said: 'The verse you wrote shows some but not all understanding. You have arrived at the front of the door but you have not yet entered it. Ordinary people, by practising in accordance with your verse, will not degenerate. But it will be futile to seek the Supreme Perfect Wisdom while holding to such a view. One must enter the door and see his self-nature. Go away and come back after one or two days of thought. If you have entered the door and seen your self-nature, I shall give you the robe and the Law.'

Shen-Hsui went away and for several days could not produce another verse.

Hui-Neng also wrote a verse ... which said:

> The tree of Perfect Wisdom is originally no tree.
> Nor has the bright mirror any frame.
> Buddha-nature is forever clear and pure.
> Where is there any dust?

and another verse:

> The mind is the tree of Perfect Wisdom.
> The body is the clear mirror.
> The clear mirror is originally clear and pure.
> Where has it been affected by any dust?

Monks in the hall were all surprised at these verses. Hui-Neng, however, went back to the rice-pounding room. The Fifth Patriarch suddenly realized that Hui-Neng was the one of good knowledge but was afraid lest the rest learn it. He therefore told them: 'This will not do.'

The Fifth Patriarch waited till midnight, called Hui-Neng to come to the hall, and expounded the *Diamond Sutra*. As soon as Hui-Neng heard this, he understood. That night the Law was imparted to him without anyone knowing it, and thus the Law and the robe of Sudden Enlightenment were transmitted to him. 'You are now the Sixth Patriarch,' said the Fifth Patriarch to Hui-Neng. 'The robe is the testimony of transmission from generation to generation. As to the Law, it is to be transmitted from mind to mind. Let people achieve understanding through their own effort.'

(Wm. Theodore De Barry (ed.), *Sources of Chinese Tradition*, Columbia University Press, 1960, p 350)

Characteristic of Zen is the refusal to give 'right answers', as though truth can be passed on just by hearing or reading a teaching. The master's skill lies in knowing exactly what the disciple requires to free his mind from attachment. Attachment may come in many forms and the mind can be freed from particular attachments in many ways. Zen stories (*mondos*) catalogue this highly practical method of teaching.

Here are two examples:

A Cup of Tea

Nan-in, a Japanese master during the Meiji era (1868–1912), received a university professor who came to inquire about Zen. Nan-in served tea. He poured his visitor's cup full, and then kept on pouring. The professor watched the overflow until he no longer could restrain himself. 'It is overfull. No more will go in!' 'Like this cup,' Nan-in said, 'you are full of your own opinions and speculations. How can I show you Zen unless you first empty your cup?'

(P. Reps, *Zen Flesh, Zen Bones*, Pelican, 1972, p 17)

Happy Chinaman

Anyone walking about Chinatowns in America will observe statues of a stout fellow carrying a linen sack. Chinese merchants call him Happy Chinaman or Laughing Buddha.

This Hotei lived in the T'ang dynasty. He had no desire to call himself a Zen master or to gather many disciples about him. Instead he walked the streets with a big sack into which he would put gifts of candy, fruit, or doughnuts. These he would give to children who gathered around him in play. He established a kindergarten of the streets.

Whenever he met a Zen devotee he would extend his hand and say, 'Give me one penny.' And if anyone asked him to return to a temple to teach others, again he would reply: 'Give me one penny.'

Once as he was about his play-work another Zen master happened along and inquired: 'What is the significance of Zen?'

Hotei immediately plopped his sack down on the ground in silent answer.

'Then,' asked the other, 'what is the actualization of Zen?'

At once the Happy Chinaman swung the sack over his shoulder and continued on his way.

(P. Reps, *Zen Flesh, Zen Bones*, Pelican, 1972, p 27)

The following story illustrates a particularly famous Zen technique, know as the *koan*, which is used to stop the discriminating mind with its reliance on intellectual understanding.

The Sound of One Hand

The master of Kennin temple was Mokurai, Silent Thunder. He had a little protege named Toyo who was only twelve years old. Toyo saw the older disciples visit the master's room each morning and evening to receive instructions in *sanzen,* or personal guidance, in which they were given koans to stop mind-wandering.

Toyo wished to do sanzen also. 'Wait a while,' said Mokurai. 'You are too young.'

But the child insisted, so the teacher finally consented.

In the evening little Toyo went at the proper time to the threshold of Mokurai's sanzen room. He struck the gong to announce his presence, bowed respectfully three times outside the door, and went to sit before the master in respectful silence.

'You can hear the sound of two hands when they clap together,' said Mokurai. 'Now show me the sound of one hand.'

Toyo bowed and went to his room to consider this problem. From his window he could hear the music of the geishas. 'Ah, I have it!' he proclaimed.

The next evening, when his teacher asked him to illustrate the sound of one hand, Toyo began to play the music of the geishas.

'No, no,' said Mokurai. 'That will never do. That is not the sound of one hand. You've not got it at all.'

Thinking that such music might interrupt, Toyo moved his abode to a quiet place. He meditated again. 'What can the sound of one hand be?' He happened to hear some water dripping. 'I have it,' imagined Toyo.

When he next appeared before his teacher, Toyo imitated dripping water.

'What is that?' asked Mokurai. 'That is the sound of dripping water, but not the sound of one hand. Try again.'

In vain Toyo meditated to hear the sound of one hand. He heard the sighing of the wind. But the sound was rejected. He heard the cry of an owl. This also was refused. The sound of one hand was not the locusts.

For more than ten times Toyo visited Mokurai with different sounds. All were wrong. For almost a year he pondered what the sound of one hand might be.

At last little Toyo entered true meditation and transcended all sounds. 'I could collect no more,' he explained later, 'so I reached the soundless sound.'

Toyo had realized the sound of one hand.

(P. Reps, *Zen Flesh, Zen Bones*, Pelican, 1972, pp 34–5)

Rinzai and Soto Zen

The branches into which Zen split, the Rinzai and Soto Zen, emphasized the koan and silent sitting respectively, as techniques for attaining this 'pure seeing' into the true nature of things. Nevertheless, these two schools are not entirely distinct in their practices. As one writer has observed:

In the Rinzai sect we find the dynamic character of the daring koan experiment and of lightning-like enlightenment, while the Soto School is characterized by a preference for silent sitting in zazen and the quiet deeds of everyday life … It appears (in Japan) … that adherence to one sect or the other is determined largely by the spiritual bent of the monks, who are inherently suited to one tradition or the other and pursue enlightenment in a way appropriate to their character. Thus one can find in the temples of the Soto sect men of brilliant wit and dynamic character who devote themselves to the koan exercises, while on the other hand certain Rinzai monks of subdued character can scarcely be distinguished from Soto disciples.

(N. Wilson Ross, *Hinduism, Buddhism, Zen*, Faber and Faber, 1973, p 156)

Zen cultural life

Japanese culture has been greatly influenced by Zen Buddhism. Its techniques pervade such arts and skills as flower arranging and archery, as well as being the foundation of traditional ceremonies, most famously the Tea Ceremony. In literature it gave birth to the *haiku*, the seventeen-syllable poem that points to the Buddha-nature, or pure-reality, being everywhere in the here and now. It illustrates the typically Zen emphasis on the paradox that the everyday and the wonder of enlightenment are but one and the same thing:

> How marvellous, how miraculous,
> I draw water
> I carry fuel.

The Tibetan Scriptures

Buddhism entered Tibet around 650 CE, but it was not until a century later that it overcame fierce resistance from the indigenous Bon religion, with its shamanic heritage and patronage of the Tibetan nobility. As so often with religious incursion, it was the support of rulership that caused changes in fortune. This was true of the spread of Christianity within the Roman world, under the reign of the emperor Constantine, and the proliferation of Buddhism in India under the emperor Ashoka. So in Tibet, once patronage moved from Bon to Buddhism, it flourished under the reign of Ral-pa-can (817–36 CE). Monasteries and temples were erected, and teachers were brought from India, which propagated the translation of the scriptures.

The relationship with the Bon tradition was not wholly one of animosity, and Padmasambhava, one of the most revered of Tibetan saints, did much as an Indian missionary to realign hostile forces, through his particular interpretation of practices and teachings. Buddhism also entered Tibet from China, though its impact was less successful; the character of Tibetan Buddhism illustrates Indian influence rather than Chinese.

It should also be noted that relations between Tibet and China have generally been full of unease, due to both Tibetan and Chinese imperialism, which has resurfaced today in the annexing of Tibet and the exile of the Dalai Lama, regarded by some as head of both religious authority and State in Tibet, though this is disputed.

Tibet has largely been isolated as a kingdom and culture over the majority of its history, and this has been both a blessing and a curse from the Buddhist point of view. The blessing is that it was able to preserve and develop the Mahayana teachings in a distinctive way over 1,000 years, with little interference. Indeed, it became recognized as a secret kingdom, seen as the repository of Buddhist wisdom by many Westerners, and was the subject of various forms of pilgrimage in the early part of the twentieth century. Westerners who came to Tibet included Heinrich Harrer, the German prisoner of war who wrote *Seven Years in Tibet*; Alexandra David-Neel, who wrote *With Mystics and Magicians in Tibet* and W.Y. Evans-Wentz who translated *The Tibetan Book of the Dead*.

The drawback was that such distinctive and ancient teachings as Tibet possessed (along with the traditions and schools which progressed from them) did not become known to the outside world until the Chinese invasion in 1959, and the subsequent dispersion of lamas and teachers to India and the West. Today there are Western scholars working with Tibetan teachers to make known the teachings and practices which had been preserved in Tibet, and Tibetan teachers and their disciples are at the head of evolving traditions in the West.

There are four main Tibetan traditions alive today: the Nyingma, Kagya, Sakya and Geluk, each of which possess a wealth of oral and written teachings. The scriptures are classified under the following titles: the *Kangyur*, meaning 'the translation of the word', which are discourses attributed to the historical Buddha; and the *Tengyur*, which are the *shastras* (commentaries on the original teachings, translated from Indian originals). In addition to these, numerous explanatory works were written in Tibetan.

The importance of Tibetan Buddhism and its scriptures is not so much that it is specifically Tibetan, but that a great deal of the corpus of Mahayana Buddhist literature, and the maintenance of its tradition, would not have survived had it not been harboured in Tibet.

Tibetan scriptures and practices can appear obscure to uninitiated Westerners; this is not surprising given Tibet's isolated history. But one of the principal emphases that underlies its tradition is the need to learn from an enlightened teacher. As one western Tibetan Buddhist writes:

> Lost in the middle of a dense, dark forest, drowning in a wild and savage sea, locked in chains in a lonely dungeon, we rely on the wisdom, power and compassion of those who can set us free. To escape from the stifling darkness of ignorance, from the raging tides of the delusions, from the iron chains of karma, we must turn to an enlightened guide. Since we need a qualified teacher to learn such simple skills as reading, writing and mathematics, how can we think to travel the long and difficult path of Dharma alone? It is absolutely essential to follow a spiritual master who has passed that way himself. Finding the right spiritual master is the most important thing in life; following him correctly is the root of the path to enlightenment.

(Nicholas Ribush, 'A Profile of Tibetan Buddhism', in P. Connolly and C. Erricker, *The Presence and Practice of Buddhism*, West Sussex Institute of Higher Education, 1985, p 72)

Another preoccupation of Tibetan teaching is the relationship between life and death. This arises mainly due to the significance of tantric teaching in Tibetan tradition. *Tantra* represents the quick path to enlightenment in one lifetime, by grasping the opportunity of a human birth not to be wasted. It also stresses the importance of confronting our negative impulses and fears during this rebirth. Death is seen as the ultimate fear or barrier, because it represents an annihilation of our identity (as we perceive it). *The Tibetan Book of the Dead* attains an especial importance, since it deals with how to find our way through the period between death and rebirth. This concept is referred to as the 'Art of Dying', which is seen as the most significant liberating experience in Tibetan Buddhist terms.

The Tibetans understand there to be a state between dying and being reborn, referred to as the *bardo* state. During this time the individual will follow a course that leads to liberation or a consequent rebirth according to his or her attachments. This journey is dependent on our last thoughts in our present life, and the course that they initiate, rather like a train of thought that is pursued, from its inception in thinking about either positive or negative impulses (for example, a day when we wake up with a negative or positive frame of mind). It is claimed that reading *The Tibetan Book of the Dead* to a dying person will initiate them into the process of dying in a positive frame of mind, and therefore ensure either a positive rebirth or freedom from rebirth entirely. Aldous Huxley is one Westerner who adhered to this philosophy and followed its practice, despite the adverse criticism that ensued from the American press and subsequent biographies.

The Buddhist rationale for such a practice is that our past thinking has determined our present status, and our present thinking will determine our future status. This is rooted in scriptural understanding and the significance of karmic influence. What *The Tibetan Book of the Dead* (*Bardo Thodol*) points to is the most significant event in our lives – our own demise – for which we have a whole lifetime either to prepare for or to ignore. It indicates the importance of preparation for the ultimate test of our earthly achievement, when all else that we rely on has passed: status, reputation and other worldly successes. We are left only with our own mind, naked and unprotected. At this point the practice of the teaching bears fruit:

> O now when the Dhyana Bardo upon me is dawning!
> Abandoning the whole mass of distractions and illusions,
> May the mind be kept in the mood of endless undistracted Samadhi,
> May firmness both in the visualizing and in the perfected stages be obtained:
> At this time, when meditating one-pointedly, with all other actions put aside,
> May I not fall under the power of misleading, stupifying passions.

> (W.Y. Evans-Wentz, *The Tibetan Book of the Dead*,
> Oxford University Press, 1960, p 203)

In conclusion

This chapter has introduced the various scriptures and schools in Buddhism and identified their salient features and differences. As a result we can now consider the following significant factors in the development of Buddhism:

- the central role of the bodhisattva in Mahayana Buddhism as a salvific force and how this contrasted with the arahant ideal in Theravada
- the poetic character of the Mahayana vision and the way it contrasted with the austere path of Theravada
- the introduction of a Buddhism of faith within Chinese and Japanese culture
- the influence of Taoism on Chinese and Japanese Buddhism, moving it in a contrasting direction based on mystical intuition
- the Tibetan interpretation of Buddhism, involving transmission from mind to mind, the need of a spiritual guide, and an emphasis on the preparation for death.

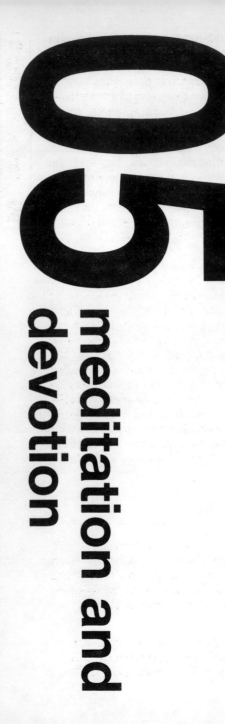

05

meditation and devotion

In this chapter you will learn:
- about different kinds of Buddhist pratice – meditation or mental training
- about how some practices are devotional, and others not.

Once, when talking to a friend about the possibility of him moving to a new place and starting a new business, I asked him whether he thought it would be good for him to make a fresh start. He replied that he had done enough travelling in his life to know that wherever you go, deep down there is no such thing as a fresh start: you take yourself and your hang-ups with you. I was looking on the outside and he was looking on the inside. My understanding of the situation was relatively superficial; his was much more profound.

Most of the time we think of the world being outside ourselves. This is the place where our actions have their effect and changes occur. If we want the world to be a better place, we have to influence it in a moral way, to create greater harmony and better communication. For Buddhists, like everyone else, this is a worthy goal; the question is, how do we achieve it? For followers of a monotheistic faith, such as Christianity, Judaism or Islam, the spiritual power for change comes from God through prayer. For Buddhists it occurs through training the mind, and recognizing our true nature or through devotion, dedication and faith. For some these can go hand in hand, with the emphasis being placed differently. For others there is a contrast between the two, with the one being of obviously greater value than the other. In order to try and tease out the continuum of different paths in this respect, I have used four classifications below: mind and heart, heart and mind, devotion as homage, salvific devotion. This is not to say these are all compatible ways of categorizing Buddhist approaches, but I hope the categories can be used as instruments for making first distinctions between differing approaches to Buddhist practice and 'self-transformation'.

1 Mind and heart

To understand this Buddhist notion of self-transformation, our conception of 'mind' has to be freed from its Western connotations. Within Indian tradition, 'mind' and 'heart' are both aspects of consciousness, and the practice of meditation, with its yogic origins, both presumes this and is the way to realizing it:

> The Buddha's path is simple and meant for ordinary people, and anyone with goodwill and determination can follow its steps toward freedom of heart and mind. Both

heart and mind have to be involved in this journey toward liberation from the 'self'. The mind understands and concludes, connects and discerns, whereas the heart feels.

> (Ayya Khema, *Being Nobody, Going Nowhere*,
> Wisdom Publications, 1987, preface)

For this reason, the words heart and mind are often used interchangeably to refer to our inner world, which we need to purify through the cultivation of mindfulness. The Buddha said:

> 'O Bhikkhus, there are two kinds of illness. What are these two? Physical illness and mental illness. There seem to be people who enjoy freedom from physical illness even for a year or two ... even for a hundred years or more. But, O Bhikkhus, rare in this world are those who enjoy freedom from mental illness even for one moment, except those who are free from mental defilements.

> (Anguttara Nikaya (ed.), *Devamitta Thera*, Colombo,
> 1929, p 276)

Here mental illness is not contrasted with an ordinary or 'normal' state of mind, but with the perfectly healthy or pure mind of one who has overcome suffering and dis-ease (an arahant). Mental defilements, which prevent this liberation, are not simply clinical conditions, but the result of a mind that is untrained and unrestrained, not functioning according to its true nature and therefore preventing happiness, contentment, tranquillity. This training of the mind is referred to in one famous Zen text as *The Taming of the Bull*. It begins with *The Search for the Bull*:

> In the pasture of this world, I endlessly push aside the tall grasses in search of the bull.
> Following unnamed rivers, lost upon the interpenetrating paths of distant mountains,
> My strength failing and my vitality exhausted, I cannot find the bull.
> I only hear the locusts chirring through the forest at night.

Following the verse is a comment:

> The bull has been lost. What need is there to search? Only because of separation from my true nature, I fail to find him. In the confusion of the senses I lose even his tracks. Far from home, I see many crossroads, but which way is

the right one I know not. Greed and fear, good and bad, entangle me.

(P. Reps, *Zen Flesh, Zen Bones*, Penguin, 1972, p 138)

Eventually the bull is tamed, and it is realized that it was nothing more than the restless activity of the 'self'. With the self now eradicated, Wisdom and Compassion arise, and attachment ceases:

> Barefoot and naked of breast, I mingle with the people of the world.
> My clothes are ragged and dust-laden and I am ever-blissful.
> I use no magic to extend my life;
> Now, before me, the trees become alive.

(ibid., p 147)

Ethical considerations are also integral to the attainment of this healthy state, since a healthy or pure mind functions according to selfless motivation, rather than through the pursuit of egotistical goals. When we put these aspects of the Buddhist analysis of mind together, we find they are summed up in the Eightfold Path: Wisdom, Morality and Mental Discipline. *Bhavana* (mental development) or meditation is the basis of living a Buddhist way of life.

Mindfulness and concentration

Ayya Khema, a Buddhist nun, writes:

> During meditation we learn to drop from the mind what we don't want to keep. We only want to keep in mind our meditation subject. As we become more and more skilled at it, we start to use the same faculty in our daily lives to help us drop those thoughts which are unwholesome. In this way our meditation practice assists us in daily living and our attention to wholesome thoughts in everyday life helps our meditation practice. The person who becomes master of his or her own thoughts and learns to think what they want to think is called an Arahant, an Enlightened One.

(Ayya Khema, *Being Nobody, Going Nowhere*, Wisdom Publications, 1987, p 11)

Formal meditation practice is like exercising the mind in the same way as we might exercise the body – in order to keep it fit and healthy, and to improve its function for a specific purpose. The basic function of the mind is concentration. Right Concentration is the eighth step of the Path, but this does not mean it is the one which comes last. Rather, we have to think of the eight steps as the development of skilfulness in eight aspects which go hand in hand, like a progressive and interdependent evolution. Most importantly, without Right Concentration, Right Mindfulness is unattainable. Thus basic exercises of concentration are the foundation of meditation. But concentration on what? The most widely used traditional practice is called mindfulness of, or concentration on, breathing (*anapanasati*).

Mindfulness of the breath

The breath is a good focus for such a meditational exercise because it is neutral. As a bodily function it usually escapes our attention, since it does not give rise to pleasant or unpleasant sensations, nor does it excite the mind. Because we take it for granted we also overlook its significance, in much the same way as we do with a life-giving substance like water. Yet it is the basis of life. Equally, its relationship with the mind is direct in a physiological and emotional sense. Breath provides oxygen, through which the mind functions. In a state of excitement we breathe fast; in a state of calm and tranquillity we breathe slowly. The breath is therefore an indicator of our mental state.

We can concentrate on the breath at various points: as it goes into and exits from the body, by concentrating on the sensation of it passing through the nostrils; by following its passage down to and returning from the abdomen; by accompanying each breath cycle with a word, such as 'Buddho' (a reminder of the relationship between concentration and enlightenment); by counting breaths, one on the in-breath, two on the out-breath, and so on up to ten.

The point is to know when concentration is focused and refined, and when the mind wanders and concentration is lost. It is important to make the distinction between the discipline of concentration and 'just thinking about something'. When the mind wanders, thoughts are arising but we are not aware of them. Concentration is a full awareness of exactly what is happening here and now, which is why it requires a discipline that thinking alone does not possess. To start with, counting is a good way to ensure you obey this distinction. If the mind wanders you may forget to count altogether, or count beyond the number at which you should return to one. Realizing you have done this is evidence of the mind having wandered. As the practice progresses, concentration should increase. It is then you begin to realize how subtle concentration can be, and how easily it can be lost. You will also realize how an excited mind finds it difficult to concentrate, and strays to objects of desire, or becomes distracted by dominant feelings. This is the learning process of meditation, which can be both frustrating and irritating. Feelings arise which are distracting, and which give rise to impatience, anger and frustration. The most simple exercise can be a humbling experience. After all, if this simple activity presents problems in a relaxed environment, how much more difficult would concentration be in the more rapid and distracting context of our everyday life?

With increasing concentration the mind becomes more tranquil, and its activity diminishes. In a state of pure calm, an awareness arises of the present moment that is undisturbed, and with it arises a moment of bliss, a lack of anxiety. When the mind is in this state, its energy is available for the purposes for which we choose to use it, unhampered by negative feelings.

Ayya Khema describes such a condition in this way:

> Once verbalization stops for a moment, not only is there quiet but there is a feeling of contentment. The mind has at last found its home. We wouldn't be very happy if we didn't have a home for this body of ours. We are equally not very happy if we haven't got a home for the mind. That quiet, peaceful space is the mind's home. It can go home and relax just as we do after a day's work when we relax the body in an easy chair and at night in bed. Now the mind, too, can take it easy. It doesn't have to think. Thinking is suffering, no matter what it is that we think. There is movement in it and because of that there is friction. Everything that moves creates friction.

> The moment we relax and rest the mind it gains new strength and also happiness because it knows it can go home at any time. The happiness created at the time of meditation carries through to daily living because the mind knows that nothing has to be taken so seriously that it can't go home again and find peace and quiet.

(ibid., pp 13–14)

Calm and insight

Insight is the goal; calm is the means. Many images have been used to illustrate this. One is of the sea, both in its calm state and in a storm. The calm sea is tranquil and serene, not only in itself, but in the effect it has upon us. Similarly, waves, foam and the sea's roar in a storm are exciting, powerful and fearful. The calm sea is like the calm mind. The stormy sea is a mind in turmoil. When the sea is calm we can see through it, but in its rough state, nothing below the surface can be seen. This ability to see below the surface is insight. We see with clarity and penetration. There is a picture by the Japanese artist Hokusai, called *The Waves at Kanagawa*. It depicts figures in small boats confronted by a huge wave, its aggressive shape about to bear down on them. They are cowering on the deck in fear. In the distance, unnoticed, and difficult to pick out in the picture, is Mount Fuji, the symbol of enlightenment in Japanese Buddhism. Its snow-capped peak resembles the waves that frame it. Reading this picture, like a Zen *mondo*, or story, the figures confronted with their fear of the wave and their death are forgetful of the path to enlightenment. Their mindfulness is distracted by the sensations of the moment. The wave may represent any fearful circumstance we face, but the message is clear. Without preparing for such moments in our life – even death itself – we shall be lost in samsara when they come. Insight is the antidote to such situations, and meditation is the way to cultivate it.

The Waves at Kanagawa, Hokusai

Meditational techniques

Accordingly, meditational techniques are divided into two types: *samatha*, which means calm; and *vipassana*, which means insight. Insight means knowing what is really happening in our minds and in our relations with others, and doing our best to create a harmonious situation in every circumstance. The significance of insight may best be described by showing how it can be obscured by negative feelings arising in the present moment. I come to each situation in a particular state of mind. Sometimes, when depressed, sad or sorrowful, I greet people in this particular state, and it colours my impression of them and the way I feel about them. This is essentially a preoccupation with myself that interferes with my concern for others and their well-being, but I say, 'I cannot help it.' Such states can be self-perpetuating and gather momentum. In my morose condition, the happy person is someone to be envied. I cannot share in their happiness and, inevitably, this shows. Then I complain about losing friends or not being wanted, and the downward spiral continues. If someone says, 'cheer up', or, 'it is not as bad as it seems', I feel even worse! Insight is the recognition of what is going on in our minds when these feelings arise, so that we may prevent ourselves from slipping back into similar mental habits time and time again. Mindfulness creates the opportunity to change these habits, by letting go of our attachment to them.

The first step on this path is to recognize such thoughts and feelings as delusion. Not because they do not exist, but because they do not constitute our 'selves'. They are not 'me', but phenomena which arise and pass away. This is the truth of impermanence that vipassana meditation makes clear. Nothing abides, nothing has to be held onto. Without this awareness the mind manipulates us, like a magician, into believing the illusions that our thoughts convey; these illusions in turn cause us distress and separate us from others.

For this reason, every sensation is a matter for awareness: those of the body, and feelings and thoughts. The contemplation of the six elements is an example of this reflection on impermanence.

The contemplation of the six elements

One considers the solid matter of the body: bones, hair, skin, nails, flesh and so on. These are the earth elements. When one dies they return to the earth elements in the universe. They are only borrowed, not one's own.

One considers the liquid elements in the body: blood, phlegm, bile and other secretions. These are the water elements. One therefore reflects, they too are not one's own.

One considers the fire element within the body: heat and energy.

One considers the air element: breath and wind.

These elements are also borrowed and will return. They are not one's own.

One considers that the space the body occupies will also be surrendered at death.

Lastly, even individual consciousness will also have to be given up at death. Each of the six elements that make up the body (earth, water, fire, air, space and consciousness) are not permanent and abiding as one's own body. Upon recognition of this, attachment to one's own body will slip away as insight increases.

Similar reflections on feelings, mind and other objects are used to the same effect; not as a means of morose introspection, but to remove attachment to that which is not abiding and untrustworthy – and, therefore, ultimately, the cause of sorrow, delusion and self-concern. As this decreases, so one's burden is lightened and Right Understanding increases.

2 Heart and mind

Metta

Another important Buddhist teaching is that one should be a blessing to the world. There is a Zen picture of a bodhisattva, who wanders with his staff visiting villages, depicted standing, smiling with children around him. The legend that accompanies the picture explains that he enters the village with bliss-bestowing hands. This expresses the purpose of what is aspired to in the Buddhist life.

Metta is the word that sums up this state of being. The *Metta-sutta*, the teaching on universal love or loving-kindness, proclaims that:

> Whatever beings there may be – feeble or strong, long (or tall), stout or medium or short, small or large, seen or unseen, those dwelling far or near, those who are born and those who are yet to be born – may all beings, without exception, be happy-minded.

Mettabhavana

This undiscriminating attitude is cultivated in a popular meditation (*mettabhavana*). It consists of five stages. In the first, one generates metta for oneself. (This is not a self-love in the sense of self-appreciation as a special person, above others, but a recognition of one's capacity to be loving to others and loveable.) At this stage one repeats: 'May I be well, may I be happy, may I progress.' In the second stage the feeling is extended to a friend, in the third stage to a neutral person, in the fourth to someone towards whom you have antipathy. In the fifth you see all these together, and then visualize the whole world of living beings and extend metta to all of them.

Thus, what appears at first to be an easy practice becomes progressively more difficult, proceeding through the stages: it confronts limitations rather than indulging preferences. As such, it also distinguishes between the notion of love which we may find appealing, and that which is demanded of us. The highest aspiration mentioned in the teaching on loving kindness is that one should love all beings just as a mother loves her child, or, alternatively, that one should see all beings as having been, at one time, one's mother. It is not a soft option, and requires much work in the training of the heart. Most importantly, it is a progressive insight into the true meaning of love and the demands which that makes. It is the path to compassion, which is often spoken of as consisting of three grades. The first grade consists of goodwill towards others. The second is friendship. The third stage, metta itself, lies beyond these and is not just an emotion but a developed skill, which progressively exposes our own weakness and vulnerability. It also has its benefits, of course. If we offer goodwill, friendship or love to others, they will feel attracted to us. But love is given not because we want to give something, or because they need it, but because the heart has been trained to do it. In other words, in time, it becomes a *spontaneous* giving rather than a difficulty. The formal practice of mettabhavana is a training for our motivation in ordinary circumstances: at home, at work and in the supermarket.

Visualization

The skill of visualization is a way both of concentrating the mind and of developing the quality of compassion. One Buddhist writer explains:

For our efforts at the spiritual life to be crowned with success not only do we need to be intellectually convinced by Buddhism, but we also need to find it emotionally attractive. We need both Truth and Beauty. Images, especially beautiful images, involve our emotions in the spiritual life and thereby make it possible for us actually to live it.

(*FWBO Newsletter*, No. 56, 1982, p 12)

Visualization is not just a development of our imagination, but a focusing of our inherent qualities for transforming ourselves and the world, through 'seeing with the mind's eye'. It emancipates us from the effect of negative emotions, thus enabling us to respond more effectively to difficult situations that we encounter. Essentially, it means that by visualizing the form of a bodhisattva (a being with higher qualities), we let go of our egotistical desires and our selfhood, and are therefore able to act in the world in a more beneficial way.

This example shows the process by which it can occur. The focus of the visualization is Kuan Yin, the Chinese form of the Bodhisattva of Compassion.

Kuan Yin

You sit down on a hill top, or anywhere high enough for
you to see nothing but the sky in front of your eyes

With your mind you make everything empty.

There is nothing there you say.

And you see it like that – nothing
emptiness.
Then you say ahhh…

But there is something!
Look there's the sea
and the MOON has risen
full, round, white.

And you see it like that
sea, silver in the moonlight
with little white topped waves.
And in the blue black sky above
hangs a great moon
bright,
but not dazzling,
a soft brightness you might say.

You stare at the moon a long
long time, feeling calm, happy.
Then the moon gets smaller,
but brighter and brighter and brighter
till you see it as a pearl, or a seed, but not so bright
you can only just bear to look at it.

The pearl starts to grow.
And before you know what's happened,
it's Kuan Yin (the Mother of Compassion) herself
standing up against the sky
all dressed in gleaming white
and with her feet resting on a lotus
that floats on the waves.

You see her
once you know how to do it
as clearly as I see you.
For her robes are shining,

and there's a halo round her head.
She smiles at you,
such a loving smile. She's so glad
to see you that tears of happiness sparkle in her eyes.

If you keep your mind calm,
by just whispering her name
and not trying too hard
she will stay a long time.

When she does go,
it's by getting smaller and smaller.
She doesn't go back to being a pearl,
but just gets so small
that at last you can't see her, then you notice
that the sky and the sea
have vanished too.
Just space is left.
Lovely, lovely space, going on forever ...

That space stays long
if you can do without you. Not you and space, you see

just space.

No you!

3 Devotion as homage

Bowing to the Buddha

It is commonly assumed that Buddhism has nothing to do with
devotion because it is concerned with self-transformation. It is
also assumed that devotion presumes an outside power or agency
to which we submit. For these reasons, Buddhist ritual appears

anachronistic. Yet there is no more pervasive devotional action performed by Buddhists than bowing, which is apparently an act of worship and submission. What lies behind this activity?

Buddhists participate in *pujas*, which is an Indian word for formal worship. It is rather like Christians attending a church service. When Buddhists enter a temple or shrine room in which an image of a buddha is installed, they may go before the image, kneel down and bow three times so that their forehead touches the floor. This is a very formal action. The three bows represent the Buddha, dhamma and sangha.

Tibetan Buddhists often prostrate themselves (an extension of bowing), by lying full length on the floor with the head pointing towards the image. There is no denying that this is an act of devotion, but it is not to be confused with worship shown towards God. Such a ritual (rather like the act of offering flowers, candles and incense which are traditional Buddhist offerings) acts as a reminder of commitment to an ideal, and a way of bringing oneself closer to that ideal. The whole person has to be engaged in this act of transformation and piety. Expressed in these forms, bowing is a means to this transformation, just as much as solitary meditation and ethical action in the world. Mindfulness is cultivated by expression of devotion as much as by these other activities. It forms part of the training of the heart, in which the emotions are touched, and the development of qualities like humility, upon which the aspiration to buddhahood and a better life depend. When Buddhists bow or make offerings, they should genuinely recognize that they aspire to progress by recognizing that the ideal lies beyond them in the present, but that it is attainable. Acts of devotion express a determination to develop the qualities embodied by the venerated image. The offerings of candles, flowers and incense express gratitude and reverence but do not imply 'otherness' (in the sense of Christian devotion to an Almighty but essentially distinct God). Flowers are a reminder of beauty and impermanence. The candles are a reminder of the light of the dhamma in the darkness of ignorance. The fragrance of incense is a reminder of the blessing of compassionate service.

Tibetan women showing devotion before the Temple at Dharamsala, India
(copyright Peter Gold; photograph reproduced from *Tibetan Reflections*
with permission of Wisdom Publications, 361 Newbury Street, Boston,
Massachusetts, USA)

In pujas, these offerings are accompanied by chanting, which
recollects the meaning and purpose of the devotion. Here are two
examples. The first is from the Thai Forest Retreat Order,
established in England by Ajahn Chah, the Thai meditation
master:

> To the Blessed One, the Lord who fully attained perfect
> enlightenment,
> To the Teaching which he expounded so well,
> And to the Blessed One's disciples, who have practised well,
> To these – the Buddha, the Dhamma and the Sangha –
> We render with offerings our rightful homage.
> It is well for us, Blessed One, that having attained
> liberation,
> You still had compassion for later generations.
> Deign to accept these simple offerings
> For our long-lasting benefit and for the happiness it gives
> us.

The Lord, the Perfectly Enlightened and Blessed One –
I render homage to the Buddha, the Blessed One.

(*Amaravati Chanting Book*, Amaravati Publications,
1987, p 9)

The second is from the *Friends of the Western Buddhist Order
Puja*:

Offerings to the Buddha.
Reverencing the Buddha, we offer flowers –
Flowers that today are fresh and sweetly blooming,
Flowers that tomorrow are faded and fallen.
Our bodies too, like flowers, will pass away.
Reverencing the Buddha, we offer candles.
To Him, who is the Light, we offer light.
From His greater lamp a lesser lamp we light within us:
The lamp of Bodhi shining within our hearts.
Reverencing the Buddha, we offer incense,
Incense whose fragrance pervades the air.
The fragrance of the perfect life, sweeter than incense,
Spreads in all directions throughout the world.

(*The FWBO Puja Book*, Windhorse Publications, 1984)

Bowing to the Buddha, making offerings and chanting constitute
the three main acts of Buddhist devotion, or puja ceremonies.
They take place before a shrine – which may vary in style
according to the branch of the tradition, but the intention is
always the same. This quotation, taken from the short ceremony
for the dedication of a shrine room in the Friends of the Western
Buddhist Order (a Western Buddhist movement), succinctly sums
up the purpose of shrine room and ceremony:

Here seated, here practising,
May our mind become Buddha,
May our thought become Dharma,
May our communication with one another be Sangha.

(*The FWBO Puja Book*, Windhorse Publications, 1984)

4 Salvific devotion

Nam-myoho-renge-kyo

In Nichiren Buddhism we meet another form of devotion based on the title of the Lotus Sutra which, in Chinese, is rendered as Myoho-renge-kyo. Devotion, or dedication, consists in the recitation of this mantra daily in order for the reciter to attain Buddhahood in their lifetime. This can be understood as a form of prayer which is not

> for the protection of the gods and Buddhas who stand above and control men. Rather the intensified spiritual force of life which forms our strong prayers reveals itself as the power of faith and the power of practice. These two powers induce the power of the Buddha and the power of the Law to function within us ... Prayer is something which causes a change in the depths of a human heart.
>
> (Daisaku Ikeda, 'On Prayer', in Jim Cowan (ed.),
> *The Buddhism of the Sun,* Richmond, UK, NSUK,
> 1982, p 71)

In this understanding it is the power of the Buddha and Law which, when invoked by faith and dedicated practice, will necessarily secure salvation.

Namu Amida Butsu

In a similar way, in Pure Land Buddhism it is stated by the Buddha Amitabha (Amida) in this scripture that:

> if those beings who in immeasurable and innumerable Buddha countries, after they have heard my name ... should direct their thought to be born in that Buddha country of mine ... if these should not be born in that Buddha country, even those who have only ten times repeated the thought ... then may I not obtain the highest perfect knowledge.
>
> (The Larger Sukhavati-Vyuha, verse 19, in Cowell, E.B.
> (ed.), *Buddhist Mahayana Texts*, Part 11,
> Oxford, Dover, 1969, p 15)

One of the great teachers of Pure Land Buddhism, Honen, defined this form of worship in his 'One Sheet of Paper' as being 'nothing but the mere repetition of the Namu Amida Butsu without a doubt of his mercy whereby one may be born into

Paradise' (Sir Charles Eliot, 1969, *Japanese Buddhism*, New York, Routledge and Kegan Paul, p 365).

Here again devotion is rewarded on the grounds that the power of that invoked is sufficient to ensure salvation or liberation, rather than that the efforts of those seeking it are, in themselves, sufficient.

In conclusion

In this chapter we have examined different approaches to meditation and devotion in Buddhist practice.

We may conclude that mind and heart, meditation and devotion, are complementary aspects of the same training in bhavana, or mental development and that this training is essentially practical, not simply intellectual or ethereal. It is creative in that it aims to ensure a better world through self-transformation and, ultimately, the transformation of the world itself. Nevertheless, we need to take account of the compatibility or otherwise of:

- significant differences in practice underpinned by philosophical and cultural shifts in Buddhism
- the influence of the Mahayana influence in the development of the idea of Buddhahood and the bodhisattva ideal
- the important shift from self-reliance within the Theravadin, Ch'an and Zen traditions to the salvific power invested in the bodhisattvas as perfected beings who can ensure salvation for those who have both faith and dedication. This differentiation in emphasis was particularly prevalent in certain Chinese and Japanese forms of Buddhism, especially in the Nichiren and Pure Land movements.

06

ethical conduct

In this chapter you will learn:
- about Buddhist ethics, which are related to the practicalities of everyday life
- about the relationship between morality and self-development from a Buddhist perspective.

Sila and skilfulness

Sila is the Buddhist term for ethical or moral behaviour, which is summed up in the three connected ethical steps of the Eightfold Path (Right Speech, Right Action, Right Livelihood, referred to in Chapter 3). At the same time, an emphasis on living well pervades Buddhist teaching and practice. This is expressed in an obvious way, in the precepts which provide everyday guidance in a simple form (simple to remember, that is, rather than simple to keep). But in order to keep the precepts successfully, Buddhists recognize the need for sustained development in themselves. We could say that the precepts provide a practical framework, for us to be guided by in our everyday activity, but the intention is to try to keep them. This intention and effort are all important, otherwise no progress can be made. Behind the precepts encompassing them is the Eightfold Path, which informs Buddhists as to how this can be achieved. Bhavana, or mental development, is what lies beneath the surface, what is happening within the person that creates this possibility. The aspiration at the heart of this is skilfulness, its effect in the world and on others – this is the cultivation of happiness and harmony.

Perhaps we can best illustrate this by returning to the physician or doctor analogy that was applied by the Buddha himself. First, there is the problem: we do not achieve in life what we wish to achieve. Our aspirations towards happiness are not fulfilled. Why is this? The prescription is that we have to reflect carefully on how we can best achieve what it is that we seek, and why we seek it. This, however, turns out to be a long-term task. It involves recognizing why we suffer the dissatisfaction we experience, and, in the course of this, through meditation and mindfulness, how we can alter our way of responding to life (which, at root, means recognizing that what we think and do isn't necessarily good for us or anyone else). Here the doctor prescribes a sustained programme that should result in a cure for the illness. This is laid out in the Eightfold Path. At the same time, we need some everyday guidance as to what we should and should not do; some rules to try to keep that will be easy to remember to keep us on track in the hurly-burly of our life, when our desires are likely to be least restrained. This is the purpose of the precepts. Similarly, the good doctor will be concerned with the root causes of our lack of health, and give us a checklist of things to do and not to do day by day. These two aspects of treating the situation go hand in hand, complementing each other. But it would be a mistake to think we could just try and follow the rules and everything would be sorted out.

Let us take a specific example. I hurt my leg badly, sustaining an injury that will take quite a while to mend. The rules are to rest, not do anything that will hamper recovery such as twisting, bending or running. At the same time, my leg will lose its strength unless I make sure that the path to recovery also includes building up the muscles, ligaments and so forth, at an appropriate time. If I carry out the first instruction as best I can but ignore the second, my leg will always be weak and liable to further injury. At the same time, I shall be unlikely ever to be able to do after the injury what I could have done previously.

The analogy ends here, because the Buddha was not concerned with rehabilitation but with improvement. Neither was he concerned with a purely physical condition, but with what we might call a spiritual one. The root of the problem is our not understanding ourselves properly in the first place, and this is more akin to a psychological disorder than a physical one. But the distinction between the two related aspects of treatment holds good – don't do yourself unnecessary daily harm, keep working at improving what you are capable of. The precepts and skilfulness work together in this way. When we look at an ethical application of this we can see how.

As a father I may say I love my children. My underlying intentions towards them are all good; I wish to bring them up well and to do them no harm. In our everyday family life, I am often in a situation where I am concentrating on something other than them: doing a job around the house that has to be done; reading to relax; or writing a letter that should have been written yesterday. It occurs to my children that they have not had their pocket money, and they interrupt me to get it – they want it now! But right now I want to relax or get this job done. How much I love my children is not uppermost in my mind; my desires and theirs clash. I hold onto mine and they hold onto theirs; the result is anger and frustration, as I tell them to go away and come back later, while they tell me if I give it to them now they will not have to bother me again. It is a trivial example, but it is one of many that will recur during the day, and during every day that we are together.

As a Buddhist, how might I deal with this situation? What can I refer to? On one level the precepts, on another level the idea of skilfulness; on a third I can recognize the application of the Buddha's teaching on dukkha itself, and the Four Noble Truths. In the immediacy of the moment I cannot decide; I need to go away and think about it, but that is impractical and not what is required. I have to act, and how I act will depend upon what thoughts and feelings arise in my mind. I may try and apply the precepts, but I cannot do this mechanically; I have to be able to overcome my own desires to satisfy my children's. I also have to make a judgement about the way their request should be treated. But if my judgement is solely based on how I feel, it is likely to be awry. After the event, all these thoughts may go through my mind, but it is too late then, and so it will be the next time, and the time after, unless I address what is going on under the surface. In practice, showing my love to my children, though it is there, becomes a much more difficult intention to perform than I might imagine.

The practicality of Buddhist ethics

Looking at Buddhist ethics in this way affirms the importance of addressing a pervasive misconception that is often held about the relevance of ethics, and the relevance of Buddhist ideas to everyday life. Both can be separated from our daily activity and treated as intellectual mind-games, but this is not the intention. The purchase of both is their utility: do they make a difference to the way we live and the world we create? This question tests their efficacy and, at the same time, helps us penetrate what otherwise may seem baffling and remote concepts. For example, the significance of anatta, the doctrine of no-self, involves an awareness only gained by the practice of mindfulness. In turn, mindfulness makes us increasingly aware of the heedlessness of much of our thought and actions. In this way, Right Speech, Action and Livelihood gain a practical significance that we can illustrate from reflection on our experience. Ignorance ceases to be a question of lack of theoretical knowledge; we can put our finger on exactly when it has determined the way we have behaved. Furthermore, we begin to realize that the view of ourselves that has prompted such actions (composed of desire and aversion) is the delusion that ensures this unsatisfactory state of affairs is maintained and replayed. I love my children, but I still behave to them in an inadequate and unskilful way. The goal of Buddhist ethics is to change this behaviour, to refine it, by increasing my capacity to create harmony and peacefulness in relations with myself and others. This is not just a matter of dos and don'ts, but rules do have their necessary place. It is not a matter of penetrating inscrutable concepts; but greater awareness involves more reflection. It is not a matter of retreating from the world, but of having a practice that prepares me for those situations in which it will be shown to be useful.

This analysis helps us to realize also that the Buddhist emphasis on intention is not about having the right sentiments or ignoring the effect of what we do. Buddhist morality is not a soft option based upon the wish to be a nice person or do good works. There is a rigour in Buddhist morality, because it conjoins both our intelligence, in the fullest sense of the term, and our feelings, in relation to what we will for ourselves and others, in progressing toward wisdom and compassion. This is why skilfulness plays such a central role, as the following Buddhist writer explains:

> According to Buddhist tradition there are two kinds of action, *kausalya* (Pali *kusala*) or skilful, and *akausalya* (Pali *akusala*) or unskilful. This is significant because the terms 'skilful' and 'unskilful', unlike the terms 'good' and 'bad', suggest that morality is very much a matter of intelligence. You cannot be skilful unless you can understand things, unless you can see possibilities and explore them. Hence morality, according to Buddhism, is as much a matter of intelligence and insight as one of good intentions and good feelings. After all, we have been told that the path to hell is paved with good intentions, but you could hardly say that the path to hell is paved with skilfulness. It just doesn't fit.

> (Sangharakshita, *A Guide to the Buddhist Path*,
> Windhorse Publications, 1990, p 140)

We can now see the moral sense of what appear at first to be simply abstract logical formulations, for example, the bare doctrinal formulation of cause and effect.

> That being thus this comes to be;
> from the coming to be of that, this arises;
> that being absent, this does not happen;
> from the cessation of that, this ceases.

> (*Majjhima Nikaya,* Vol. II, quoted in H. Saddhatissa,
> *Buddhist Ethics*, Wisdom Publications, 1987, p 28)

This can now be applied on both the grand scale (spelt out in the teaching on 'dependent origination', the theory of karma and the pictorial expression of the Buddhist world view in the Wheel of Becoming), and also in the minutiae of thought and action between one moment and the next. It is this second application that makes sense of things on a larger scale, and reveals ethics, the issue of how to live well or appropriately, to be the core of the Buddha's teaching. Nirvana may appear to be a wonderful dream – or a hideous annihilation – when viewed in a speculative fashion, but neither view is of any significance whatsoever. Chase nirvana or run away from it; such thoughts, conceptions and actions are as erroneous as seeking a first cause or beginning. What matters is the here and now of separating delusion from understanding, and recognizing the effect of doing so; what arises and what ceases, what is wholesome and what is not. This is at the heart of Buddhism and Buddhist ethics. It is the dharma and the path to happiness, or what is also termed 'quietude of heart'.

Working on yourself and benefiting others

This may be introduced in the form of a story. My younger daughter has a habit, when being castigated for a mishap she has performed, such as breaking a cup or mislaying her recorder, of responding with the refrain, 'I didn't mean to.' I believe her complaint is authentic; she is not just using it as an excuse, but really saying she doesn't believe she is truly at fault. However, as an adult, it is clear to me that 'not meaning to' does not solve the problem. Something more is required of her (and of me) if we are not to repeat the situation. I may reflect that the inadequacy lies in her thoughtlessness: if she were more aware of what was required of her, such things would happen less often! If she maintains the same stance in adulthood she will not receive a lot of sympathy. The point is this: whether you mean to do something or not relies upon being aware of what is required in being responsible for the cup or the recorder. When we take this into account, we cannot view doing the right things as just an impetuous activity – well-meaning but not well-considered, or as an unreflective wish to concentrate on that which we prefer to think about, in the moment, without regard to other things that also need to be considered. The answer to this problem lies in recognizing responsibilities I may find more onerous, and in executing tasks in a way that requires more discipline than I would normally exercise. In other words, I have to work on *myself* in order to be of benefit to others. A well-meaning person with little regard to the effects of their action may be about as much use as a bull in a china shop! This applies whether we are talking about the home environment, aid sent to catastrophe areas across the world, or diplomatic efforts to resolve crises.

'Working on yourself' in terms of awareness and discipline is of fundamental importance but, from a Western point of view, coloured by our own cultural context, it can appear to have an individualistic emphasis, contrasting thinking of others with thinking of oneself. If this is also related to the traditional Buddhist communal form of monasticism, then is might appear as a retreat from social obligation; a form of self-obsession and introversion. But this is not the case. Self-development and the recognition of personal and social responsibility are inseparable. The principle holds good on the individual and the global scales; what matters is to keep the balance. In traditional Buddhist countries, the balance is kept by regarding monastic and lay life as interdependent aspects of the social order. In the West we have some difficulty with this, due to a very different social history. Nevertheless, it is important to consider what external environment, what pattern of daily life and what time spent in quietude to address issues, is necessary. This is one of the vital challenges to Buddhism today, as it spreads to the West and reconsiders its role in an increasingly Westernized Asiatic world. For the Westerner wishing to understand the Buddhist view, the important issue to consider may be how the Buddhist accent on self-development, or bhavana, can enrich the Western emphasis (in real terms) on altruism. For Buddhists of course, at least in theory, the two are not distinct, since the one flows from and enriches the other, but that is not to say that Buddhists always get it right, or that social structures in one society necessarily serve the same ends in another. What must be confronted, however, is the naïve criticism that Buddhism falls short, morally speaking, where other traditions succeed. If anatta, mindfulness, skilfulness, wisdom and compassion are properly understood in relation to each other, there are no grounds for levelling such a criticism. Indeed, we might say that such scrutiny should be cast the other way.

The precepts and the dharmas

The precepts outline what to abstain from, and the dharmas are the qualities to cultivate. They go together, and it is important to recognize that while abstaining from the one negative state of mind resulting in negative action, the other, positive, state is encouraged. The precepts have already been mentioned in Chapter 1. The basic dharmas, or ethical principles, are also five in number:

Abstaining from acts of harmfulness is an encouragement of metta, or loving kindness.

Abstaining from taking what is not given is an encouragement of *dana*, or generosity.

Abstaining from sexual misconduct is an encouragement of *santutthi*, or contentment.

Abstaining from false speech is an encouragement of *sacca*, or truthfulness.

Abstaining from intoxicants of the mind is an encouragement of *sati*, mindfulness or awareness.

Here, then, is the foundation of Buddhist practice (bhavana), the qualities without which no progress is possible. The precepts are held up as the fundamental code of Buddhist ethical life, not because they stop you doing what you might want, but because only to the extent that they are adhered to can the discipline required to progress be made possible.

Let us look at this discipline in more detail, this time using the fourth precept: abstention from false speech. As with all the others, false speech is rooted in craving, hatred or fear. False speech is a protective device which ignores truthfulness. The more you lie, the more acceptable the habit becomes, and the less important it is to be truthful. False speech goes further than direct lying, of course. Outright lies are its gross form, but it is also connected with many levels of communication. Right Speech, the fourth step of the Eightfold Path, is speech generated by affection and guided by discernment. It is to say something which is helpful in a given situation, and to a particular person or group of people. It is not the expression of anger, but equally it should not be talking for talk's own sake. It should be useful, and, by virtue of this, be meaningful also. Put bluntly, it means you should think carefully about what you are going to say and how you are going to say it. This requires self-restraint – another important quality for Buddhists. There is much that stands in the way of achieving this goal with all its implications, but perhaps the root of the matter is the need to develop honesty; not just the idea of being honest with others, but of being honest with oneself. Let us try an example.

I am in conversation with a friend, and we talk about what we have been doing during the week. My friend tells me that she applied for a job, went to the interview yesterday, and was told she had got it. Now she is wondering whether to accept it, but is obviously very excited at the prospect. She explains that, on the strength of this success, and because she will earn more money and have more status, she went out this morning and bought some new clothes. She wants to show me the clothes and tells me about all the new people she will meet, the places she will be travelling to, and the projects she will be in charge of.

When my friend knocked on my door this morning I was pleased to see her. Now I am not so sure. I want to feel pleased for her but I am finding it difficult. I want to say the right thing, but I lack the conviction to say it with any spontaneity. I have been doing mundane chores, and here is someone speaking of the excitement I would wish for my own life. Feelings arise that are difficult to suppress and, though my responses are conventionally appropriate to my role as friend, my heart is not in it.

We have all been in situations which give rise to such difficulties. But notice the levels on which Right Speech has to be addressed in order to be accomplished. Maybe the best I can do now is put on a good face, say the right things. But true affection and the capacity for sympathetic joy will require much more work in addressing the underlying reasons for my own dukkha which prevent me offering them to the world – or in this particular case, my friend. Restraint, discernment, awareness and acceptance all have to be available to me. Fundamentally, I must recognize that life will not present itself to me as I would wish it, and I must address and recognize my wishes for what they are – desire, aversion and fear – if I am to be able to communicate with real generosity. So the example of Right Speech also serves as an example for the other precepts. In this I must recognize that every action is as it is because of the thoughts that gave rise to it, and that progress on the Buddhist path is a matter of disciplined improvement, and of the cultivation of those qualities that will eventually make such situations no longer onerous, because the negative states that bring them about will have been replaced by positive ones. Ultimately we may even be able to replace our own dukkha with insight. As we listen, we discern the need of the other person and respond freely. Such a capacity to listen and respond is referred to as 'giving the gift of the dharma', and this is a blessing to the world, freely given for its own sake and resulting in transformation.

We may view this progress from the one state to the other not in terms of a sudden transformation, but rather as the development of a skill. If I were learning to drive, swim or juggle, it would not be so different. I must recognize what I am getting right and getting wrong, and acknowledge what is improving as well as investigate what is not quite right. With all these things there are sudden breakthroughs. At first I am pretty useless; nothing goes right. Then a number of things come together, and something I once could not do at all is now possible. All of a sudden it seems effortless, and there is nothing in the way. That is how it is. When we think of this on a grand scale we can start to understand the Buddhist idea of the bodhisattva, one who aspires to be a buddha, and who acts for the weal of the world, to relieve its suffering.

Buddhism does not, of course, simply think in terms of individual ethics. A question which is often asked, especially by individuals who feel disempowered, is 'What can I do to change the whole situation?' Wars, famines and global catastrophes constantly confront us, in the news and in the media generally. While we need to know about such events, we also have to feel able to respond to them, rather than retreat from them. In this respect the first precept is particularly significant. Most religious and ethical traditions make firm statements about not killing in a needless way, not murdering and abjuring senseless violence. But the first precept, abstention from harming living beings, is a commitment to non-violence. While in theory this is a very noble aim, we would be mistaken to say it is not contentious.

We have so far illustrated situations in which we may wish to do the right thing but encounter difficulties in putting such a motivation into practice; this emphasizes the importance of skilfulness in Buddhist ethics. We are often confronted by situations in which our ideals are overrun by a desire for revenge or a wish to inflict pain and retribution. Everyone may regret times when they acted impetuously and hurt someone else, perhaps physically but more often emotionally. Yet most of us recognize times when violence appears a necessary preventive measure in order to stop further suffering. Why should Buddhist teachings stand so resolutely against such a common-sense necessity? If I act out of a good motive, isn't my action thereby exonerated? In a Christian context, this is the point at which the Sermon on the Mount would be weighed alongside the Ten Commandments. The first is a much more radical teaching than the second, and the first precept aligns itself with this radical alternative.

So we start with the situation we find ourselves in, and accept that we are working on ourselves to influence the overall world that we live in, with the aspiration to be virtuous in all things. Ultimately this aspiration is to achieve harmlessness, but at present it is to be as kind as possible. On the one hand we may take this example from a Thai monk working in a particularly difficult area of Thailand, where there are pirates and fishermen who may be seen as rather rough and cruel people. We are told: 'Murder is quite common among them. So this monk just tries to encourage them not to kill each other. When these people come to the monastery he doesn't go round raising non-killing to the level of, "You shouldn't kill anything – not even a mosquito larva", because they couldn't accept that. Their livelihood depends very much on fishing and the killing of animals' (Ven. Ajahn Sumedho, *Cittaviveka: Teachings from the Silent Mind*, Amaravati Publications, 1987, p 25). His teaching aims at gradually sensitizing them in their everyday life to be less violent.

At the other extreme, we consider the situation of the Dalai Lama, exiled in this present life from his country; many of his people are undergoing repression, and in some cases, torture. His response to such a dilemma tests the credulity of listeners across the world. He continues to eschew violence as a means to repatriation and freedom for his people, and his views can only be honoured on the basis of his personal integrity and stature. While other calamities of a similar kind have evoked military reprisal and quests for violent intervention, the present incarnation of the Bodhisattva Avalokiteshvara (the embodiment of compassion) still affirms the need to seek peaceful ways of overcoming present injustice. The focus of the Buddhist view goes broader and deeper, more than just a response to immediate affairs. The dharma, virtue, the precepts and the Eightfold Path cannot be affirmed if there is no practice of sila (Right Speech, Right Action and Right Livelihood) and, as a consequence, going for refuge may entail facing up to difficult responsibilities within a world driven by karmically negative forces.

Renunciation

No account of Buddhist morality would be complete without dwelling on the concept of renunciation, which is so central to the Buddhist view. It is apt to be misunderstood when it is seen as a curtailment of freedom and opportunity, but this is largely due to a reductionist understanding of such a rich concept. The important question is, 'What does renunciation entail?'

Once the Buddha had set in motion the Wheel of the Law (dharma) by preaching his first sermon, he spoke of having entered on the course that will make an end of suffering, and he stated that, 'The road was declared by me when I had understood the removal of the darts.'

The darts (*salla*) are the hindrances or fetters that bind us to the round of rebirth. They symbolize lust, hatred, delusion, pride, false views, grief and indecision. When Buddhists speak about renunciation it is in relation to these things. Buddhist decisions about morality are necessarily undertaken with the knowledge that virtue itself lies in the renunciation of these things, and that whatever situation arises Right Action or Livelihood cannot be motivated by any of these forces. While in humanitarian terms we may recognize fairness, or even retribution, as a way of dealing with the balance of events in life (on a personal or global scale), that course can never be the proper motivation of a Buddhist sensibility. Whatever takes place here and now is determined by the ongoing effect of karmic conditioning, and the eradication of this can only be initiated by the renunciant ideal. A short-term re-balancing of affairs, from a moral point of view, is not necessarily an improvement in the overall context of human history. We may witness this in the fact that the ending of one war or period of violence does not end violence altogether. The seeds of one conflict may be sown in the conclusion of a previous one. Necessarily, therefore, the ideal of renunciation has to take account of the continuous possibility of present suffering, while holding fast to the motivation that renunciation imposes. As with all ethical ideals found within the great religious traditions, the conflict between pragmatism and idealism is pronounced; but Buddhism, perhaps, identifies it more obviously than others, since renunciation brooks no compromise. Its strength lies in its overall vision but, understandably, this involves a commitment that is not easy to sustain.

Renunciation is intimately related to skilfulness, and thus to the notion of transforming the mind. There is an evolutionary sense to this interconnection, which is well expressed in the following passage by two Tibetan teachers:

> There are many ways of transforming the mind. The method presented here is intended to turn the mind from non-virtue to virtue. For instance, if we set about training our body, first we feel stiff and awkward. After performing physical exercises, however, our body becomes supple and agile and can adopt many postures which previously would have been difficult. It is evident

that the body can gain a greater degree of flexibility by applying the appropriate exercises, and the same is true for the mind. Initially, we may have to endure many difficulties and hardships, but by making a concerted effort we can make our mind very supple. Endowed with this quality we may then engage in a great many skilful activities.

(Geshe Rabten and Geshe Dhargyey, *Advice from a Spiritual Friend*, Wisdom Publications, 1984, p 25)

Neither skilfulness nor virtue is gained from complacency. There is little to offer from such a safe haven that will benefit others. Helping people by saying things that renew them, and allow them to face difficult situations, inevitably arises from sharing our own difficulties with them. We may not think we are speaking with wisdom, but rather voicing our own inadequacies; but the effect is more vitalizing than platitudes of commiseration. Given that circumstance does not let us live exactly as we would wish according to our desires, this makes good sense, but we must often be pushed into realizing it. This struggle is one that we must have with ourselves; but it is a creative one, the benefits of which become tangible in practice. The Buddhist scriptures offer advice as to how to accomplish it. Here are some verses related to transforming anger. The purpose of recollecting such advice is to remove the obstacles to generating metta (loving kindness).

Admonition to Oneself

The fourth method: if, however, in spite of one's efforts, irritation continues to arise, one should think thus:

Suppose an enemy has hurt you
In what is now his domain,
Why try yourself as well to hurt
Your mind? That is not his domain.

This anger that you entertain
Is gnawing at the very roots
Of all the virtues that you guard –
Where is there such a fool as you!

Another does ignoble deeds,
So you are angry – how is this?
Do you then want to copy, too,
The sort of acts that he commits?

Suppose another, to annoy,
Provokes you with some odious act,
Why suffer anger to spring up,
And do as he would have you do?

If you get angry, then may be
You make him suffer, may be not;
Though with the hurt that anger brings
You certainly are punished now.

If anger-blinded enemies
Set out to tread the path of woe,
Do you, by getting angry too,
Intend to follow heel to toe?

If hurt is done you by a foe
Because of anger on your part,
Then put your anger down, for why
Should you be harassed needlessly?

Since states last but a moment's time,
Those aggregates, by which was done
The odious act, have ceased, so now
What is it you are angry with?

Whom shall he hurt, who seeks to hurt
Another, in the other's absence?
Your presence is the cause of hurt;
Why are you angry, then, with him?

> (*Visuddhimagga* 308, copyright H. Saddhatissa.
> Reprinted from *Buddhist Ethics* with permission of
> Wisdom Publications, 361 Newbury Street,
> Boston, Massachusetts, USA.)

In conclusion

It will have been noted how Buddhist ethics dwell on practicalities and attention to the everyday, and a process of improving our sensitivity in the way we live and treat others, both humans and other creatures. In looking forward to the next chapter on moral issues, it is worth noting that from a Buddhist perspective:

- there are no absolute laws, only principles to be borne in mind
- there is no absolute authority or set of commandments handed down by a divine being
- there is no idea of punishment, only the karmic injunction that you reap what you sow in terms of both the effects you create in the world and the concomitant effects you create for yourself.

As a result, we cannot speak of a systematic set of Buddhist ethics that applies in all situations for all individuals. This is in part because there is no arbitrator or judge upon the individual in the Buddhist scheme of things. Also, generally speaking, Buddhism has no eschatology: there is no salvific plan for how things will work out overall despite the way in which we behave. One way of understanding this is that we make our own destiny, there is no other imposed upon or delivered to us. When we examine Buddhist approaches to moral issues in the next chapter the result of this will become clearer.

07

moral issues

In this chapter you will learn:
- the Buddhist principles –
  related to the natural world,
  the animal world and human
  society – that inform moral
  behaviour
- about issues central to the
  concerns of present-day
  society.

For Buddhists, all moral issues are approached with the following in mind:

- Purifying the Mind and Developing Wisdom.
- Following the Precepts.
- The Law of Karma and Rebirth.
- Intentionality and Skilfulness.
- Developing Loving Kindness and Compassion.

These are not separate considerations but rather the factors which ensure that what one does is a blessing to the world, rather than a corruption of it. Sila (ethical action) is the expression of dharma (truth); carried out in the course of everyday life and moral decision making, it frees the world from dis-ease and confusion.

However, for Buddhists, there is no overall authority that legislates right and wrong on particular issues. There is guidance, and there are limits, but the task of making difficult decisions, within the framework of the precepts, is the individual's responsibility. The following issues have been chosen to illustrate this, and to represent particular focuses of Buddhist concern.

The natural world

Animal welfare

Rebirth, when aligned to the doctrine of harmlessness, leads Buddhists to emphasize compassionate attitudes to all living things. The *Culla-Vagga*, verse 6, states that:

> Creatures without feet have my love,
> And likewise those that have two feet,
> And those that have four feet I love,
> And those, too, that have many feet.

> May those without feet harm me not,
> And those with two feet cause no hurt,
> May those with four feet harm me not,
> Nor those who many feet possess.

> Let creatures, all, all things that live,
> All beings of whatever kind,
> See nothing that will bode them ill!
> May naught of evil come to them!

The *Buddhist Declaration on Nature* affirms:

> The fact that (animals) may be incapable of communicating their feelings is no more an indication of

apathy or insensibility to suffering or happiness than in the case of a person whose faculty of speech is impaired …

There is a striking similarity between exterminating the life of a wild animal for fun and terminating the life of an innocent human being at the whim of a more capable and powerful person … [Buddhism is a] system which propagates the theory of rebirth and life after death, it maintains that in the continuous birth and rebirth of sentient beings (not only on this planet but in the universe as a whole) each being is related to us ourselves, just as our own parents are related to us in this life …

We regard our survival as an undeniable right. As co-inhabitants of this planet, other species too have this right for survival. And since human beings as well as other non-human sentient beings depend upon the environment as the ultimate source of life and well-being, let us share the conviction that the conservation of the environment, the restoration of the imbalance caused by our negligence in the past, be implemented with courage and determination.

(*Buddhist Declaration on Nature*, Assisi,
29 September 1986)

The *Sutta Nipata* echoes these sentiments:

> May creatures all abound
> in weal and peace; may all
> be blessed with peace always;
> all creatures
> weak or strong,
> all creatures great and small;
> creatures unseen or seen,
> dwelling afar or near,
> born or awaiting birth,
> – may all be blessed with peace!
> Just as with her own life
> a mother shields from hurt
> her own, her only, child, –
> let all embracing thoughts
> for all that lives be thine,
> – an all-embracing love
> for all the universe
> in all its heights and depths
> and breadth, unstinted love,
> unmarred by hate within,
> not rousing enmity.

Ecology

The Buddhist emphasis on harmony and ecological balance is extended to the whole of the natural world. Buddhists see a need to ensure the balance of nature as an ethical priority. In the *Buddhist Declaration on Nature* at the Conference of World Faiths in Assisi they stated:

> Hence Buddhism is a religion of love, understanding and compassion, and committed towards the ideal of non-violence. As such, it also attaches great importance to wildlife and the protection of the environment on which every being in this world depends for survival.

In the West, where ecological issues have gained some prominence, Buddhist initiatives have also been in evidence. For example, in 1979, The English Sangha Trust bought an area of West Sussex woodland for a Forest Retreat Sangha. This is now the focus of a conservation project based on the Buddhist idea of harmony with all forms of life. The wood is being restored to its original character having previously been exploited commercially, by the implementation of a monocultural system of agriculture, wherein are planted trees of a species suitable for growing as a cash crop. The wood is now seen as a place of peace and tranquillity, where monks and nuns can engage in solitary meditation and retreat, and where indigenous wildlife can flourish.

In 1991 the Samye Ling Tibetan Centre in Scotland launched the 'Holy Island Project'. This has resulted in buying Holy Isle, just off the Isle of Arran, to use as a place of spiritual retreat and as a nature reserve. Four hundred years ago, the island was the site of a monastery, and the project intends to restore it to its former use, but as an interdenominational retreat centre as well as a facility specifically for Buddhist practitioners.

Vegetarianism

Given the first precept, it might seem logical that all Buddhists are vegetarian; however, this is not always the case, as this comment demonstrates:

> 'Is it permissible to eat meat?' I asked a learned and holy Tibetan lama. 'Certainly, although if you are practising meditation on compassion it could be counterproductive.'
>
> 'Is it not the case that the one who eats meat bears responsibility for the killing?' The holy man looked

astonished. Patiently he explained to me basic Buddhist truths which I should have mastered lives ago. Of course not. The one who eats meat a) intends to eat, and b) may or may not intend to eat meat. Meat is, as a matter of fact, what is being eaten. But nowhere in the mental states of our reverend gourmand is there an intention to kill. In fact, in the Tibetan tradition, by the monk reciting suitable formulae over the juicy curry, the goat may actually obtain a more favourable rebirth than would otherwise be the case. Thus, even while eating meat, our monk can generate compassion and do good towards a creature which was already dead, and dead through no wish of the monk himself.'

> (Paul Williams, in C. Erricker (ed.), *Teaching World Religions*, Heinemann, 1993, p 46)

Nevertheless, in the West especially, some Buddhists do make out a strong case for encouraging the vegetarian viewpoint.

In *A Buddhist Case for Vegetarianism*, Roshi Philip Kapleau cites his own students often asking the question, 'Does Buddhism prohibit meat-eating?' He includes a letter illustrating the dilemma that many Westerners face when trying to convert Buddhist principles into practice, which runs thus:

> We were drawn to Buddhism by its teaching of respect for all forms of life, human as well as non-human. But being new to it, we are confused and concerned about one thing. To practise Buddhism correctly, is it necessary to give up eating meat? There seems to be no agreement among Buddhists on this point. We've heard that in Japan and Southeast Asia lay Buddhists and even monks and priests eat meat, and that teachers in the United States and other Western countries do the same. But here in Rochester we're told that you and your students are vegetarians. Do the Buddhist scriptures forbid the eating of meat? If so, for what reasons? If they don't forbid it, why, may we ask, are you a vegetarian? We would become vegetarians ourselves if we were sure that by doing so we could become more deeply involved in Buddhism. But if that were not the case, we'd rather not give up meat, partly because all our friends eat it. Also, we do have some reservations from a health standpoint about a vegetarian diet.

> (Roshi Philip Kapleau, *A Buddhist Case for Vegetarianism*, Rider, 1983, p 4)

Underlying this concern is the idea that meat gives strength and energy, and contributes to a balanced diet. Kapleau cites the American philosopher, Thoreau, in answer to such a question:

> When asked by a farmer, 'I hear you don't eat meat. Where do you get your strength (read 'protein')?' Thoreau, pointing to the husky team of horses drawing the farmer's wagon, replied, 'Where do they get their strength?' Kapleau further contends that according to modern medical opinion, the issue is now beyond speculation. Vegetarians, it seems are on the side of the angels.
>
> (ibid., pp 4–5)

He goes on to cite the pain and suffering involved in animal slaughter, and in the way in which animals are reared and transported in environments solely conditioned by economic greed. Vegetarians would maintain that meat eating represents a tacit acceptance of human greed, and a complicity in its process. So, one may ask, should Buddhists not therefore align themselves with the principle of vegetarianism? The issue can be extended further, as this sentiment from an ancient Chinese verse indicates, linking animal slaughter to bad karma:

> For hundreds of thousands of years
> the stew in the pot
> has brewed hatred and resentment
> that is difficult to stop.
> If you wish to know why there are disasters
> of armies and weapons in the world,
> listen to the piteous cries
> from the slaughterhouse at midnight.
>
> (ibid., p 17)

Of course, the principle of rebirth also plays a part in this argument. In Mahayana Buddhism, one of the themes for contemplation is that, in the endless cycle of rebirths, not a single being has not been our mother, father, husband or other relative in some way. This breaks down the species division between humans and non-humans, and does not allow us to think of other creatures as separate, inferior life forms. All life therefore becomes sacred.

Nevertheless, traditionally, Buddhism is not exclusively vegetarian. One contemporary Buddhist, of the Tibetan tradition, in answer to the question 'May monks eat meat?' replies:

Strictly speaking, from the point of view of the *vinaya*, a monk should not eat meat. However, most Tibetan monks do eat meat and I have been influenced by them so I eat it too. Originally, when I was first ordained and living in a monastery in Nepal most of my time was spent in study and meditation so I didn't eat meat. We tended to get up early and go to bed early and a vegetarian diet made sleep lighter and the mind clearer for meditation. But when I started travelling and leading a more 'normal' lifestyle – working – I just found that I was too hungry at night and did not feel so strong. So I started eating meat.

(P. Connolly and C. Erricker, *The Presence & Practice of Buddhism*, West Sussex Institute of Higher Education, 1985, p 111)

So the answer to the question, 'Are Buddhists vegetarian?' is this: some are and some are not. However, Western Buddhists are certainly sensitive to this issue, and many see a sensitizing of our way of life as a commitment to vegetarianism.

There is a caveat to this, however. Monks, as mendicants, when presented with *dana* (their meal of the day, put into their alms bowl by lay Buddhists), are expected to accept such generosity unquestioningly. Traditionally, giving meat is often seen by lay Buddhists as a generous gesture, and it would not be appropriate for the monks to refuse.

Human society

Capital punishment and imprisonment

In principle, and following the first precept, Buddhism deplores the taking of life under any circumstances. However, in some Buddhist countries, notably Thailand and Burma, the death penalty is exercised in certain cases. One of the most important teachers in Buddhist history, Buddhaghosa, considered the act of killing and murder as follows:

'Taking life' means to kill anything that lives. The precept says that you should not strike or kill any living being. 'Anything that lives' is anything that has what is called the 'life-force'. This includes all members of the animal kingdoms as well as humans. 'Taking life' means killing or trying to kill deliberately, by word or action.

With regard to animals, it is worse to kill large ones than small ones. This is because you have to make a much greater effort to kill large ones. Even where the effort is the same, the difference in importance has to be taken into account. When it comes to human beings, the killing is considered to be worse if the person killed was a good (virtuous) person. Apart from that, the seriousness of the offence is also measured by how much the murderer wanted the killing to happen.

(quoted in J.Rankin et al., *Religion and Ethics*, Longman, 1991, p 152)

While the act of killing is effectively prohibited in principle, the important issue is to be compassionate in any circumstance. Given this, one should offer this compassion to anyone, whatever their circumstance and whatever acts they may have committed.

One Buddhist mission which promotes this principle is a chaplaincy service for prisoners in the United Kingdom. The purpose of this venture is to bring some serenity, contemplation and desire for altruistic action into prisoners' lives. 'Buddha groves' (areas for contemplation in which Buddha images have been placed) have been established in some British prisons. The director of the British Prison Chaplaincy Service explains:

My purpose in encouraging the placing of these simple Buddhist shrines in the prisons is twofold and has nothing to do with proselytizing or trying to win converts to Buddhism. The Prison Service admits that prisoners should be allowed to practise their religion and that places of worship should be provided for the prisoners of all religious faiths. Our first objective then, in a very modest way, is to help meet that standard by providing the few Buddhist prisoners with a focus for their devotion and meditation practice. And, secondly, for those who are not Buddhist we hope that having the opportunity to rest their eyes on something as serene and peaceful as a Buddha-Rupa will help them quieten their minds and bestow a little respite from the turmoil so often about and within them.

The particular results of their efforts are exemplified thus:

Inmates in Risley (prison) fasted recently so that the money that would have been used to feed them could be diverted to the starving in Rwanda.

(Ajahn Khammadhammo, *The Forest Hermitage Newsletter*, September 1994)

Abortion and mercy killing

In this area, the Five Precepts once more prevail as guiding principles – especially the first, which is linked with the quality of compassion. However, given that there is no overriding authority in ethical matters in Buddhism, each individual must make his or her own decision about the circumstances in which they find themselves.

Abortion, in principle, is to be avoided, though, as the following comment shows, it is not absolutely forbidden:

> Although abortion appears to, perhaps really does, abrogate the first principle, it might on balance, and in particular circumstances, yet be considered a necessity for compassionate reasons.

> (General Secretary, The Buddhist Society)

However, groups motivated by the Buddhist principle of compassion do tend to attach a particular significance to birth – despite it not being linked to a doctrine of creation – as is demonstrated here with regard to doctors and midwives:

> Every birth is Holy. I think that a midwife must be religious, because the energy she is dealing with is Holy. She needs to know that other people's energy is sacred.

> (Ina May Gaskin, *Spiritual Midwifery*, The Book Publishing Co., 1980, p 282)

War

It hardly needs stating that every world religion is, in principle, against violence. But, in practice, the question of course remains as to what to do when violent action is required to preserve a particular faith or culture.

When a British mission, led by Younghusband, sought to enter Tibet by force at the beginning of the twentieth century, the Tibetans put down their arms and retreated from their borders. This might be seen as an act of cowardice, but the Buddhist motivation was to reduce the amount of harm incurred by conflict. The message of the Dalai Lama, in exile today, echoes this action. Politically naïve as it may appear, Buddhists have generally taken this stance of non-resistance in most violent situations (although armed resistance to the Chinese has been organised by some Tibetans within Tibet, with the involvement of the CIA).

Scripture and tradition both point to social harmony being the result of inner peace. The *Dhammapada* states:

> Though one man conquer a thousand times a thousand men in battle, he who conquers himself is the greatest warrior ...

> Better than sovereignty over the earth, better than the heaven-state, better than dominion over all the worlds is the first step on the noble path ...

And:

> Hatred does not cease by hatred, hatred ceases only by love. This is the eternal law.

Of course, the ideal is not always matched by the actuality, as the problems faced by Tamils in Sri Lanka in recent years have demonstrated.

Suicide

Suicide is not a moral fault, properly speaking, because morality is directly concerned with what we do to others. The great Buddhist teacher Nagarjuna explained:

> According to the *Treatise on Discipline*, suicide is not murder. Fault and merit result respectively from a wrong done to others or the good done to others. It is not by caring for one's own body or killing one's own body that one acquires merit or commits a misdeed.
>
> (*Buddhist Studies Review*, Vol 4, No. 2, 1987, p 106)

However, if one person incites another to suicide, that is a different matter:

> If a monk, with deliberate intent, takes with his own hands the life of a human being ... if he himself gives him a weapon and tells him to kill himself; if he praises death to him; if for example he says to him, 'Fie on you! What good does this miserable life do you? Far better to die than live', in such a way that the other conceives in his heart a delight in dying; if in these various fashions he tells him to die or praises death to him, and later that man, because of this, dies, that monk is blameworthy of a very grave offence and should be excluded from the Community ...
>
> (ibid., p 105)

Suicide is, however – like all conscious or voluntary acts – subject to the law of karma. Suicide is folly, insofar as taking one's own life is the outcome of the desire to annihilate oneself; for the fruit of that act is a rebirth in the samsaric realm, and hence further suffering.

Nevertheless, suicide is justified in the case of the 'Noble Ones', who have already cut off desire. There can be no possible further fruition to their actions. Death is a way of severing their last link with this world and passing into nirvana, since they have done what had to be done. A test case is that of Valkali: Valkali was a disciple of the Buddha who became sick and experienced great suffering. The Buddha was told of this, and came to where Valkali lay:

> The Master approached and said to him: 'Do not move, Valkali, there are seats quite near and I shall sit there.'

> Having sat down, he went on: 'Friend, is it tolerable? Is it viable? Are the painful feelings you are experiencing on the decrease and not on the increase?'

> 'No, Master,' replied Valkali, 'it is neither tolerable nor viable. The painful feelings are on the increase and not on the decrease.'

> 'Then have you some regret and some remorse?'

> 'Yes, Master,' confessed Valkali, 'I have much regret and much remorse.'

> 'Does your conscience reproach you for something from the moral point of view?'

> 'No, my conscience does not reproach me for anything from the moral point of view.'

> 'And yet,' stated the Buddha, 'you have regret and remorse.'

> 'This is because for a long time I have wanted to go and look at the Master, but I do not find the strength in my body to do it.'

> 'For shame, Valkali!' cried the Buddha, 'What good would it do you to see my body of filth? Valkali, whoever sees my Doctrine, sees me; whoever sees me sees my Doctrine.'

> Having spoken thus, the Buddha went to the Vulture Peak, while Valkali had himself carried to the Black Rock on the Seers' Mount. During the night two deities warned the Buddha that Valkali was thinking of liberating himself and that, once liberated, he would be delivered.

The Buddha dispatched some monks to Valkali to tell him:

'Blameless will be your death, blameless the end of your days.'

'Return to the Master,' said Valkali, 'and in my name prostrate yourselves at his feet. Be sure and tell him that I no longer feel any doubt regarding the transitory, painful and unstable nature of all the phenomena of existence.'

The monks had hardly left when Valkali 'took the knife' and killed himself. The Buddha, being doubtful about this, immediately went to the Black Rock in the company of several disciples. Valkali lay dying on his couch, his shoulders turned to the right, for it is thus that the Noble Ones die. A cloud of black dust moved around him.

'Do you see, O Monks,' the Buddha asked, 'that cloud of dust which is drifting in all directions around the corpse? It is Mara, the Malign One who is seeking the whereabouts of Valkali's consciousness. But Valkali's consciousness is nowhere: Valkali is in complete Nirvana.'

Hence the Noble Ones who have triumphed over delusion and eliminated passion can, once their task is done, speed the hour of deliverance by voluntarily taking their own lives. Whatever the means used, act of will, recourse to the supernormal, or quite simply the rope or knife, their suicide is 'blameless'.

(ibid., pp 110–11)

Altruistic sacrifice

Equally, Bodhisattvas who gave their life altruistically for other beings were regarded as noble and blameless; one such was the Bodhisattva Vessantara, whose action towards the hungry tigress in the *Vessantara Jataka* is recorded in Chapter 4.

Auto-cremation

There is another form of religious suicide, known as auto-cremation. The burning of their own bodies by Buddhist monks in Vietnam, as a protest against the regime, arguably falls into this category. The important point in these events is, of course, not the act itself, but the question of its motive or intention, and the state of mind in which it was carried out.

Gender and equality

In all the major religious traditions of the world this is a vexed issue, largely for historical and social reasons. In the times of those who founded traditions the status of women tended to be subservient to that of men. In Indian culture, the caste system provided a rigorous definition of a woman's role. For example, the question of a dowry, to be paid by the wife's parents to those of the husband, was also an indication of what was expected of her in the future.

In Buddhism the caste system was abolished, even though the monastic nature of the movement made the Buddha reticent to receive women into the order. The segregation of males and females was strictly observed in the context of renunciation, which emphasized the importance of avoiding situations that could inflame lustful desires.

However, women were accepted in both lay and monastic environments. The role of the mother, as one who gave and who was worthy of compassion, was stressed. The notion of rebirth actually accentuated the recognition that gender difference was not a fundamental determinant of identity. As the tradition evolved, so women played their part. When Buddhism extended beyond India to Sri Lanka, an order of nuns was requested for the island. Nevertheless, conservative social influences have tended to ensure that, on the whole, the role of women in traditionally Buddhist countries today is not equal to that of men, whether in the monastic sangha or lay life. In the Theravadin tradition there is some difficulty regarding the status of nuns, since full ordination died out in the lineage over the course of time, and Western female Buddhists who decide to take up the monastic life are duly prevented from achieving fully ordained status. Therefore they are, at present, subservient in status to any ordained monk, regardless of the number of years they have been in the sangha. This is an issue that the Western branches of Theravada Buddhism are constantly seeking to address.

In other branches of Buddhism the issue has evolved differently. A woman was made spiritual head of the reformed Soto-Zen Church, as Abbess of Shasta Abbey in California, and Throssel Hole Priory in the United Kingdom. The Reverend Jiyu-Kennett was certified as Dharma Heir and fully licensed teacher by her master, the Very Reverend Keido Chisan Koho, Zenji.

In Tibetan Buddhism there have always been female bodhisattvas, who have been the subject of devotion. Green and White Tara, embodying compassion, are the most obvious examples. Kuan Ying (the female form of Chenrezig or Avalokiteshvara, in Chinese and Japanese Buddhism) is also venerated. However, as often tends to be the case, this esteem is not wholly transferred to the status of women in these societies! As far as equality is concerned, there is still a way to go, but Western Buddhism could provide the lead in this respect, because it is such a significant issue in Western society. The FWBO acknowledges, with some qualification, the value of the feminist movement:

> Feminism ... could be described as a movement that demands – or insists – that women should have access to all the facilities they require for their development as human beings; it asserts that they should not be confined or limited to any particular range of facilities or activities; and it encourages them to take more initiative, be more independent, and to function as individuals in their own right, rather than being mere extensions or supports to the men in their lives. Feminism of this sort is quite compatible with Buddhism and the spiritual life ...

> At the hub of the FWBO we therefore find a unified Order of women and men; everything in the Order is open to women and men; they take the same ordination and vows; they exercise the same functions at public centres; they practise the same meditations, study the same texts, and so on. In the FWBO we feel that no one should be excluded from the process of higher human development, whether on the grounds of sex, race, colour, level of education, or social position.

> (*Golden Drum*, Windhorse Publications, No. 7, November–January 1987/8, p 13)

In conclusion

In this chapter we have covered Buddhist responses to a number of moral issues. However, as noted in the previous chapter, Buddhism does not have a systematic philosophy of ethics, as a result:

- While there is a rich tradition of moral reasoning in Buddhism, it is not possible to state 'what Buddhism teaches' about specific moral issues.
- The emphasis on 'moral enquiry' in Buddhist tradition tends to set up something equivalent to a 'case law' to be drawn upon, rather than absolute injunctions.

- Because Buddhist approaches to moral issues are based upon applying a principle, such as compassion, to a situation, it is possible for the outcome (the action taken or not taken) to vary. In this respect we could classify Buddhist morality as being 'situational' rather than rule abiding.

08
the social order

In this chapter you will learn:
- about Buddhist monastic and family life
- about the Buddhist rites of passage, in particular about the distinctiveness of the Buddhist understanding of death and rebirth.

Ordination

Ordination generally entails taking up the mendicant life and 'going forth' as a monk or nun. In the Theravada tradition this is known as *bhikkhu ordination*, and follows on from the procedure first established by the Buddha when he ordained his first disciples, saying, '*Ehi bhikkhu!*' ('come bhikkhu!') after his first sermon in the Deer Park at Sarnath.

Candidates for ordination will already be *semaneras* (novices). The ceremony will take place within a *sima* (a specially defined area). An *upajjhaya* (preceptor) must officiate. He will be a senior monk, head of an order or senior incumbent of a monastery, invested with this responsibility. The candidates must be able to recite the *Patimokkha* (rules of discipline). Before the ceremony, new robes will have been made for the candidates, dyed brown or saffron. After it, they will be bound by the 227 rules of the monastic community and the Ten Precepts. In the Mahayana tradition the conventions and ceremonies vary, but the commitment is essentially the same. The robes worn are black in the Zen tradition and maroon in the Tibetan.

Celibacy

The *Vinaya* (Code of Discipline) orders monastic life, which demands celibacy. It is worth noting, however, that in certain Korean and Tibetan orders it is possible for monks and nuns to marry, and that this is the norm for Japanese monks. The Western Buddhist Order does not, strictly speaking, have monks and nuns. They may be married with families or be single. However, celibacy is practised by some Order members. Those with families may still choose to live in single-sex communities, as this comment by a Western Buddhist Order member illustrates:

> Some people are surprised that I have a child and that I am an Order member who has gone for refuge to the Buddha and Sangha. Chastity, living in a community of men, and having a child, with the mother living in a women's community with the child, is cooperatively worked out. All Order members are working towards happy celibacy, contentment. That is certainly what I'm working toward. The primary thing is that I remain clear about being a Buddhist first and a parent second, for the sake of myself and the child. If I lose sight of that I'm lost really. What

children need is clear positive emotion from the adults around them. I need the conditions to support positivity and clarity.

(FWBO member)

Weddings and marriage

Marriage is regarded in Buddhism as a social and civil matter. Monks therefore do not officiate at weddings, nor are they allowed to be present at the ceremony. Monks will bless a marriage as a separate event, after the ceremony, but the distinction between this and the ceremony itself is quite clear. As one Theravada Buddhist puts it:

It's not according to the *Vinaya*, which is the code of conduct for the monks. They are excluded from taking part in these ceremonies, because the Buddhist monk is a person who has renounced worldly life. He is working on his own salvation, and he is in a monastery which has been provided.

(John Bowker, *Worlds of Faith*, BBC, 1983, p 207)

Family life

Since Buddhism is traditionally centred upon monastic life and the quest for liberation, it might seem that Buddhists would have little to say about married life and bringing up children. However, more than ninety-five per cent of Buddhists are lay people, with these issues very much at the centre of their lives.

Sangha has a larger meaning than just 'monastic community', indeed, had the Buddha not spread his message to lay people the tradition would not have developed in the way that it has. The importance of the interdependent relationship between monastic and lay society was always emphasized by the Buddha, and with good reason, since, given the doctrine of rebirth, our station changes in successive lives and the merit accrued by good karma in one life is the only means to elevation in the next. Thus the significance of how one lives life as a lay person, and the way in which children are nurtured are important issues in Buddhist society which have led to the observance of specific rules and customs.

The Buddha said: 'A wise man should avoid unchastity as if it were a pit of burning cinders. One who is not able to live in a state of celibacy should at least not break the purity of another man's wife' (*Suttanipata*, v. 396).

The importance of the family

In the Buddha's Discourses there is much advice to householders on the importance of family life and how it should be conducted. The *Rukkhadamma Jataka* compares the strength of family life to the trees of the forest, which are able to withstand the force of the wind, when a solitary tree, however large, cannot (*Jataka*, Vol. 1, v. 329).

The metaphor is apt for the significance of both family life and sangha generally, suggesting that family ties and spiritual friendship encourage growth in the dharma and resistance to samsaric conditions. The *Sigalovada Suttanta* gives the most specific advice on lay society and family life. Sigola was a young man who showed no interest in the dharma, but who was entreated by his dying father to worship the six quarters of the earth and sky. Ignorant of the meaning of this, he was met one morning by the Buddha taking this advice literally, worshipping in every direction. The Buddha explained the six quarters to him as parents, teachers, wife and children, friends and associates, employees, religious teachers and priests. In each of these relationships certain duties pertain.

Parents and children

In the relationship between parent and child, the child should:

- support his or her parents
- perform their duties for them
- keep up the family and family traditions
- be worthy of his or her heritage
- offer alms in honour of departed relatives.

The parent should:

- restrain the children from evil
- direct them toward the good
- attend to their education
- see them married at a proper age
- hand over their inheritance.

(*Digha Nikaya*, Vol. III,180, quoted in H. Saddhatissa, *Buddhist Ethics*, Wisdom Publications, 1987, p 118)

This description of duties can be complemented by a story illustrating the spirit of the relationship between parents and children that Buddhism seeks to develop:

Red Beans and Rice

There was once a director of a big company in Japan. He was elected president of a special club for businessmen. At the fancy dinner party to celebrate his election he served all his guests a dish of red beans and rice. In Japan, this dish is served when you want to wish someone well-being in the future. But at this grand dinner, this dish seemed out of place. The director was moved to explain why he had served the dish. He told everyone that it commemorated an incident in his life.

He was born and lived in a very poor farming family. His family was so poor that he grew to realize that however hard he might work on the land, he would never be able to produce enough from it to be able to care for his parents in their old age or to try to help educate his brothers and sisters. He decided that he would have to go to a town to find some other work. However, he was very aware that in Japan for an elder son to leave the land and his family was a source of great sadness. After much thought he resolved to make his departure at night, secretly. So he packed a small bundle for travel.

Long before dawn he made ready to leave his home. He was just about to slip out of the kitchen door when he saw that his mother, who was normally asleep at that time, instead was up and working in the kitchen. Without turning to look at him she spoke.

'I've prepared some red beans and rice for you. Eat it before you go.'

He sat down in front of it at the small kitchen table. His mother brought over some hot soup as well. He was so close to tears that he could not eat anything. Seeing this his mother said, 'Maybe since you've just got up you may not be hungry. I'll take the rice from your bowl and make it into rice balls which you can carry with you and eat later.'

He received the rice balls from her and left the house into the dark of the night. Following the dark road to the station, he cried all of the way. He went off to the town and worked very hard. Even though he made a fortune, he could never forget that dish of red beans and rice. If he thought about doing something bad, the memory of the red beans and rice stopped him.

At the dinner party, the businessman said, 'There are many people here who are much finer than I am, but in spite of that I have been elected as president. What gave me this honour is red beans and rice. Therefore I would like you also to eat it.'

When an old Zen teacher heard this story he was very moved. Not only by the maternal love that was demonstrated, but by the superb wisdom of the mother shown by her willingness to let him go. Somehow, she knew exactly what her son was thinking and what it was that he had to do.

(Ven. Morinaga Soko Roshi, *Rainbows Magazine*, Amaravati Publications, July 1994, p 4)

Husband and wife

In the relationship between husband and wife, the husband should:

- be courteous to his wife
- respect her
- be faithful
- hand over authority to her
- provide her with clothes and adornments.

The wife should:

- perform her household duties well
- be hospitable to relatives
- be faithful
- protect the family income
- be skilled and industrious in her duties.

(*Digha Nikaya*, Vol. III, 190, quoted in H. Saddhatissa, *Buddhist Ethics*, Wisdom Publications, 1987, p 120)

Spiritual friendship

The idea of spiritual friendship underpins relationships within Buddhist community life, and is of particular importance in the bond between husband and wife:

If the matter of selection of the family into which one is born in the present existence is closely connected with the karmic effects of previous lives, the selection of one's friends is clearly more directly associated with the circumstances and acts of the current life. Physiologically, the world is perpetuated by the family relationship, but the Buddha has also given the quality of making friends as one which is instrumental in 'making the world go round'. The person who is kindly, who makes friends, makes welcome, is free from avarice, is understanding, is a conciliator, such a one obtains good repute. Generosity, kindly speech, doing good to whatever person, fairness in all things, everywhere as is fit and proper, these are indeed the means on which the world turns, just as a chariot moves on quickly depending on the pin of a wheel axle.

(*Digha Nikaya*, Vol. III, 192, quoted in H. Saddhatissa,
Buddhist Ethics, Wisdom Publications, 1987)

The *Sanyutta Nikaya* says:

It is not easy to find a being who has not been your mother, or your father, your brother, your sister or your son or daughter ...

(*Sanyutta Nikaya*, Vol. II, 189)

From this we can see that all relationships are meant to be approached in the same way, and with the same virtues and conduct in mind. Spiritual friendship is the key to this, whether for monk or for lay person, but in considering the relationship between husband and wife this is the essential quality – the pin that turns the wheel of family life. As one Buddhist, a member of the Friends of the Western Buddhist Order, explains:

Perhaps the most radical changes in our attitudes to marriage occur when we begin to develop spiritual friendships, for here we discover the delights, the joys, of a truly human relationship in which there is no longer the aspect of two insecure people trying to prop each other up. Instead we find ourselves striving toward the same sublime ideal as our friend. We can face up to difficulties in our friendships by trying to bring more and more of our ideals into our communication with each other. We urge each other on to become more independent, to let our qualities shine out, to overcome weaknesses.

(*Golden Drum*, Windhorse Publications, No. 7, p 7)

Birth and upbringing

Traditionally, before her baby's birth, a mother-to-be may visit a temple to receive blessings from the monks. Soon after the birth, too, babies are taken to the temple to receive blessings. Many Buddhists give their children names which begin with auspicious sounds, and a monk may be consulted as to suitable names. Some Western families may wish to give Asian names to their children. Later on in their lives, boys in Burma and Thailand may take temporary ordination as part of their education. This will last for only a matter of weeks in most cases. This rite of passage is unavailable at present to Buddhists in Western countries. Some efforts are being made, however, to establish a ceremony marking children's commitment to a Buddhist way of life:

Coming of Age: A Buddhist Way

On March 12th, I celebrated my 13th birthday at the Devon Vihara. I decided to do this because my cousin and my friend are both having a Barmitzvah this year. (A Barmitzvah is a Jewish ceremony celebrating coming of age.) I decided that I wanted to find a Buddhist way to celebrate my 13th birthday and the beginning of my adult years. So I talked with Ajahn Santacitto at the Devon Vihara and he liked the idea very much.

The day before the event I stayed at the Vihara and helped with various jobs. I was also preparing myself for the day ahead. I wore white clothing which represents purity and was trying to keep the precepts. For the celebration itself, I invited lots of people to come along.

The day started with the offering of a dana meal to the monks, followed by Paritta chanting, precepts and a short Dhamma talk by Ajahn Santacitto. All of these I requested in Pali by myself. After the chanting and the Dhamma talk, other people offered reflections on what it is to be a man. The ceremony ended by planting a Douglas Fir tree outside. It came from our front garden so it felt like part of our family was left at the Vihara. It was nice to plant something living that would grow big and strong. It felt symbolic of the day and we could see it year after year and remember the occasion.

Lots of people gave me nice presents including the monks at the Devon Vihara who gave me a Buddha rupa.

I enjoyed the whole day and thought it went really well. I especially enjoyed staying at the Vihara by myself beforehand.

(*Rainbows Magazine*, Amaravati Publications,
July 1994, p 5)

Religious observance

Observing Buddhist families keep a Buddha statue in the home, prominently positioned and well above the ground. This acts as a shrine; in some family homes there may be a separate shrine room. As in the monastery or temple, pujas or short services will be conducted here daily, and especially on full moon or festival days. Offerings of flowers, candles and incense are given and the precepts and refuges taken. Food is placed in front of the Buddha as a sign of generosity.

Families may also attend the local monastery or temple on observance days, when they will take the traditional offerings (dana, or food for the monks and nuns in the Theravadin tradition), and re-affirm their commitment by taking the refuges and precepts. This may be followed by meditation and chanting.

Religious observance is directly linked to the idea of merit. Particularly in the Theravadin tradition in traditional Buddhist societies, one of the major distinctions in the social order was that between the monastic sangha and the wider sangha, or lay population. While the monastic sangha pursue enlightenment based on meditative practice, the lay population is expected to support the monastic presence by providing for them materially and by following the precepts laid down by the Buddha. By doing both these things a store of merit is gained, producing good karma, which in turn influences rebirth. Thus we have two complementary systems at work, which function at a social level to support the monastic–lay division in society, but which also provide two differing forms of practice in progression toward enlightenment. From this point of view, *dana* (generosity or giving) becomes a highly meritorious act, and providing food for the monastic sangha, becomes a quintessential expression of this and clearly demarcates the differing roles and functions of the monastic and lay populous. As we shall see later, this distinction has not been as closely observed as Buddhism has developed in the West. Westerners in contemporary society who are attracted to Buddhism most often see Buddhist practice as a way of improving themselves, thus meditation is a key feature of this attraction. At the same time there is no institutionalized social order in the West into which the monastic–lay distinction obviously needs to fit. We shall return to this issue later when specifically focusing on Buddhism in the West.

Children's education

In traditionally Buddhist Asian countries a child's schooling includes a basic outline of Buddhist values. The *Sigalovada Suttanta* gives five ways in which a pupil should conduct him- or herself towards the teacher, and five in which the teacher should conduct him- or herself towards the pupil:

> The five devolving on the pupil are stated in Pali terms which may be construed literally and figuratively. In the literal sense, 1) the pupil should rise from his seat in salutation, 2) wait on the teacher, 3) desire to hear him, 4) render him personal service, and 5) honour him by reception. Figuratively these may be taken as displaying energy, understanding the teacher, paying attention, showing obedience, and preparing the work thoroughly.

> The teacher should show his compassion, or love, for the pupils by teaching and training them well and happily, seeing that they grasp all the arts and crafts equally and thoroughly, teaching them in the respectful manner he adopts towards friends, and by making them secure in every way.

> (*Digha Nikaya*, Vol. III, 189, quoted in H. Saddhatissa, *Buddhist Ethics*, Wisdom Publications, 1987, p 127)

In the West the situation is different:

> Struggling to find our own way and balance in daily living – what about the children? Should we be establishing Buddhist schools? Some people are investigating this possibility and feel the need to provide a Buddhist orientated education. Others feel that the way forward is through integration. What is clear at the moment is that there is no form of western Buddhism to point to and say, 'This is how we will all do it'. True to the teachings themselves, everything is uncertain, but at this particular juncture in the development of Buddhism, incredibly exciting.

> (*World Religions in Education*, The Shap Working Party, 1986, p 23)

A Buddhist school has now been established for primary school children in the UK, at Brighton, in Sussex. Summer schools and family days are run by various Buddhist groups. The following extract from a children's newsletter illustrates the sort of activities that take place, in the words of a nine-year-old child:

A Day at Amaravati

A nun told us a story about a monkey, an elephant and a partridge. They tried to remember a tree to see who was the oldest and it was the partridge because he could remember he dropped the seed that grew into the tree.

We did paintings and drawings of that and after that we went out to the Stupa in the field and we had a joss stick each and held it like a prayer and we had to walk around three times and each time we came to the front we did three bows and then we stuck the joss sticks in the ground near the flowers and lit them … Then we did meditation. Ven. Amaro lit a candle and we sat cross-legged with our knees on the ground and were very quiet and looked at the candle and thought about who was our best friend and I thought I couldn't really say my brother because he is my best friend, so I thought about Charlie instead and then I thought of my brother who I love and my mummy and daddy and then Ven. Amaro banged a little gong and we woke up.

(*Rainbows Magazine*, No. 7,
Amaravati Publications, 1986)

There is some debate as to how Western Buddhist groups should educate their children, as one Buddhist observes:

Parents think different things about what we should do. Some think it should be like a Buddhist Sunday school. Others think we should leave them completely alone. My view is that I don't want to inject children with adult ideas. I want them to grow up with some healthy appreciation of the law of karma, of cause and effect; a healthy appreciation of others and that there is more to life than the material surface. There's a depth to life. What I don't want is a dead Dharma being injected in some way into children.

(FWBO member)

Death and dying

Death and dying are of particular significance in the Buddhist world view, because they are part of the cycle of rebirth, and therefore directly connected to birth itself (rather than being at the other end of life's events). It is important to die well, but also to live every moment as if it were one's last. This is not a morbid outlook. As one Tibetan teacher has said, 'Death is a great adventure'. Of course, fear of death *does* induce morbidity, and Buddhism addresses this issue. All is impermanent in the samsaric realm, and we must accept that. Rebirth is a consequence of this impermanence. Death is the event in the chain of cause and effect that induces rebirth. Sogyal Rimpoche, a Tibetan Lama who has written on the subject of death and dying, examines the issue thus:

> At the moment of death our life becomes clear. Death is our greatest teacher. But, unfortunately, people in the West think of death only when they are dying. That is a little bit late.

He also makes the point that:

> Life is nothing but changes, which are little deaths.

> (Interview in the *Observer* 22 November 1992, p 55)

These teachings are complemented by Ajahn Sumedho in talking about khamma (karma) and rebirth:

> By being mindful we free ourselves from the burden of birth and death, the habitually recreating pattern of khamma and rebirth. We recognize the boring, habitual re-creations of unsatisfactoriness, the obsessions with worry, doubt, fear, greed, hatred and delusion in all its forms. When we're mindful, there's no attachment to ideas and memories of self, and creativity is spontaneous.

> (Ajahn Sumedho, *Cittaviveka*, Amaravati Publications, 1987, p 92)

Cleverness, of course, is concerned with how we make progress in the world in our present lifetime. Wisdom is about how we understand the prospect of living well in a wider context. And perhaps the advice given to Siddhartha by the Buddha in Herman Hesse's book is directly applicable here: 'Cleverness is good, but patience is better.'

This points to the need to accept and learn from the inevitable results of our karma, of which impermanence and dying are a part. In *The Tibetan Book of the Dead*, an account of how to approach death, and the journey to rebirth, emphasizes this event as a creative and practical process focused on mindfulness, through which ignorance can be overcome.

Such a positive approach to the inevitable event of death complements the work of hospice movements, and is borne out in Sogyal Rimpoche's statement that what we need to ask is, 'How can I help someone who is dying?' and 'Can you help someone who has already died?'

Funeral rites

When a person is dying it is usual for a monk or lay person to recite appropriate scriptures to them, to remind them of the Buddha's teaching and to calm their mind. In Tibetan Buddhism *The Tibetan Book of the Dead* is often read to prepare the dying person for the journey through the bardo state, from this life to the next, with the hope that it will result in either liberation or a meritorious rebirth. It is important for the dying person to know that the state of mind in which they die will influence their rebirth.

At funerals, monks conduct the services, giving a talk and chanting scriptures on the theme of impermanence and the transitory nature of life. The ceremony does not dwell on bereavement, but on the qualities of the dead person. In the Soto Zen tradition the funeral is an ordination ceremony, in which the dead person's faith can be strengthened to help him or her face the Eternal Buddha without fear.

The relatives of the deceased person have a duty to arrange a memorial service with an alms offering at a temple or a monastery, or at home. This ceremony is meant to confer the transfer of merit to the deceased person. On anniversaries of death similar ceremonies may also be arranged. Relatives may also make gifts of money, books or objects to the temple or monastery.

The usual way of disposing of the body is by cremation. When great teachers die it is usual to preserve their relics in the same way as the Buddha's, and to distribute them to monasteries or centres set up by that teacher, where a *stupa* will be built to house them. These may then become centres of pilgrimage and be regarded as holy shrines. This has been done recently with two teachers who established branches of the Buddhist tradition in the West: the Thai teacher Ajahn Chah and the Tibetan Lama Yeshe. In both cases, relics and stupas can be found at centres which they founded in Western countries.

Chorten (stupa) at Sarnath

Ajahn Chah's Funeral

On 16 January 1993 the body of Ajahn Chah was burned in a beautiful furnace specially built at the monastery where he had lived and taught. It was inside a great white circular building called a chedi or stupa which had a large arched doorway facing each of the four directions.

People came from all over the country and from abroad to climb the steps and go inside the stupa to see the ornate mother-of-pearl coffin in which Ajahn Chah's body had been kept for exactly a year since he died. (It had been specially treated so that it would keep that long and give everyone a chance to pay their respects to such a special person.)

Nearly half a million people including the King of Thailand, the Sangharaj (the head of the Thai Sangha) and Luang Por Sumedho assembled by the stupa to chant blessings, listen to talks, and sit in quiet reflection for many hours that day and night. At midnight the furnace was lit and many climbed the steps to see this final moment of Ajahn Chah's physical existence. White smoke curled out of the top of the tower on the stupa and drifted into the sky.

(*Rainbows Magazine*, Amaravati Publications, 1993, p 3)

After three days, a chosen number of bhikkhus presided over the extraction of the relics from the crematory. Most were locked up for safe-keeping; three large relics, white and honeycombed like coral, were placed on the shrine for public view. When we left, the Sangha were still using the chedi for their group meditation practice.

(*Forest Sangha Newsletter*, Amaravati Publications, No. 234, April 1993, p 5)

Rebirth

In the Tibetan tradition, when a great teacher dies, a search is made for his *tulku*, or reincarnation, at the request of the Dalai Lama. Lama Yeshe's tulku was found to be the son of two of his Spanish disciples. Once this identity is established the child will be brought up and educated according to Tibetan practice, in the belief that he will continue the work he performed in his previous life.

The procedure for finding a tulku is established in Tibetan lore. This account of the search for the present Dalai Lama (the fourteenth) serves as an example.

Lama Yeshe and his tulku

Searching for the Dalai Lama

After certain signs had been observed as to the direction and location in which he would be found, over a period of two years, an official group was sent out to find him. They carried with them objects that belonged to the thirteenth Dalai Lama. They disguised themselves and visited houses in which they might find the child. Eventually they came to a house that corresponded to one seen in a vision of the Regent concerning the child. The two-year-old boy in the house was subjected to the prescribed examination:

> He was first shown four different rosaries, one of which – the most worn – had belonged to the thirteenth Dalai Lama. The boy, who was quite unconstrained and not the least bit shy, chose the right one without hesitation and danced round the room with it. He also selected out of several drums one which the last Incarnation had used to call his servants. Then he took an old walking-stick, which had also belonged to him, not deigning to bestow a glance on one which had a handle of ivory and silver.

(Heinrich Harrer, *Seven Years in Tibet*,
Rupert Hart-Davies, 1953, pp 269–70)

In this way the present Dalai Lama was found.

The idea that the dying teacher knows of his own rebirth is part of the uncanny logic of this whole process, to which we cannot all be privy. When Lama Yeshe met the parents of his tulku, prior to his death, he is said to have given a small pearl to the mother with the words, 'This is for your next child.'

'But I have enough children already,' she replied, 'I shan't be having another, fifth child.'

He gave her the pearl saying, 'Just in case, wait and see.'

In conclusion

In this chapter we have surveyed ways in which Buddhism has traditionally fitted into and influenced the social order in different Buddhist countries and examined the associated teachings and practices. This has raised issues as to how and whether, as Buddhism spreads and as societies change, Buddhism will also need to adapt. These issues will be further addressed in later chapters, but we can identify the following at this point:

- Buddhism has integrated itself into a number of traditional Asian societies and the monastic–lay structure of Buddhism has been influential in the construction of social roles and values.
- Buddhist beliefs and teachings have been instrumental in determining specific social practices in relation to birth, upbringing, rites of passage and death rituals.
- Buddhist understandings of karma, rebirth and social responsibility have had a shaping effect on the social order.
- The spread of Buddhism in the West and changes in societies as they modernize are likely, in turn, to be reflected in the way Buddhism engages with different societies in the future and the forms Buddhism takes.

09

festivals and ceremonies

In this chapter you will learn:
- about the different kinds of Buddhist festivals and ceremonies, the reasons for them and the ways they are celebrated
- about the cultural influences on festivals celebrated in different countries.

There is great diversity in the range of Buddhist festivals and ceremonies because Buddhism has spread into a number of very different cultures in the course of its history. According to the type of Buddhism represented, these festivals tend to focus on the Buddha Sakyamuni, the significant events in his life, his teachings and the Buddhist community, or range wider by including saints, bodhisattvas and other Buddhas and beliefs. What also differs is the way in which these events are celebrated, for each culture brings to them its own particular style and form and a specific calendar year. For these reasons, it is best to divide Buddhist festivals into four main groups, representing the Theravada tradition, the Tibetan tradition, the Chinese-Japanese tradition and the Western Buddhist Order.

All Buddhist religious festivals follow the lunar calendar, and most of the important ones are celebrated on full-moon days. Knowing exactly when a particular festival will occur is not such an easy task. The solar calendar varies year by year, so just like Easter in the Christian tradition, Buddhist festival days fall on moveable dates. Buddhists rely on printed calendars for their information, and the festival celebration itself will occur on the appropriate full-moon day (or sometimes on the weekend closest to it in non-Buddhist countries).

Theravada festivals

The traditional importance of monastic orders in Buddhism has a strong influence on the character of Theravada festivals. The monastic calendar is marked by two important events: *uposatta* days, which occur weekly, and the Rains Retreat, which occurs annually. Devout lay people may also follow the monks' observance of uposatta days.

Uposatta days

Originally, uposatta days were times when monks met on the full moon and new moon to re-affirm their monastic code and confess their shortcomings to one another. They subsequently developed into days of religious observance for lay people as well. Occurring weekly, they function in a similar way to the Sabbath in Judeo-Christian practice, but since the full moon is the most auspicious day (because it marks the Buddha's birth, enlightenment and death), this is treated as far more important than the others, with the new moon also being more significant than the other two.

It is worth noting how full-moon observance actually keeps Buddhists in touch with natural rhythms as well; this is not just coincidental, for samsara is a notion that unites the cycles of the natural world with those of human destiny. The moon acts as a symbolic reminder of both the samsaric round of human life and the presence of the dharma, or truth made available by the Buddha, which is also ever-present. Thus the full moon gains a magical quality, pointing to the need for diligence and offering the hope of liberation.

The pattern of observance on these days involves visiting a monastery or temple, listening to the teaching given by a monk, chanting from the scriptures, taking part in meditation and re-affirming the precepts. For a devout lay person this is an opportunity to gain merit by performing acts of generosity, donating money to the monastery and showing reverence to the Buddha, through performing acts of devotion before buddha images. Another common practice is to take the Eight Precepts for the day, rather than the usual five, and to pursue the precepts more diligently. So, for example, they may abstain from eating meat or fish, practise sexual abstinence, not eat after noon or forego the use of adornments and usual forms of entertainment. In short, they are re-acquainting themselves with the renunciant life, behaving temporarily like members of the monastic order. Buddhist festivals tend to be less a matter of festivity, more a matter of remembrance and re-affirmation.

New Year

Occurring on 13 April (Western calendar) in Sri Lanka and Thailand, but on the 16 April in Burma, this festival is really secular, and often somewhat irreverent, but socially significant. In Sri Lanka it operates rather like the Western Christmas. It is a time for visiting relatives and friends and giving presents; in Burma and in Laos people buy and release fish as an act of compassion. In Thailand it is a water-throwing festival. Veneration is also shown to Buddha images, revered teachers and respected grandfathers, by sprinkling or bathing them with water. The festivities continue for three days. Temporary sand stupas are erected in temple grounds, which are later levelled to create new sand surfaces. Robes are placed on Buddha images and are used afterwards by the monks. Pranks are also played, for it has its light-hearted side.

Wesak

Wesak celebrates the Buddha's birth, enlightenment and death, which are all, according to Buddhist tradition, supposed to have occurred on the same day of the year; as such, this is the most important Theravadin festival. It takes place on the full-moon day of the second month in the Indian year, which, in the Western calendar, occurs in late May or early June. The Indian name for this month is Vaishakha, which, translated into Sinhalese, becomes Wesak, and in Thai, Visakha. Thus the festival is named after the month. Emphasis is placed on the enlightenment of the Buddha, which is the pre-eminent event, since it marks the point at which the dharma was rediscovered by the historical Buddha Sakyamuni. It is customary to put up decorations in local temples and to light lamps after dark, symbolizing enlightenment coming into the world. Wesak lanterns are made by pasting thin paper over light wooden frames. At temples Bodhi trees and stupas are often ringed with oil lamps, and people send Wesak cards to their friends, rather like Christmas cards. These usually depict memorable events in the Buddha's life.

Other activities are reminiscent of lesser Buddhist festivals, with lay people visiting local temples or monasteries, listening to darsanas and staying up through the night in meditation. In the Thai tradition, it is customary to circumambulate the monastery three times, recognizing the importance of the Buddha, dharma and sangha (the Three Jewels). Observance of the precepts in a more rigorous way also entails abstaining from agriculture or other occupations which may harm small living creatures. Dana (generosity) is also encouraged, which results in lay families often bringing sumptuous dishes to the monastery or temple in recognition of their duty to the monastic order, and as a further way of expressing the festive spirit of the occasion and the importance of the whole sangha. This also confers merit. In Burma, though it is not recognized as a festival of light, as in Sri Lanka, the importance of the occasion is marked by watering the Bodhi tree in a local monastery or temple.

At this point it is worth reflecting on the significance of festivals for Buddhists; which do not necessarily parallel their importance in the Christian tradition. For example, even the pre-eminent festival of Wesak is not necessarily seen as of great importance for Buddhists, in the context of striving for enlightenment and moral improvement, as the following passage indicates:

Wesak is all right: it's a day which commemorates the birth, the Enlightenment, and the passing away of the Buddha. But why make extra effort for one particular day? For the feeble-minded, perhaps a day like that would be of much benefit. But to me, every day should be a day of effort – should be such a day. Why just one particular day?

(John Bowker, *Worlds of Faith*, BBC, 1983, p 159)

a Buddhist family at Wesak with *dana* for the monks and nuns

Poson

Poson is a peculiarly Sri Lankan festival which occurs on the next full-moon day after Wesak, in June or July. On this day, in the year 250 BCE, the emperor Ashoka's son, Mahinda, who was a Buddhist monk, is supposed to have arrived in Sri Lanka to convert the island to Buddhism. Religious processions, called *perahara*, are organized, in which a particularly venerated person or object is conducted through the town, with great pomp and noise made especially with drums and fireworks. Often an image of Mahinda is constructed and placed on a cart or float-like vehicle. At Mihintale, near the ancient capital of Anuradhapura, where Mahinda is said to have arrived, these festivities are at their grandest.

Asala

Asala, normally in July, marks the beginning of the Rains Retreat (called *Vas* in Sinhalese) and recalls the preaching of the Buddha's first sermon, the Turning of the Wheel of the Law. Since this marks the beginning of the Buddha's ministry, monks preach sermons recalling the event. In the latter half of the month Sri Lankans stage the Asola Perahara, a spectacular procession in which the relic of the Buddha's tooth is processed through the streets of Kandy. Relics of the Buddha, or of great Buddhist teachers, are usually to be found wherever Buddhist missionary activity has founded new centres. But the history of this event is primarily nationalistic rather than religious. This ceremony marks the importance of Buddhist identity within Sinhalese nationalism, acting as a display of the legitimacy of the power of the king. The legacy of this is a contemporary exhibition of a distinctively Sri Lankan festival, with sumptuously decorated elephants, dancers, festivity and fireworks that have the character of a mardi-gras. It is a local pageant which really has little to do with Buddhist ideals and is the prerogative of the laity rather than monks.

Rains Retreat

The Buddha preached and spent his life travelling northern India and throughout the sub-continent in general. Life is regulated between the months of June or July through to the end of September by the monsoons. Travel during this season was, at the least, uncomfortable and often practically impossible. It became a habitual practice that during these periods wandering monks would settle down in one sheltered place. This developed into the strict monastic rule that monks would not leave their monastery during this period, and this provided a time for more intense devotional practice. Correspondingly, today the normal availability of monks to the laity is curtailed.

At the end of the retreat, monks hold a special ceremony confessing any fault or offence, and asking forgiveness of their fellow order members. On the final day of the retreat, or within the following month, the relationship with the laity is re-established with the *Kathina* ceremony.

In Burma and Thailand lay men often take temporary ordination at the beginning of the retreat and live as monks for the next three months. There are also no Burmese weddings during this period. At the end of the retreat the Burmese celebrate the festival of *Thitingyut*, which lasts three days and is their festival of lights. Everyone is expected to visit elder relations and friends, to pay respects and give small gifts. Lamps are put up (traditionally consisting of candles inside paper lanterns) all over the house and on shrines of local deities (*nats*), in big trees, which are specially venerated, and around stupas. The lights are said to illuminate and welcome the Buddha's descent from heaven after preaching to his mother. In Thailand lay people use candles to light lamps in the monastery, which will burn for the three months of the retreat.

Kathina ceremony

Held in October or November of the Western calendar, Kathina is organized by lay people in order to present monks with new robes. One robe is ceremonially presented as the Kathina robe to the head of the monastery, to be given to the monk who is, at least in theory, to be the most virtuous. He will be chosen by the abbot. This story illustrates the origins of the practice:

> The scriptures relate that thirty monks were travelling together with the intention of spending the retreat season with the Buddha. However, when the full moon of July (the start of the retreat) arrived, they had not reached their destination, and according to custom they were required to stay where they were. So, it is told, the monks were disappointed, and spent the three-month retreat away from their teacher.
>
> At the end of the retreat the monks finished their journey to see the Buddha. Coming to hear of their disappointment, he was moved to give them a teaching that would uplift and inspire them. He suggested that they should make a new robe together. The lay supporters living near the Buddha gladly offered cloth and the monks set about sewing a robe. In those days the method used involved spreading the pieces of cloth on a frame and stitching them together. This frame was called a *kathina*.

> (Bhikkhu Thitapanne, *The Kathina Festival*, in C. Erricker and V. Barnett (eds), *World Religions in Education: Festivals*, The Shap Working Party, 1987, p 21)

The robe is made, according to ceremonial prescription, by sewing patches together in such a way as is said to imitate the patchwork of the paddy fields familiar to the early monks on their travels. The community first presents the cloth for the robe, which is marked, cut out and sewn by the monks on the same day, before being given back to the laity for presentation. Another meaning given to the word 'kathina' is 'difficult', which suggests the arduousness of the vocation of a disciple of the Buddha, and the tenacity required to follow the dhamma.

The robe-giving ceremony is also a reminder of the interdependence of the monastic order and the laity; the monks offer spiritual example and teaching to lay followers and, in return, the laity satisfy the mendicants' basic needs. This interdependence was stressed by the Buddha, and has certainly been a vital factor in the survival and continuation of Buddhism as a living tradition. Its importance is highlighted by the fact that this ceremony is the only one involving the laity that gains its authority from the earliest Buddhist scriptures.

This sensitive description of the robe-giving ceremony, by a British Buddhist, conveys its essential meaning:

> Now began one of the simplest and most moving ceremonies that I have been privileged to witness. The Kathina robe was presented on its own special stand in front of the Shrine and the resident Bhikkhu was invited to receive it. The reverence of the ritual by which the recipient made that robe his own shed a whole new light on the significance and virtue of giving. The robe was unwrapped and examined as if each fold and thread was to be personally known.
>
> Next the robe was marked in one corner. The significance of this action has been lost over the years. It could be that the marks were originally a means of identifying the robe, serving the purpose of a name tag. Or it is possibly a deliberate defacing of the newness of the robe, making it come with built-in wear and tear and therefore, losing the sense of pride that new things invariably bring. Finally, the new robe was placed between the folds of the old robe and the two were stroked together. The symbolism of this action was as if the one was being made a natural continuation of the other. The new robe became endowed with the qualities of the old – the one was never actually cast aside and the other never actually replacing. The two merged as a continuance of purpose.
>
> (Gwen Nodder, *First Make Your Shrine*, in C. Erricker and V. Barnett (eds), *World Religions in Education: Festivals*, The Shap Working Party, 1987, pp 22–3)

Burmese custom emphasizes that girls weave the monks' robes. Along with the robes, toy trees are offered, representing the mythical trees of heaven. On their branches the lay people pin banknotes, as an offering to the monastery.

Loi Kratong

Loi Kratong is the main Thai festival of lights, held on the full moon of November. Like Asala in Sri Lanka, this is not centred on the temple, and has only tenuous connections with Buddhist origins. Gates and doors of houses are decorated with palm leaves, banana stalks, coloured lanterns, lamps and candles. The monastery grounds are similarly decorated with paper flags and sets depicting scenes from the *Vessantara Jataka* recalling the previous life of the Buddha as the compassionate Prince Vessantara, and his selfless generosity. There are also offerings to the river spirits, consisting of floating trays with lighted candles, coins and food. In return for these the spirits will rid people of misfortunes. These offerings are processed to the rivers accompanied by fireworks, drums and gongs. The river comes alive, the variety of craft launched upon it ranging from huge floats to tiny trays of plaited banana leaves.

Ajahn Sumedho, a Theravadin monk, wearing robes

Magha Puja

This Thai festival marks All Saints' Day, or Dharma Day. It commemorates an event three months before the Buddha's death when, before 1,250 of his enlightened disciples, he predicted his demise and gave them the *Vinaya* (the code of discipline for the monastic sangha), which all monks are now supposed to recite every fortnight. In Northern Thailand and Laos this day is the festival of lights, when the *Vessantara Jataka* is read through in one day. It is also marked by a great fair.

Tibetan festivals

Tibet provides a distinctive culture for Buddhist life, and the terms 'Tibetan' and 'Buddhist' are synonymous within the Tibetan world. Before the invasion of Tibet by China in 1959, little was known of this way of life, but since then, Tibetan Buddhism has established itself in India and across Europe and the United States, with the diaspora led by the present, fourteenth, Dalai Lama and a number of important Buddhist teachers, or lamas, around whom communities have grown. The centre of 'Tibet in exile' is the small town of McLeod Gange, above Dharamsala in the Indian foothills of the Himalayas, where the Dalai Lama has his palace.

The Tibetan calendar is lunar and divided into twelve months; to keep in step with the solar year it is necessary to add a month during certain years. To keep in phase with the moon some months are less than thirty days. Some Tibetan festivals commemorate the usual events related to the Buddha's life; others have a peculiarly Tibetan significance.

Losar

Losar is Tibetan New Year, which falls in February. Lasting for fifteen days, it commemorates the Buddha's early life, through to his enlightenment and his efforts to establish the dharma during his teaching career. Within Tibet monks sat their examinations for higher degrees on the fourth day, called the Great Prayer (*Monlam Cheamo*). The fifteenth day is the full-moon day, *Chonga Chopa*, when Tibetan culture comes into its own with the remarkable butter sculptures for which it is famous. These are usually of scenes in the Buddha's life, coloured with different dyes. Tibetans also put on puppet shows on the same themes. Traditionally, the monks of two famous monasteries called the Upper Tantric School (*Gyuto*) and Lower Tantric School (*Gyume*) are responsible for these displays. They are now located in India, and the celebrations take place in Dharamsala.

The sense of the New Year as a time of trial and conquest in the Buddha's life is echoed in the Tibetans' understanding of its significance for them. It is a time of overcoming and renewal, as this commentary on its rituals and celebrations taking place at Dharamsala shows:

> The New Year must be borne decisively from out of the ashes of the old. Negative thoughts, deeds, and misfortunes accumulated during the previous year are purged from community, home, and individual lives through prescribed rituals by clergy and members of the household.

> The ushering in of *losar*, the New Year, begins on the evening of the twenty-ninth day of the last month of the old year. Tibetan friends and family gather together to partake of *gutuk*, the 'special nine soups'. Contained within are sculpted and stuffed dumplings, which signify the fortunes for the coming year of every person present. The person who chooses a dumpling stuffed with salt might gain renown and lead a virtuous life during the coming twelve moons. Whoever gets the chilli pepper will be angry and argumentative. And woe be it to he or she with the lump of charcoal, for that person will be cursed with a black heart. This provides many laughs for most and frowns for a few.

> Each person finishes all but a little of his soup. The leftovers, along with old food, coins, pieces of clothing lint, a candle, and a *khatag* greeting-scarf are put together into a large bowl along with a humanoid-shaped *torma* sculpture known as *lu*. These serve as ransom offerings to attract the accrued evil and misfortune of the past year away from the household. The men carry the items to a lonely spot along the road by torchlight, crying 'Come out! Come out!' to the evils. The job done, they quickly return without ever looking back, for to do so would cause the evil to return with them. This act, it occurs to me, is a powerful metaphor to a central notion in the Tibetan experience, that one must continue on life's path without looking back. 'No attachments, no regrets', a lama once observed.

> (Peter Gold, *Tibetan Reflections*, Wisdom Publications, 1984, pp 82–3)

Following this, a procession of monks carries special New Year *zor tormas*, which are huge constructions in which the community's bad karma of the previous year is symbolically enclosed by ritual prayers. On top of these conical edifices are death's heads. The torma is paraded towards a large mound of straw, a pyre on which the physical manifestation of evil will be burned.

Tibetan New Year has its own special place in the calendar and, as on other celebratory occasions, the Tibetan love of colour and ritual is evidenced by an abundance of coloured prayer flags and the sounds of Tibetan instruments.

Saga Dawa

This festival, held on the fifteenth day of the fourth month (the full moon of May in the Gregorian or Western calendar), recognizes the Buddha's birth, enlightenment and death (the equivalent of Wesak). This is the strictest observance day in the Tibetan calendar, when no meat is eaten and lamps are lit everywhere. Circumambulation is another feature of this festival; devotion is shown by going round Buddhist monuments in a clockwise direction, by means of prostration – measuring out the distance with the body and standing where the head faced the ground in a continuously repeated process. Devout Buddhists will also take a vow to fast and be silent for seven days, which symbolizes both the significance of abstinence in Buddhist practice and the Buddha's passing.

Dzamling Chisang

This is a day of purification which falls on the full-moon day of the fifth month (June). Fire offerings are made to guardian spirits who protect individuals, families and places of importance and who act as national deities. Shrines are erected next to Buddhist temples. Tibetan belief in spirits goes back to their bon ancestry (the indigenous religion preceding Buddhism). The spirits are seen as having been converted to Buddhism and becoming its protectors. Since they are vegetarian, burnt offerings are made of favourite Tibetan dishes such as roast barley mixed with butter, and Tibetan sweets. The offerings are made by lay people, who abstain from meat for three days beforehand.

Chokhor

This festival commemorates the Buddha's first sermon, the Turning of the Wheel of the Law. Occurring in June or July, on the fourth day of the sixth month, it is a summer festival, associated in the Tibetan climate with fine weather and colourful celebration. The community would carry *xylographs*, scriptures engraved on long, rectangular wooden blocks, and statues, in great processions with a carnival atmosphere. This signified the spread of the dharma through the Buddha's teaching. Afterwards there would be picnics, often with traditional Tibetan brew of *chang*, an equivalent of beer based on the fermenting of wheat, which facilitated hospitality and festivity.

Lhabap

On the twenty-second of the ninth month (October), Tibetans celebrate the Buddha's descent from the Tushita heaven where he preached to his mother. It occurs at the same time as the end of the Rains Retreat in Theravada countries. It represents his return to earth, when temples are visited and feasts occur.

Ngacho Chenmo

This event is the anniversary of the death of Tsongkhapa on the twenty-fifth day of the tenth month, falling in November. Tsongkhapa founded the Yellow Hat School of Tibetan Buddhism, which includes the Upper and Lower Tantric Schools. Possibly the most influential figure in Tibetan Buddhism, Tsongkhapa was a monk famous for his learning and the strictness of his monastic discipline. As a mark of mourning, Tibetans eat a special porridge containing lumps of dough, and lamps are lit in his memory. In Lhasa, his image used to be carried in a torchlight procession. This day also marks the end of the Rains Retreat period, when new robes are offered to monks.

Guru Rimpoche's birthday

Guru Rimpoche's birthday occurs in July, and celebrates one of the greatest of Tibetan figures. The title means 'precious teacher', and was given to Padmasambhava, who converted many Tibetans to the practice of Buddhism as one of the first Indians to bring the dharma to Tibet. It is celebrated with a *tsok* ceremony; food and light are offered to the Buddha in beautifully decorated shrine rooms in which highly colourful pictures, known as *thangkas*, hang round the walls, and statues of buddhas are placed around the room. Flowers and incense also create a celebratory atmosphere, in which chanting and silent meditation take place. At the end of the ceremony food which has been offered is shared amongst the worshippers.

The following description of a statue of the guru in the Himalayan hillside around Dharamsala recalls his significance for Tibetan Buddhists:

> A huge, glaring statue of the *guru* himself sits carved into eighteen feet of gilded rock. A *dorje* (thunderbolt-scepter) is held incisively in one hand, skull staff in the other. Huge eyes pierce one with the legendary power he manifested to the independent mountain people to the north, powerful enough to consolidate their beliefs and enlist their native gods into a distinctively Tibetan form of Buddhism.

> (Peter Gold, *Tibetan Reflections*,
> Wisdom Publications, 1984, p 76)

Stories of Padmasambhava recall his great power, and sometimes miraculous feats, as with this episode occurring in the present-day Indian village of Rewalsar:

> There he meditated in a cave high over a massive valley, and took one of the local king's daughters as his consort. The king of Zahor, being angered by his daughter's uncomely behaviour, condemned Padmasambhava to be burned alive. The fire was ignited but he was not even scorched. And the flames, turning into water, overspilled to form a beautiful oval lake which Tibetans call *Tsopema*, the Lotus Lake.

> (Peter Gold, *Tibetan Reflections*,
> Wisdom Publications, 1984, p 75)

Japanese and Chinese festivals

Buddhist influence has waned in China since its peak 1,000 years ago, when it combined with Taoist and Confucian indigenous tradition. In recent history, the Maoist revolution and China's present communist government have repressed Buddhist practice, but not eradicated it. It still survives, particularly in the provinces close to Tibet. Though the Western calendar is influential today, the Chinese still use lunar months, which operate in a similar way to the Tibetan system. Chinese tradition is especially concerned with the remembrance of dead ancestors and the celebration of birthdays, and this influences their Buddhist festivals.

Japan received Buddhism via China, so it is not surprising to find similarities, though variations of Buddhism in Japan have flourished in connection with Shinto, the earlier Japanese religion (which bears similarity with Confucianism in its respect for ancestors, and filial and state order are of great importance). The two main festivals in both countries share common themes. The names referred to here are the Japanese versions.

Gautama Buddha's birth

This is known as *Hana Matsuri* in Japan, where the Buddha's enlightenment and death are remembered separately. It occurs on 8 April, and, correspondingly in the Chinese calendar, on the eighth day of the fourth month. The themes of flowers and water are prevalent, reflecting the mythology of the Buddha's birth itself:

> The beautiful queen Mahamaya had a dream. She saw a young white elephant with six great tusks descend from the sky and enter her womb. The gods told her that she was going to give birth to a son which would become a buddha. The queen told her husband the news and they were both very happy. When the time for the birth of the child was close, the queen decided to travel to her parents' house, as was the custom at that time. On the way she visited a beautiful garden called Lumbini Grove. The garden was full of flowers and singing birds. Suddenly, the queen started to give birth and so the Buddha was born in a beautiful, flowering garden.
>
> After the birth two streams of water appeared from the sky. One was cool and refreshing; the other was warm and perfumed. They bathed the Buddha and his mother.
>
> The infant Buddha stood up as soon as he was born. Shaded by a white parasol held over him by the gods, he faced north and took seven steps. Then, looking in each of the other directions, he said, 'I am the chief in the world, I am the best in the world. This is my last birth, I will not be born again.'
>
> (Peter and Holly Connolly, *Religions Through Festivals: Buddhism*, Longman, 1989, p 32)

At Japanese temples different aspects of the story are shown in displays:

> A large papier-mâché white elephant reminds people of the queen's marvellous dream. The infant Buddha stands, to remind people that he could walk as soon as he was born and the setting represents the Lumbini Grove. Bowls of delicately perfumed tea are poured on to the Buddha's image by Japanese Buddhist children. This is a way of honouring the Buddha and remembering that the gods provided perfumed water from heaven for his first bath.
>
> (Peter and Holly Connolly, *Religions Through Festivals: Buddhism*, Longman, 1989, p 33)

The festival coincides with the flowering of the cherry blossom in Japan, and stalls selling food and gifts are set up in temple courtyards. Folk dancing and acrobatics form part of the celebrations.

The following description of a Chinese ceremony also recalls the bathing of the Buddha by the gods:

> After hymns and offerings the monks poured spoonfuls of water over a tiny image of the infant Sakyamuni, standing in a low basin of water. Sometimes each of the [lay] visitors was allowed to pour a spoonful too.
>
> (Holmes Welch, *The Practice of Chinese Buddhism*, in Alan Brown (ed.), *Festivals in World Religions*, Longman, 1986, pp 57–8)

The Festival of the Hungry Ghosts

This festival honours dead ancestors. According to Buddhist cosmology, samsara is divided into realms, through which living beings pass. The realm of the hungry ghosts is one of these. In effect it parallels All Soul's Day, but with special significance due to the importance of ancestors in Japanese and Chinese tradition. Occurring in July, or the seventh month in the Chinese calendar (July or August), it lasts for three and seven days, in Japan and China respectively. It recalls the story of Maudgalyayana, or Mulien, one of the Buddha's chief disciples who had special powers, through which he was able to visit other realms. On one of his journeys he found his mother in one of the hells. In some versions she is described as one of the hungry ghosts, who typically suffer from distended stomachs and tiny mouths (illustrating their incapacity to satisfy their desires). The story recounts that he saved her by offering a feast to all buddhas and monks, and by virtue of this act of merit she was raised out of hell by the Buddha using a rope.

The theme of this story is mirrored in the following Chinese ceremony of the 'release of the burning mouths', performed on the full-moon day:

> This was a Tantric ritual lasting about five hours and always held in the evening when it was easier for hungry ghosts to go abroad. The presiding monks wore red and golden hats in the shape of a five-pointed crown. Before them was a collection of magical instruments – mirrors, sceptres, spoons, and so on. The monks assisting them – usually six to eighteen – were equipped with ... bells (which sounded, when rung together, rather like a team of reindeer). In the first half of the ceremony the celebrants invoked the help of the Three Jewels. In the second half they broke through the gates of hell, where, with their instruments and magic gestures, they opened the throats of the sufferers and fed them sweet dew, that is, water made holy by reciting a [prayer] over it. They purged away their sins, administered the Three Refuges [declaring one's trust in the Three Jewels], and caused them to take the Bodhisattva resolve. Finally they preached the *dharma* [the Buddha's teachings] to them. If all this was properly done, the ghosts could be immediately reborn as men or even in the Western Paradise.

> (Holmes Welch, *The Practice of Chinese Buddhism*, in Alan Brown (ed.), *Festivals in World Religions*, Longman, 1986, p 57)

In Japan fairs take place with food, shows, dancing and games – especially tug-of-war, a reminder to them of the Maudagalyayana story. Ancient Japanese customs are included. On the first day of the festival, 13 July, freshly gathered herbs are placed in front of the family shrine, candles are lit and food is offered to attract the spirits of ancestors into the homes. On 14 July families celebrate the reunion of their ancestors with the living with traditional folk dances. Buddhist monks visit homes and read scriptures before the shrines as a mark of respect. On 15 July the spirits return to the other realms, and fruit and flowers are offered to the Buddha with requests for blessings on the family and ancestors in future life.

Western Buddhist festivals

The Friends of the Western Buddhist Order celebrate the Buddhist year with three main festivals: Buddha Day, Dharma Day and Sangha Day, representing the Three Jewels.

Buddha Day is held on the full moon in May, and celebrates the Buddha's enlightenment. Dharma Day is in July, and Sangha Day in November, according with Kathina. These are times for the Western Buddhist Order to come together with friends or *mitras*, interested Westerners are also welcome. The gatherings take place in FWBO centres, which are usually large houses or halls converted to Buddhist purposes. Ceremonies take place in a shrine room, decorated for the occasion, and include a talk from a senior Order member, a puja with chanting and meditation, and the sharing of food. Sometimes special events are held for children. Mitra ceremonies are often held after the puja on Dharma Day, when new members of the community, wishing to affirm their commitment do so by taking the Three Jewels, and offer flowers, candles and incense in front of the shrine. On Sangha Day mitras make these same three offerings as a re-affirmation of their commitment.

shrine at FWBO festival, Buddha Day

In conclusion

In this chapter we have noted how festivals in Buddhist countries and those influenced by Buddhism take on diverse cultural expressions and are linked with differing beliefs, practices and histories. We can conclude the following:

- Diversity is an accepted part of the history of Buddhism as it has spread into new cultures.
- Festivals are expressions of the cultural importance of Buddhism in those societies where it has been influential.
- As societies change and as Buddhism spreads into the West, in which there is little prior Buddhist influence except within immigrant sub-cultures, further adaptation will need to take place and some consideration will need to be given to how Buddhism establishes its cultural roots.

10

Buddhism today: East and West

In this chapter you will learn:

- about the spread of Buddhism
- about the presence of Buddhism across the world
- about how different types of Buddhism are responding to contemporary challenges and influences.

The spread of Buddhism

Today Buddhists are spread across the world; however, as with peoples of other faiths, such as Christianity, it is not always easy to identify them.

Buddhist monks and nuns, who have been ordained into the monastic sangha, wear saffron robes if they belong to the South-East Asian (Theravada) tradition, maroon robes if they are Tibetan, and black robes if they are Zen monks. However, their conspicuousness does not identify the far larger number of lay Buddhists. We might say that to identify monastics as the whole Buddhist community would be rather like identifying clergymen as the sole representatives of Christianity. Let us consider the presence of Buddhism in Asia, the United Kingdom and the United States today.

Buddhism in India

Buddhism began in India but eventually declined there and, through missionary activity, spread north, south and east. In India Buddhism met opposition from the Hindu caste system and especially from the high-caste Brahmins with whom the Buddha himself disputed. As a result, after the rule of King Ashoka, who had converted to Buddhism and propagated it, Buddhism declined in India. Sun Shuyun, in her book *Ten Thousand Miles Without a Cloud* (London, Harper Perennial, 2004) traces the journey of the Chinese Buddhist monk Xuanzang from Xiang in north China to India in order to retrieve scriptures that revealed the true teachings. He accomplished this arduous and protracted journey in the seventh century BCE and, as a result, wrote his *Record of the Western Regions,* which gave significant observations on the state of Buddhism in India at that time and complemented Fa Xian's *Record of Buddhist Countries* in providing the first historical map of Buddhist India during its first 1,000 years. These were used by British Orientalists, and Alexander Cunningham in particular, during the imperial rule in India in the nineteenth century to excavate important Buddhist sites, in Bohd Gaya and Sarnath in particular, and to re-establish the importance of Buddhist monuments such as the stupa at Sarnath, the site at which the Buddha gave his first sermon (see Shuyun, pp 224–8).

The revival of Buddhism

Today the Buddhist tradition survives in India, largely through the conversion movement of Dr Bim Ambedka among the *dalits* or untouchables (or, as Gandhi named them, *harijans* – Children of God), which has expanded since its inception in 1956 to at least three and a half million.

The Buddhist mission to the untouchables was originally started by Ambedkar, himself an untouchable, who conducted a campaign for social reform as a lawyer and member of the Indian parliament. He presented the 'Hindu Code Bill' to the Indian parliament in the late 1940s and early 1950s. Its rejection led him to seek an alternative religion for both himself and fellow untouchables. This brought him into contact with Ven. Sangharakshita, leader of the Friends of the Western Buddhist Order (FWBO), who was also concerned with the role of religion in establishing a just society and spiritual renewal. They were both of the opinion that a new Buddhist movement was required to be the vehicle of this vision. At its centre was the concept of the 'dhamma worker', committed to realizing the social ideals of Buddhism, unrestricted by the traditional monastic code.

Ambedkar converted to Buddhism in October 1956, taking the refuges and precepts from the most senior monk in India, along with 5,000 of his followers. This number increased to about four million in the following months. Dr Ambedkar, however, was a sick man and died just five weeks after his conversion, leaving the movement without a leader. Sangharakshita committed himself to holding the movement together, despite vituperative opposition from sections of the Indian press.

Buddhism and social justice

Focusing on the state of Bihar, home to the majority of Buddhist sites and the Buddha's travels, and the place from which Ashoka ruled, we get a sense of the contemporary unrest that involves this Buddhist movement. In her book, Shuyun comments that she was advised not to go there. She records how her dalit guide at Bodh Gaya, Ashoka, named after the original Buddhist King following his conversion to Buddhism through the Ambedkar movement, explained the situation today from a dalit Buddhist perspective:

> Buddhism was a rejection of Brahminism and caste ... In the Sangha, everyone is treated as equal, whether you are a Brahim or a sweeper. It is revolutionary, the first of its

kind. It shows the world how a community based on equality can work ... The Sangha here does not mean the usual assembly of monks and nuns. It means everybody who embraces Buddhism.

(Shuyun, 2004, pp 227–8)

The unrest in Bihar was a result of the untouchables rejecting the political impositions and inequalities of their high-caste governors. Ambedkar's Buddhism, though non-violent and in pursuit of democracy, has radicalized Buddhism by rejecting two of the traditional tenets of Buddhism closely aligned with the Hindu worldview: karma and rebirth. Shuyun explains:

Ambedkar did not want his followers to have any crutches, any false hope. You must fight to improve this life, he believed, not some imaginary future one. Hinduism was based on karma and rebirth too ... Under it dalits were expected to perform their prescribed duties ... The reward might come in some very distant future ... No wonder Ambedkar totally rejected the doctrine of karma, rebirth and the intervention of divinities on his people's behalf.

(Shuyun, 2004, pp 309–10).

In India, under the inspiration of Ambedkar, the resurgence of Buddhism has become a social phenomenon stripped of its metaphysical acoutrements and accents the Buddha's message of equality, democracy and social reform.

The involvement of the FWBO

The FWBO's involvement in this movement in India has been significant. It elaborates in one of its newsletters on the plight and prospects of the untouchables in a way that complements the comments of Ashoka above:

The Untouchables are a class of being who are outside caste altogether. A vast congeries of communities and tribes, they are traditionally regarded as being less than human: unfit for education or religious instruction, often even refused the use of the roads. They live in ghettoes just outside the villages and towns, cut off from the rest of the people, expected to perform the most odious tasks, such as scavenging, cleaning lavatories, performing execution, and burning the dead. 'Polluted' from birth, their duty is to perform all the chores that would otherwise bring pollution to the caste Hindu. Above all they must not allow themselves to pollute him through physical, or even visual, contact.

(Nagabodhi, FWBO Newsletter No. 54)

After 1977 the FWBO was a prime motivating force sustaining the missionary activity begun by Ambedkar in India. The movement is known as Trailokya Bauhdda Mahasangha Sahayak Gana, and its main centres are in Pune and Ahmedabad. Its teachings emphasize spiritual practice and the relevance of Buddhism in the modern world. In contrast to other forms of traditional Buddhism, it is particularly socio-politically oriented, with a strong emphasis on ethical teachings, social identity and the need for vernacular preaching and teaching. Its character is well illustrated by the following passage:

> The local group usually meets weekly or monthly to recite simple texts ... sometimes in Pali, more often in Marathi or Hindi, and to listen to explanations of Buddhism. In villages the converts still live in their special area outside the village proper; the temple or shrine of their deity, usually the goddess Mariai or Mariamma, goddess of smallpox and cholera, has in most cases been changed into a Buddhist mandir, small statues and pictures of Buddha and Ambedkar replacing the shapeless stone of the goddess. In cities the majority cluster in slums, where a small hut is set aside for the same purpose.
>
> (H. Dumoulin and J. Maraldo (eds), *Buddhism in the Modern World*, Collier Macmillan, 1976, p 143)

The writer goes on to remark, however, that such converts often retain a hatred of Hinduism as the cause and symbol of their former degradation, despite the Buddhist doctrines of universal love and compassion, which accords with views expressed earlier.

Buddhism in South-East Asia

In the main, Buddhism in South-East Asia is Theravadin, following its initial spread in a southern direction from India. The following commentary highlights how it has been affected by modern influences that have impacted from Western ideas, nationalistic influences and a revival of missionary activity.

Modern influences

The most significant effect on South-East Asian Buddhism has been the impact of Western society and values in the twentieth century and now in the twenty-first century. Modern influences have stressed the need for Buddhist teachings to be seen as scientific, and adaptable to worldwide social conditions. In major urban centres its 'religiosity', and its adaptation over the course of its history to folklore and local belief, has been played down in order to make it acceptable to Western ways of thinking. The Buddha has been presented as 'the greatest discoverer and scientist of all time', and 'a social reformer bent on liberalizing the Brahmanical society of his own day' (J. Kitagawa and F. Reynolds, in H. Dumoulin and J. Maraldo (eds), *Buddhism in the Modern World*, Collier Macmillan, 1976, p. 47). The Buddha's teachings have been slanted towards the social purpose of modernizing society and effective social reform, rather than the pursuit of the transcendental goal of enlightenment in traditional Buddhist South-Asian societies as they have embraced modernization. Effectively, as in the United Kingdom with Protestant Christianity, Buddhism has tended to shed its cosmological doctrines and meditative emphasis in favour of a more acceptable and pragmatic vision. In effect, this amounts to a form of 'Protestant Buddhism', which presents the Buddha as the exemplar of modern knowledge, as the following illustrates:

> The Buddha was the first great scientist to appear among men. The Buddha discovered what scientists have only now discovered, that there is nothing called matter or mind existing separately in this world but they are the result of forces which continually cause them to come into operation and that they dissolved and came into operation again ...
>
> (G.P. Malalasekera, in R. Gombrich (ed.), *Theravada Buddhism*, Routledge and Kegan Paul, 1988, p 196)

Nevertheless, as Theravada Buddhism has spread from this region to the West, there has been a dramatically increased emphasis on meditation and a renewed belief in the possibility of attaining nirvana. This is one of the paradoxes involved in the transplantation of ideas from one culture to another and the revision of the interpretation of the tradition that ensues.

Buddhism and nationalism

In traditionally Theravadin countries like Thailand, Burma, Sri Lanka and Laos, the question of the relationship between religion and national identity has always been important. In a shrinking world that has seen major political and economic changes during the twentieth and twenty-first centuries, the role of Buddhism has been an important feature of the development of these countries. The monastic sangha's role, in particular, has been a matter of concern in the face of modernization, given the possibility of marginalization.

Efforts have been made to ensure that Buddhism remains a significant intellectual and cultural influence. In Sri Lanka, Thailand and Cambodia, attempts have been made to set up Buddhist universities. Five have been established since the Second World War; students are encouraged to relate Buddhist doctrines to their contemporary situation as training for effective service in society.

There has also been a rebirth of religious vitality among lay people. In Thailand in particular, a programme of dhamma education has increased significantly in modern times. Equally, meditation-orientated sanghas in Burma and Thailand have sought to revive lay practice. Since the Second World War over 200 meditation centres have been established in Burma. During the 1960s and 1970s this revival spread to Thailand and was reinforced by teachers establishing monasteries, where disciplined meditation practice is seen as reviving the vitality of the monastic sangha. One example of this is the Forest Retreat Order of Ajahn Chah, referred to earlier, which is now established in the West.

Missionary activity

Buddhist mission has also been a focus of renewal. Initially, its main concern was to restore Buddhist holy places in India; this developed into the re-propagation of Buddhism in India and the publishing of Buddhist literature in English. This mission has now developed to include seeing the West as an important area of missionary activity. The impetus for this emerged most obviously from the Sixth Great Buddhist Council, where two themes dominated: first, that Christianity and Western culture were declining, and Buddhism's 'scientific' approach made it the religion most acceptable to modern society. Second, that Buddhist ethics provided a stabilizing influence in a world of continual conflict.

There have been setbacks to all these initiatives, however. Laos and Cambodia have been engulfed by political turmoil. Sri Lanka and Burma have both experienced social and political difficulties that have destabilized national progress. In Burma the Buddhist democratic leader Aung San Suu Kyi provides the most celebrated case. Here, the country has been ruled by army generals for four decades, since 1962. When elections took place in 1990, Aung San Suu Kyi won more than eight out of ten of all the votes. However, the army did not let her form a government or take her position as leader, and have never allowed voting since then. Aung San Suu Kyi remains under house arrest in her home, despite being given the Nobel Peace Prize in 1991.

Thailand has to remain wary of the influence of Western capitalism on its social fabric and values. Nevertheless, Buddhism still exists as a vital force in the national identities of these nations, and is becoming recognized in the West as an alternative source of vision and values.

Tibetan Buddhism

Tibetan society

The single most dramatic historical event to have an effect on Buddhism in the twentieth century was the Chinese invasion of Tibet, and the subsequent exile of the Dalai Lama in India since 1959. At this time Tibetan society was still feudal in nature, and half its six million population were nomadic. One-third of its labour force worked on the land. The third largest group were the monks, fifteen per cent of the population. Otherwise, the most conspicuous group was professional beggars. This was a recognized way of life with set traditions. Because alms giving was an obligation of the faithful, begging did not have the sort of disapprobation attached to it that we find in the West. One group of beggars (the *ragyapa*) was traditionally assigned the role of disposers of the dead. Corpses would be taken to nearby peaks and cut up, with the flesh laid out and bones pulverized so that they could be eaten by vultures and wild animals. Alternatively, the poor would be placed into swiftly flowing streams, to be eaten by the fish. In this way, the discarded body became food for fellow creatures. It was the performance of a generous and meritorious deed.

Only renowned teachers' and high lamas' bodies were treated differently. The formers' relics would be placed in *chortens* (stupas) as a memorial and reminder of their teachings. The latter would be embalmed by the monastic community.

Tibet had harboured no militaristic or expansionist ambitions in the previous 1,000 years of Buddhist influence. Its balance of payments with regard to imports against exports, such as they were, was healthy. It was, essentially, a highly conservative society that saw no need for change. Once villages had provided themselves with the physical necessities of life, any spare income was used in making offerings to temples and monasteries and the poor. There was no unemployment in the accepted sense, and social advancement did not fit the scheme of things. Since a century before Columbus, the most influential figure had been the Dalai Lama, the first being born in a nomad's tent on the plains of eastern Tibet. The order of Tibetan society was ordained by the same law that decreed the Dalai Lama always to be an incarnation of the Bodhisattva Chenresig (Avalokiteshvara).

Today Tibet has been shaken by the political, military and social changes of Chinese insurgence. Monasteries have been destroyed, resistance has been systematically subjugated and, most significantly for Tibetans, the Dalai Lama himself is absent. Tibetan Buddhism in exile has had to consider its adaptation to a larger world.

Tibetan Buddhism in exile

The key figure in this adaptation is the Dalai Lama himself. His residence is situated in the small town of McLeod Ganj near Dharamsala, in the Himalayan foothills of India, which hosts the largest number of Tibetans in exile within one place. This is regarded as the centre of Tibetan Buddhism while exile continues. However, he also travels the world, balancing the twin needs of sustaining the fabric of Tibetan life in exile and acting as ambassador for its cause and promoting world peace. At the same time he remains a Buddhist monk.

Ever since the invasion, His Holiness (as he is known to Tibetans) has appealed to the United Nations on the question of Tibet. This has resulted in three resolutions being adopted by the General Assembly, but China has repeatedly refused to respond positively to the various proposals offered to alleviate the Tibetan situation. It is remarkable, and yet consistent, that the policies advocated by the Dalai Lama to solve the Tibetan problem have always been based on non-violence. This gained him worldwide recognition in 1989 when he was awarded the Nobel Peace Prize. However, it has not resulted in substantial political backing from the international community. The Dalai Lama's concern for the plight of Tibetans remaining in their mother country is made clear in the following statement:

> On this anniversary, I pay homage to the brave men and women of Tibet, who laid down their lives for the freedom of our country, and I call upon every Tibetan to renew our dedication until we have regained our rights and freedom.

> (*His Holiness the Dalai Lama's Visit to the United Kingdom*, The Office of Tibet, May 1993, p 6)

Meanwhile, the continuance of Tibetan Buddhism, uprooted from its historical environment, is sustained by various means. Tibetan refugees have been resettled in India, Nepal and Bhutan with 83 schools established for children across the world. Across the world 117 monasteries have been established. In Dharamsala a Tibetan Medical and Astrological Institute, a Library of Tibetan Works and Archives and a Tibetan Institute of Performing Arts have been founded. There is also a school in Dharamsala to promote the education of Tibetan culture for the young born in exile. Such initiatives not only sustain the cultural and religious life of an exiled community, but also offer enrichment to a wider world. This helps, albeit in a small way, to compensate for the deaths of 1.2 million Tibetans, the imprisonment and torture of thousands of religious and political prisoners, the destruction of 6,000 monasteries and the outlawing of the teaching and study of Buddhism in Tibet.

Personal encounters

It was an ironic experience to be offered a children's book on the life of the Buddha, produced by a Buddhist publishing group located at a Tibetan Buddhist Centre in the United Kingdom, in the Tibetan Institute at Sarnath. It was also humbling to be thanked for my interest in the Buddhist religion, when I had taken the time of an important Tibetan official and was, myself, no more than a passing Westerner possessing equal amounts of curiosity and cheek. In answer to my question of how the situation of suffering, domination and exile could best be dealt with, he replied: 'By continuing to spread the word of what was happening, pray and hope for the future.' A salutary and gentle response that, in its unexpected character, faced me, with my own Western conditioning, as a matter for reflection.

meeting on the rooftop at Dharamsala reporting on the situation in Tibet

A world away, in the offices of Wisdom Publications in London, I was introduced to the tulku of Lama Yeshe. He was already known to me through talking to a nun at one of the western centres that he had established. In her broad Lancashire accent, and while making tea, she described to me the transition, in her later years, from neighbourhood life in a Lancashire town to ordination as a nun in Tibetan robes. In the telling, her respect and affection for the lama who ordained her became apparent.

It comes as something of a shock to a Western mind to accommodate the relationship of these two events from a Buddhist perspective, and to become aware of the karmic significance involved. After all, without the Chinese invasion of Tibet, none of these small, anecdotal circumstances would have occurred. Such is the mystery of things, and the influence of large-scale political change on individual lives as it ripples across the globe.

The propagation of the dharma

On a broader front, Western Buddhists in the Tibetan tradition are engaged in producing materials in the form of videos and books for educational and study purposes, in the hope that Mahayana Buddhism may become known to future generations, and be better understood by adults in the modern world. They are also engaged in the question of lineage, since the preservation of the teachings is a matter of the relationship between guru and disciples. Given that Tibetan is not a language generally available to a worldwide audience, much effort is being spent in providing translators of Tibetan origin to disseminate the speeches of Tibetan lamas in English and other languages. At the same time, the teachers themselves are attempting the transition to a new means of communication. The difficulty of the Tibetan situation has raised some debate as to the adaptation of Tibetan Buddhism to Western society as well as the influence of modern society on Tibetan Buddhists. As one commentator critically observes:

> Some Tibetan lamas have succeeded in establishing themselves in the Western world, where they have discovered the existence of a potential following among Western 'truth seekers' with predilections for Buddhist or general theosophical ideas. The successful ones seem to be those who have learned to adapt their ideas and teachings to what is expected of them – namely, a minimum of intellectual preparation and the practice of meditation in order to achieve a kind of equipoise in the affairs of this world.

This would seem to be quite desirable so far as it goes, but it is something rather different from the main preoccupation of Tibetan Buddhist practice, which has always offered a transcendent – not a this-worldly – ideal to those who are intellectually and morally prepared, and to those who are not so prepared the prospect of improved this-worldly conditions in a future life, achieved by the accumulation of personal merits. These are the ideals still kept in mind by the majority of Tibetans in exile, and these are mainly simple folk, whose religion is quite properly one of faith in the Buddhas and supporting divinities and of the practice of meritorious acts. The reciting of invocations to chosen divinities as one tells one's string of 108 beads, the turning of the prayer wheel in supplication to the Lord of Compassion, Avalokiteshvara, and the making of offerings to those who are qualified to recite the scriptures on one's behalf remain the main religious occupations of Tibetan lay folk in the settlements established in India. The few who feel the need for a higher ideal and are free to pursue it must needs go on pilgrimage looking for a suitable teacher, who is certainly still to be found, although the circumstances of life in exile make such a quest far more difficult than it ever was in Tibet itself, and it must be remembered that those who might once have gone on such a quest now tend to go in pursuit of modern forms of education.

(David Snellgrove, in H. Dumoulin and J. C. Maraldo (eds), *Buddhism in the Modern World*, Collier Macmillan, 1976, p 291)

Tibetan Buddhists outside their tent

Buddhism in the West

Buddhism in the West has emerged, partly through immigrant communities arriving in Europe and North America but also through Westerners discovering Buddhism or becoming Buddhist monks in Asia and returning to the West as part of Buddhist missionary activity in the twentieth and twenty-first centuries.

Buddhism in the United Kingdom

Although Buddhist ideas were studied in late Victorian Britain, the religion was brought to public attention by a Buddhist monk, Ananda Metteyya (the Englishman Alan Bennett). The Buddhist Society of Great Britain and Ireland was founded in 1907 as a vehicle for his teaching. It was succeeded in 1924 by the present Buddhist Society, the founder president of which was the late Judge Christmas Humphreys, who largely created the climate in which Buddhism began to take root and flourish in the West. In 1926 the London Buddhist Vihara was established in Chiswick, West London – the earliest Buddhist temple in Britain.

Since that time, many different branches of Buddhism have been established, originating in such countries as Thailand, Tibet and Japan. As a result, Britain today has a great variety of Buddhist groups and communities – far more than would be found in any one 'traditionally Buddhist' country. The *Directory of Buddhist Groups*, produced by the Buddhist Society, reported 74 groups in 1979; eight years later there were 191, and this number has continued to grow. The four largest are illustrated here.

Theravada Buddhism

The Theravada tradition is the branch of Buddhism predominant in South-East Asia and Sri Lanka. In Britain there are a number of Theravadin communities. Those from Sri Lanka have their main centre at the London Buddhist Vihara (monastic residence). There is also a Thai temple in the London area, as well as a Burmese vihara.

Perhaps the most significant Theravadin movement in Britain is the Thai Forest Retreat Order, established by the late Luang Por (venerable father) Chah, with its main activities at 'Amaravati', a Buddhist Monastery in Hertfordshire and 'Cittaviveka' in Sussex. The names 'Amaravati' (meaning 'deathless realm') and 'Cittaviveka' (meaning 'silent mind') give clues to the aspirations of all Buddhists. The monks and nuns in this order in Britain are Western converts to Buddhism. As a young monk, Luang Por Chah was disaffected with the state of Buddhism in Thailand; the study of doctrine and texts and the laxness of monastic training brought him no closer to realizing the one aim of the Buddha's teaching: the cessation of suffering. His founding of the Forest Retreat Order was meant to be a return to the original practice of the Buddha's Sangha (monastic community) and its strict rules of conduct, the Vinaya. During the course of the 1950s through to the 1970s Westerners became attracted to the order when they discovered it through travels connected with military service (the Korean and Vietnamese wars) and the 'hippy trail'. This led to a specific monastery being set up for Westerners in Thailand in 1974. In 1977, an invitation from the English Sangha Trust to establish an order of Western Buddhist monks in Britain brought the Forest Retreat Order to Britain, led by Luang Por Chah's senior Western disciple, Ajahn (now Luang Por) Sumedho. Eventually, Cittaviveka and then Amaravati were established as the main monasteries, but other smaller viharas have also been founded, notably in Devon and Northumberland. Other branch monasteries now also exist in New Zealand, Switzerland and Canada.

Another key development in the Forest Retreat Order's activity in Britain has been the establishment of a Buddhist prison chaplaincy service by Luang Por Khemadhammo (Ven. Chao Khun Bhavanatisa), run from the Forest Hermitage in Warwickshire. The chaplaincy is called Angulimala, named after a robber who was converted to Buddhism by the Buddha. Its website is at www.angulimala.org.uk.

Tibetan Buddhism

The Tibetan tradition has all four of its branches represented in Britain: the Manjushri Institute at Ulverstone in Cumbria, Samye Ling Buddhist Centre at Eskdalemuir in Dumfriesshire, and the Madhyamika Centre, near York, are the largest.

The New Kadampa movement based at the Manjushri Institute has attracted particular attention and some controversy. New Kadampa was established there in 1991, led by Geshe Kelsang Gyatso who was born in western Tibet, left in 1959 with the Chinese occupation and travelled to India and Nepal, spending much of his time in meditational retreat. In 1977 he was invited to become resident teacher at the Manjushri Institute, which had been founded by the students of Lama Thubten Yeshe in 1976 with Lama Yeshe as its first spiritual director.

The lineage of New Kadampa proceeds from the Indian Buddhist Master, Atisha (982–1054 CE), the founder of the Kadampa tradition, through the fourteenth-century Buddhist Master, Je Tsongkhapa, founder of New Kadampa and the Gelug tradition in Tibet. The emphasis in New Kadampa is on the union of *sutra* and *tantra* for the training of the mind.

At the Manjushri Institute disputes occurred over the spiritual direction of Geshe Kelsang and Lama Yeshe. Central to these was the emphasis Geshe Kelsang placed upon the inclusion of Tantric Buddhism. With Lama Yeshe's death in 1984, the New Kadampa Tradition (NKT) under Geshe Kelsang's spiritual direction has flourished. This has involved more radical and exclusive teachings and policies. Geshe Kelsang took the view that the Gelug tradition had been corrupted since the time of

Tsongkhapa and that his disciples should separate from it. This has involved an iconoclasm that discourages veneration of other lamas and their teachings, including the Dalai Lama. New Kadampa regards itself as promoting the pure teachings of Tsongkhapa, with Geshe Kelsang as his spiritual heir. Its centres have spread throughout Britain and within Europe.

Soto Zen: Serene Reflection Meditation (Tsa'o-Tung Ch'an)

The Japanese Soto Zen tradition has established itself as the Serene Reflection Meditation movement with a monastic centre at Throssel Hole Buddhist Abbey near Hexham in Northumberland, a smaller centre in Reading, Berkshire and two further centres in Britain. There are also a number of affiliated groups around the country, known as Serene Reflection Meditation Groups. This form of Soto Zen Buddhism migrated from Japan to establish Shasta Abbey in California and then Throssel Hole Abbey in the north of England. The Abbess at Shasta Abbey and spiritual leader of the whole movement was Jiyu Kennett, who was born in England and eventually became foreign guestmaster at the Sojiji Temple in Yokohama before establishing the Serene Reflection Meditation movement in California, then later in Britain.

The teachings are based on the lineage from Bodhidharma, the Indian Buddhist monk who brought Buddhism to China as a direct transmission of the truth through just sitting. In Japan this legacy was continued through Dogen Zenzi and his teaching of transmission from mind to mind rather than through scriptures. The teachings and disciplines laid down in Dogen's Shobogenzo (The Treasury-Eye of the True Teaching) are the basis for monastic practice.

Distinctively, the Serene Reflection Meditation movement has taken on adapted forms of practice suited to Western culture. For example, at Throssel Hole the daily services are in Gregorian Plainsong and the movement refers to itself as a church, with its ordained leaders given the title reverend. At the same time, the traditional Japanese monastic routines and disciplines are adhered to: the main daily meal is conducted in silence, the monks sleep in the main hall with thin mattresses taken from wall cupboards, times for ablutions at the start of the day are strictly adhered to and formal meditation is conducted in the traditional zazen manner, facing the wall with eyes open. Emphasis is placed on the development of compassion and wisdom expressed in daily life. Its openness to the gender of monastics is significant. Men and women, regardless, are called monks.

The Friends of the Western Buddhist Order (FWBO)

The FWBO deserves its own separate entry here, with a more extensive commentary, due to its more radical and controversial interpretation of how Buddhism needs to be adapted to the modern world.

The Friends of the Western Buddhist Order differ from most other forms of Buddhist organization in many respects, the most important being that they are specifically committed to the ideals and practices of Buddhism in a form that is effective in the conditions of modern Western industrialized society.

the Three Jewels emblem of the FWBO

It was founded in 1968, by the Ven. Sangharakshita, as a Western sangha. At the heart of the organization is the Order itself. This consists of men and women who have gone for refuge to the Three Jewels, and accepted Sangharakshita as their spiritual teacher. In this sense, the Western Buddhist Order has established its own tradition, not dependent on, but related to, other branches of Buddhism.

Upon ordination, members are invested with a *kesa*, a strip of white brocade worn around the neck, with the emblem of the

Three Jewels embroidered on it. If Order members have undertaken to follow a celibate life, the kesa is gold in colour. These are worn at FWBO gatherings, and on occasions when an Order member is representing the FWBO. An Order member also receives a new name, taken from Sanskrit, to signify spiritual rebirth and their belonging to the sangha. It indicates their aspiration to progress in the spiritual life. Thus, for example, 'Bodhananda', meaning the 'Bliss of Enlightenment'.

Male Order members are known as dharmacharis, and female Order members as dharmacharinis, meaning 'dharma farers' or 'those who practise the dharma'. Order members are not monks or nuns in the traditional sense of being mendicants, but neither are they lay members. The lifestyles of Order members vary, and there are no rules apart from the precepts. Some Order members work full time for the FWBO, usually teaching and running centres; others work in Right Livelihood businesses, attached to the organization and seeking to promote its aims. These may be connected with publishing, running bookshops or cafes, and so on. This is a form of outreach, concerned with living an ethical life and supporting the Order itself. Other Order members may work outside the movement, but seek to bring their Buddhist commitment to their professional life, as this comment from a hospital psychiatrist shows:

> If my bleep goes off I use it as a cue to check my breath. I find that useful, like building up little islands of mindfulness into my day.

Sangha and spiritual friendship

The FWBO believes that the sangha should not be mendicant, because this will hinder the spreading of the dharma. As one Order member explains:

> For instance, monks aren't allowed to handle money. So, if you're a monk, and you want to travel around the country giving talks on Buddhism, you have to make elaborate arrangements to pay your train fares. The rule is a hindrance. Anagarika Dharmapala (the founder of the Mahabodhi Society) had this problem. Thinking that following the full Vinaya might hamper his work, he did not take the Bhikkhu Ordination. He followed a much simpler form of ethical code, which he thought would allow him to be as effective as possible. After all, what is

important is that you are really able to practise Buddhism, and not that a tenpenny piece never crosses your palm.

(Dharmachari Vessantara, in P. Connolly and C. Erricker (eds), *The Presence and Practice of Buddhism*, W.S.I.H.E., 1985, p 60)

They also feel that it encourages exaggerated deference to a group seen as the religious professionals, diminishes the expectations of the lay person, and is not conducive to a sense of inherent spiritual equality.

The sangha is therefore understood in a distinctive way, as the following passage explains. It is:

The totality of those who have 'Gone For Refuge' … the spiritual community. It is the absolute contrast to the social group which is a network of need-based relationships. The Sangha comes into being when people experience together their common commitment to the highest of ideals and feel a mutual concern and friendliness. It is only to the extent that there is real metta, true friendliness, that there is Sangha. And it is this spirit of friendship which is the crucial element in the spiritual life.

(Dharmachari Subhuti, *Buddhism For Today*, Element Books, 1983, p 87)

Mitras

Mitra is the word for 'friend', and denotes Friends of the Order. These are individuals who form an association with the Order without being full Order members. They declare their openness to the movement, and Order members reciprocate by accepting them as mitras. Their involvement may vary from occasional contact through attending classes, to going on retreats or working in one of the FWBO cooperatives, and living in a community. However, it is a positive commitment to practising meditation and learning about the dharma. Mitras are expected to follow the Buddhist Path and support the development of the movement in an active way. There is a small ceremony for new mitras, at which they make an offering of a flower, a candle and incense before the Buddha image, during a puja.

Positive Buddhism

The FWBO believes that the Buddha's message should be presented in a positive way, such that it is seen as enhancing the society it is in, rather than being separate from it. They emphasise the positive counterpart of each precept. So, for example, the first precept, 'I undertake to refrain from harming living beings', is balanced by 'With deeds of loving kindness I purify my body.' In concert with this, it welcomes Western literature (such as the work of Goethe and William Blake) which represents teachings seen as supporting the Buddhist vision. It accentuates qualities such as good communication, creativity and active involvement in society as ways in which the aim of spiritual evolution can be achieved:

> While we don't ignore the Buddha's teachings on dukkha, we stress that Buddhism is a Path leading to higher and more satisfying mental states. For instance, one traditional formulation of the Dharma which we often talk about is the 'spiral path'. It begins when you see the unsatisfactoriness of ordinary mundane life, which gives you confidence in the Buddha's analysis of the human predicament. With that confidence you practise the precepts and meditation wholeheartedly. This purifies your mind and leads to higher mental states: joy, rapture, calm and bliss – each state higher than the last – until a total psychic integration is achieved. On the basis of this arises insight into the nature of Reality. This enables you to 'see through' mundane life, so you no longer cling to it. Its waves no longer overwhelm you, or even ruffle your mind. The path culminates in the knowledge that you are completely free from even the subtlest predisposition to future suffering.

> (Dharmachari Vessantara, in P. Connolly and
> C. Erricker (eds), *The Presence and Practice of
> Buddhism*, W.S.I.H.E., 1985, p 67)

Buddhism in the United States

In the United States Buddhist influence has been felt more keenly in certain areas than in other Western countries. This is partly due to its proximity to Asia on the west coast. At the end of the nineteenth century, Japanese and Chinese families settled in California; the Japanese also settled in Hawaii during the twentieth century after the enforcement of strict immigration laws in California in 1902. Hawaii also became the focus of Buddhist missionary activity in the United States, which in turn led to temples and meditation centres being established on the mainland. In the process of this transference from their original cultural setting, Buddhists have adapted their organizations and forms of service. Buddhist influence has also spread into American cultural life, beyond classically Buddhist institutions, through its attraction as a spiritual philosophy, and a meditative practice.

To some degree, the spread of Buddhism in the United States – especially along the west coast – has only a tentative relationship with the religion as it has developed in traditionally Buddhist countries, such as Japan. Young Western liberals, anxious to find an alternative to establishment thinking, propagated Zen as a life-enhancing but essentially individualistic philosophy of life. This can be recognized, for example, in the writings of Alan Watts who (although British) lived and worked for the majority of his life in the United States, and was related to the beat movement of the late 1950s and early 1960s, typified by Jack Kerouac and Allen Ginsberg. Such love affairs with Buddhist ideas, while exhilarating, could not be responsible for rooting Buddhism in a new culture. The seeds of Buddhism in America were more obviously sown as a result of the World Parliament of Religions in Chicago in 1893, where Anagarika Dharmapala spoke as founder of the Maha Bodhi Society and, as he became later towards the end of his life, as a practising Buddhist monk in the Theravada (South Asian) tradition.

The proliferation of Buddhist centres during the latter half of the twentieth century owes much to the work of established Japanese teachers, such as Shunryu Suzuki and his American disciple Richard Baker, who received his entitlement to teach from his Japanese master. By transferring this traditional lineage to a new socio-cultural environment, Buddhism may well establish a lasting presence on new soil while remaining true to its own principle of spreading the dharma.

However, while the last sentiment may, in due course, come to pass, these are still somewhat turbulent times. We cannot record the history and contemporary form of Buddhism in America, and more specifically in the United States, in the same way as was done above with regard to Britain. It is, perhaps, a reflection of different national castes of mind. For example, migration to the United States has been an ongoing phenomenon driven by the idea of becoming American. In Britain migration, often a result of decolonization, has been much more a matter of keeping a separate identity while still being British by nationality. To some degree this may have influenced the way in which tradition, linked to previous forms of Buddhism in Britain, has continued but been adapted. In the United States the record of the arrival and integration of Buddhism has been far more eclectic. Rather than being grouped around separate Buddhist traditions it has been grouped around particular individuals, and what we might call the making of Buddhism in America is a different sort of project. Below I summarise, necessarily briefly, aspects of this development under the names of a few influential figures who represent different approaches and facets of Buddhism in the United States.

Thomas Merton

Although a Catholic monk, Merton had a significant impact on the West's recognition of Buddhism. He recognized the connection between his own contemplative practice and, in particular, that of Zen. In his late fifties he had a productive correspondence with D.T. Suzuki, whose prodigious publications on Zen Buddhism had been influential in the West, and met him in 1964. Merton's aim was to cross those fault lines of religious tradition to open communication between contemplatives in their different monastic orders. His hope was that this could influence a world that desperately needed spiritual invigoration. To this end he saw communication between the spiritual traditions of East and West as instrumental. This 'lateral' communication was a driving force. As Merton put it:

> as a pilgrim who is anxious to obtain not just information, not just 'facts' about other monastic traditions, but to drink from ancient sources of monastic vision and experience. I seek not only to learn more about religious and monastic life, but to become a better and more enlightened monk myself.
>
> (from 'Mystics and Zen Masters' in Rick Fields, (ed.) *How the Swans Came to the Lake: a narrative history of Buddhism in America*, third edition, Shambala, 1992, p 297)

On 4 November 1968 Merton met the Dalai Lama in Dharamsala. Their conversation included focusing on the Madhyamika concept of sunyata and later on the way in which monks could be living examples of the transformation of the way in which humans could live.

Shortly before his death from electrocution after a shower in Bangkok, Merton travelled to Pulonnaruwa in Sri Lanka where he observed the sculptures of the Buddha in *paranirvana* accompanied by Ananda and a Buddha seated in meditation. He commented: 'Looking at these figures ... an inner clearness ... became obvious ... everything is emptiness and everything is compassion ... I mean I know and have seen what I was looking for (Fields, 1992, p 300)

Chogyam Trungpa

Chogyam Trungpa arrived in North America in January 1970. He had previously resided at Samye-Ling monastery in Scotland. Soon he was preaching that 'America suffered ... from spiritual materialism: "deceiving ourselves into thinking we are developing spiritually when instead we are strengthening our ego-centricity through spiritual techniques" ' (Fields, 1992, p 309).

Trungpa diagnosed the American spiritual condition as dependent upon spiritual excitement. His style was laconic and relaxed but developed into establishing the Vajradhatu organization, situated at the Rocky Mountain Dharma centre and, later, the Vajradhatu Seminary, which took place at a hotel in Jackson, Wyoming. Trunpa's exposition of the vajrayana became the apotheosis of his teachings, introducing tantric practices which he explained as 'just the same old Buddhist stuff in many ways. But the whole basic thing creates a lot of power ... We should be very careful' (Fields, 1992, p 312).

Nevertheless, eclecticism remained a driving force. Trungpa Rimpoche set up the Naropa Institute based on the model of the ancient Indian Buddhist University of Nalanda, to introduce the intellectual critical mind of the West to the intuitive meditative practice of the East. Here a mixture of experiences was brought together that extended beyond the Buddhist tradition and embraced Ram Dass, the previous Harvard psychology professor, and other luminaries who offered differing spiritual experiences.

Jack Kornfield

Jack Kornfield first studied under Ajahn Chah in Thailand (see references to the Thai Forest Retreat Order above). He returned to America as a saffron-robed Bhikkhu – but found it impossible to keep his vows as a forest monk and returned to lay life. He established the Insight Mediation Centre with Joseph Goldstein, based on vipassana meditation techniques. This resulted in becoming aware of the differences in training Westerners. Motivation and progress were different in following this traditional practice when comparing Westerners wtih Burmese students who attended. The real difference appeared to be one of concentration and faith in the practice. This, in turn, connected with a lack of Western belief in traditional tenets of faith: karma and rebirth. Mahasi Sayadaw, one of the Theravadin elders who visited the centre, remarked: 'All you can do is preach what the Buddha said. It is not only in America. Few practise. Even in Burma there are more people who do not practise meditation than people who do' (Fields, 1992, p 322).

Kornfield's experience is quite unusual in the context of the United States. He sought, with his partners, to set up a practice that was closely aligned with the tradition he had been immersed in, rather than broadening it to include a more eclectic experience. One of the results of this was to identify the difficulties Westerners have in subjecting themselves to an established tradition rather than taking on a more flexible spiritual practice with eclectic elements that, despite the value of variety, does not require the same rigour.

Thich Nhat Hahn

While never taking up residence in the United States, Thich Nhat Hanh nevertheless has had a significant influence due to his connection with the Vietnam war. He is a Vietnamese Buddhist monk who worked for reconciliation between North and South Vietnam. In 1966 he was exiled, at the age of 40, by being banned by both the Communist and non-Communist governments. Objections to Thich Nhat Hahn were based upon his non-violent resistance and his championing of 'engaged Buddhism', which we shall return to in our final chapter. His phrase, 'Don't just do something; sit there', indicated the way in which he believed that the practice of meditation and the cultivation of mindfulness could be powerful tools in opposing social injustice.

In exile he embarked on a mission to spread Buddhism around the world. On his visits to the United States from 1966 onwards he presented his own views on how to end the conflict in Vietnam. He also organized rescue missions for Vietnamese seeking to escape political repression. His idea of an enlightened social consciousness that was not complicit with the status quo struck a chord for Americans who were at odds with their own government's propagation of a war which many thought unjust and wasteful. It was a call to do something effective without resorting to violence. It also made the link between Buddhism as a path for personal spiritual development, through meditation, and social action. Embrionically, it created a new perspective on the idea of snagha as a community of individuals acting together to improve society. Thich Nhat Hanh explained that rather than see contemplation and action as separate things they should be viewed as necessarily complementary.

> I think in Buddhism, these two cannot be separated. To meditate is to be aware of what is going on – in yourself and the world. If you know what is going on, how can you avoid acting to change the situation?

> (Fields, 1992, p 375)

His efforts to generate peace led Martin Luther King, Jr to nominate him for the Nobel Peace Prize in 1967. Now, nearing seventy, he continues to visit the United States every other year from his community based in France, and draws large crowds to listen to his message of peace, social action and reconciliation. Perhaps, more than any other Buddhist figure apart from the Dalai Lama, his teachings and actions provide the basis for Buddhist engagement with ecumenical dialogue and social renewal in the twenty-first century.

In evaluating the American experience we have to admire the enthusiasm for incorporating Buddhist practices into an American vision of cultural change and the openness to differing forms of expression of the contemplative life. At the same time there is a need to register the difficulties this involves in terms of commitment to practices that are rooted in alien cultural traditions which require adaptation to a new environment.

In conclusion

We may say that the twentieth century was a time of upheaval and progressive change for Buddhism, as its traditional centres were subjected to different political and economic influences. Its missionary activity has increased, but it is too early to say whether it will ultimately have any significant effect. Its contacts with communism, capitalism and advances in scientific knowledge have placed it in a position similar to that of other world faiths in a world of rapid change. This discussion of the influence of Buddhism worldwide once again points to the importance of establishing a sangha or Buddhist community, as the tradition spreads from one country to another. Taking account of the customs and mores of different societies is a recurring theme in Buddhism. The relevance of the Buddha's teaching, however, does not seem to have diminished. The twenty-first century is already replete with suffering. Attacks on the twin towers in New York, reprisals in Afghanistan and the war that has been waged on Iraq do not suggest we are any nearer to accomplishing what the Buddha hoped the world would achieve. Summarily, the commentary in this chapter indicates that:

- There are significant differences between the Buddhist presence in the East and that in the West, but change is evolving in both, partly as an effect of globalization.
- Adaptation of Buddhism in the United Kingdom and the United States has been different but, being still in a position of transition in both countries, that may well change in the future.
- The diversity of Buddhism has never been more obvious, as the traditionally Eastern forms from different countries start to become manifest in and adapted within the West, and as the East and West develop greater connection with, and influence upon, each other.
- There are signs that certain movements within Buddhism are engaging more specifically with social change and issues of social justice. At the same time, certain traditional metaphysical tenets of Buddhism and traditional roles, for monks and laity, are becoming subject to change.

transition, adaptation and influence: prospects for Buddhism in the twenty-first century

In this chapter you will learn:

- more about the prospects of Buddhism in the twenty-first century
- how Buddhism is adapting to different movements and responding to different issues
- about ways that Buddhism is being renewed and reinterpreted in the West.

This chapter follows on from the last but attempts to probe the themes highlighted in the chapter title in greater depth and, in doing so, identify specific examples of ways in which Buddhism is facing up to, or being forced to adapt to, issues and circumstances of particular contemporary significance.

Into the twenty-first century

Chapter 10 concluded by indicating that the relevance of the Buddha's message does not seem to have diminished. However, in the late twentieth and the emergent twenty-first century social change and the influence of globalization present new challenges for any religion. Political and economic shifts always impinge on religious communities and often test the resolve of those communities to be involved in the world's affairs rather than just retreating from the wider social order. In this way Buddhist traditional reliance on a monastic sangha is called into question. Does monasticism separate itself off from the most significant issues the modern world faces such that it makes Buddhism peripheral to the interests of that world and marginalizes the impact of the Buddhist message? This is a complex question, partly because Buddhism has many differing forms and attitudes towards engagement; partly because there is a real question as to whether the dharma needs to be, or is best expressed, as 'religious' in a world beset by secularization. If the Buddha's teaching *is* still relevant today how can it *be seen* to be relevant to today and influence the world we create in the future?

In his study of the world in the twentieth century Clive Pontin concludes that:

> Given the way the world evolved in the twentieth century and the distribution of economic and political power at the end of the century, it seems likely that, as in the past, the world will, over the next few decades, continue to be characterized by progress for a minority and barbarism for the overwhelming majority.

(Clive Pontin, *The Pimlico History of the Twentieth Century*, Pimlico, 1999, p 546)

The Boer War saw the invention of the concentration camp, by the British, at the beginning of the century. The First World War introduced the impact of modern armaments, capable of mass killing, into trench warfare. Both these developments led eventually and respectively to the Holocaust of the Second World War and the atom bomb, which was used not against the military but against large civilian populations. At the end of the century ethnic cleansing had become a widely favoured solution to settling disputes within nation states and across contested borders. The major economic powers, the wealthy Western nations, have done little but offer rhetoric and sanctions (in some cases) in response. At the same time, economically, they have been careful to maintain their privileged position in a rampant free-market economy, through the World Bank and the G8 group, which has excluded countries in the periphery (the Third World), and by ensuring that arms sales remained a major export priority.

Passing into the twenty-first century, the major economic powers are multinational global corporations. Their effect on communities and values across the globe and in specific countries has been well documented by Naomi Klein, in her publication *No Logo*, and George Monbiot in his book *Captive State: the Corporate Takeover of Britain*, amongst others. The exploitation of child labour in peripheral countries has increased, not diminished. The perpetrators of this exploitation are those who most influence the 'branding' of lifestyles and 'individuality' in the West; for example, Nike and Adidas. This double exploitation of the worker and the 'customer' is the prevalent value base for commercial success and 'cool' image. The real customer is the shareholder and the bargain struck is based on the promise of ever-increasing return on the dividend invested. This is the prevailing situation to which Pontin is referring.

What are the Buddhist responses to this state of affairs? The responses have depended on the specifics of localized situations and priorities in those situations that, in some cases, have had a much to do with socio-cultural and political factors as they have had to do with simply religious ones. To illustrate, here are two different, contrasting examples of the way in which Buddhism has been involved in and been affected by the affairs of nation states. They are case studies in one of the most pressing contemporary problems, that of migrant and indigenous minorities. In the first example Buddhists are the minority in question, in the second Buddhism is the state religion.

Migrant Buddhism and the Japanese experience

In Chapter 10 I briefly alluded to Japanese migration to the United States. Here I report the experiences and issues that faced those Japanese Buddhist communities in more detail.

In Tetsuden Kashima's study of Japanese Buddhists in the United States (*Buddhism in America: the Social Organization of an Ethnic Religious Institution*, Greenwood Press, 1977), we find a story which can be paralleled by other immigrant groups' histories, for example, those of Vietnamese Buddhists, Bangladeshi and Khojas Shi'a Ithnasheeri Muslims and various Hindu and Sikh communities. The author is of Japanese extraction and the son of a priest, the Reverend Tetsuro Kashima, of the Japanese Buddhist Churches of America. In this study we can trace an example of Buddhist ethnic transference to the West, which is comparatively rarely documented in Buddhism, as opposed to the transmigration that has occurred with ethnic groups in other religions.

Kashima remarks on how 'The Buddhist Church of America (BCA) represents an alien religion in America – one that has continued for seventy-six years.' It is predominantly Jodo Shinshu of the West and East School varieties and most emigrated from the Hiroshima area (Prefecture), representing a quarter of the total of Japanese migrants (84,562). The Buddhist Church of America (BCA) represents Jodo Shinshu (Amida Buddhism or Pure Land) with its headquarters in San Francisco. It was inaugurated under this name in 1944 after the traumatic events during the Second World War when almost all the Japanese and Nisei (first-generation Americans of Japanese ancestry) were interned. This resulted in a complete dislocation of habits and lifestyles. A continual theme in the history of the institution is its importance as a force for ethnic solidarity: 'The Buddhist Church is a place for the Japanese to meet other Japanese' as one Nisei father stated. In this respect it existed solely for the Japanese and their offspring since 1899. The use of the word Church became increasingly problematic for its members during the later decades of the twentieth century since it does not reflect the purposes or structures of an inherently Japanese Buddhist religious community. As Kashima points out, temple or *dojo* ('a place where the Way is cultivated') is a more proper description of its place of worship, and sangha is a more exact description of its membership (Kashima, 1977, p 187).

The history of Japanese immigrants bears some familiar features. Prejudice and wilfully ignorant racism such as that propagated by the Western Central Labour Union in Seattle in 1900 whose propagation for restrictions on immigration led to such descriptions of Japanese Buddhists as having the 'treacherous, sneaking insidious, betraying and perfidious nature and characteristics of the Mongolian race' (Kashima, 1977, p 18).

Kashima suggests that the use of the word 'Church' was probably an attempt to mitigate against anti-Japanese agitation and is evidence of the Americanization of second- and third-generation Japanese.

The Japanese bombing of Pearl Harbor in December 1941, despite its condemnation by the Buddhist Mission of North America (as it then was), led to internment. Most of those interned were Buddhists. Even before the bombing 'Many Japanese destroyed items that might be regarded as incriminating: some burned sutra books, while others concealed their family Buddhist altars' (Kashima, 1977, p 48, quoting from Ryo Munekata (ed.), *Buddhist Churches of America*, Vol. 1, Nobart Inc., 1974).

With generational change from Issei to Nisei to Sansei (third generation, but second generation American born) the membership declined in relation to the size of the Japanese-American population since the BCA never systematically proselytized and successive generations did not have the same need for its support as members of an ethnic minority. Also, those who still belonged to and supported the organization did not necessarily practise Buddhism. One Nisei minister commenting on why there was continued Nisei involvement with their church suggested:

> Perhaps it could be guilt or family pressure. What my parents have done for the temple, and therefore ... I must carry on. And the other one would say I must do it for my children. These may be some of the reasons why they do it. But not so much from the religious standpoint. (Kashima, 1977, p 188)

And one Nisei said, 'I don't know anything about Buddhism, I'll come not to the service but to other things. To carnivals, but not to study class or the *Hondo* [temple hall]' (Kashima, 1977, p 188).

Kashima remarks on the differences among the three generations as highlighted by the Reverend Koshin Ogui:

As history shows, the Issei had to work to support their families, nothing but work. The Nisei were educated by the Issei to build up their lives the same as the *hakujin* [Caucasian] people. So you see the majority of Nisei people out to buy cars and homes. They don't think about spiritual matters. They are more satisfied with fancy cars and homes. The Sansei are raised in such a background and getting tired of it. Of course, they respect their families. But they're looking for more importance in life – to go forward to fight for human rights, against racial discrimination and to help the community instead of building up their abundance. (Kashima, 1977, p 197)

If this proves to be the case and the BCA extends its involvement with other non-Japanese Shin-Buddhists, the spiritual heart of the organization could be revitalized. But Kashima's judgement is equivocal: 'Looking ahead we may conceive of many futures for the BCA, which is really just another way of saying that the future is uncertain.' He also refers to the remarks of the historian H.A.L. Fisher as being highly applicable to this situation:

One intellectual excitement has ... been denied me. Men wiser and more learned than I have discovered in history a plot, a rhythm, a predetermined pattern. These harmonies are concealed from me. I can see only one emergency following another, as wave follows upon wave, only one great fact with respect to which, since it is unique, there can be no generalization ... the play of the contingent and the unforeseen. (Kashima, 1977, p 205, from Robert A. Nisbet, *Social Change and History: Aspects of the Western Theory of Development*, Oxford University Press, 1969, p 284)

Kashima suggests that possible futures depend on how a number of present problems are resolved. He cites five: decreasing and changing membership; the ethnic character of membership; economic problems; the proper techniques for teaching Buddhism; interrelated problems with the ministry. All of the problems are ultimately interconnected, as he observes (see Kashima, 1977, p 207). He also posits that if the BCA comes to include a wider racial representation, as its leaders envision, then 'Buddhism will indeed become fully Americanized' (Kashima, 1977, p 220).

What is interesting, in this study, is the way it fits within the issues discussed at the beginning of this chapter. The close but shifting connections between ethnicity (Japanese), nationality (American), and religiosity (Buddhist) represent the equation that the community has to balance across three generations. For each generation the balance between these factors is different, in terms of priority. Migration was one of the dominant features of the twentieth century and is likely to be no less dominant in the twenty-first. It determines the issues of particular importance to this Buddhist group, it creates future uncertainty, discrimination, and problems in distinguishing the relationship between religion and culture, a relationship that changes across generations. Is being Buddhist important, as an aspect of identity, in a secularized American environment? Is it better to shed it in the movement towards becoming fully American, or is it the vital commitment to be retained and nurtured, against all others, to preserve identity and values? What does being Buddhist actually mean for this community and how does it relate to the larger issues introduced above concerning the spiritual and moral condition of a globalized world in the twenty-first century? What does the propagation of the dharma mean for this kind of community when its initial concern for the first, migrant, generation was economic survival and ethnic identity, then, for the next generation, wealth creation and assimilation? The questions that emerge for an immigrant group of this kind differ to those posed for Buddhists in other situations. When Kashima speaks of anticipating Buddhism becoming fully Americanized what sort of Buddhism will this be? We cannot know, but the twenty-first century will tell us. The third generation's concern with social issues fits a particular pattern of increasing Buddhist interest and activity, again touched on in Chapter 10, that we return to more fully later.

Buddhism, nationalism and the Sinhalese question

The second example is taken from the Sinhalese situation, again referred to earlier in the last chapter. Buddhism is not immune from ideological systems and, in the case of Sinhalese nationalism, it is a motivating force. The reasons behind this are, as always, complex and consist of economic, cultural, political, mythological and historical factors working together. As Tambiah announces at the beginning of his study (Stanley Jeyaraja Tambiah, *Buddhism Betrayed? Religion, Politics and*

Violence in Sri Lanka, University of Chicago Press, 1992):

> Frequently during my travels in the United States colleagues, friends and acquaintances ask me the discomforting question, 'If Buddhism preaches nonviolence, why is there so much political violence in Sri Lanka today?'

(ibid., p 1)

Sri Lanka is a small, highly populated island with a poor agrarian economy. It is seeking to develop its economic base in the context of high unemployment. It is populated by both Buddhists (the majority and heirs to its ancient classical past) and Tamils (the minority). Resultant Sinhalese nationalism seeks to recover its past glories as a civilization by calling on its Buddhist heritage and aggravating anti-Indian sentiment. This alienates the Tamil population which, as a result, fights for independence of rule. Opposing militant political factions developing within a situation of economic scarcity thus bring the development process to a halt and exacerbate the influence of ethnic and religious, in the cause of ideological conflict. The need, as Tambiah envisions it, is for 'a greater amount of pluralist tolerance in the name of Buddhist conceptions of righteous rule ... that can accommodate minorities' (ibid., xii, xiv). As he indicates, this attitude stretches back to the Emperor Ashoka's rule in India and that of the early Buddhist kings in south-east Asia as a model for contemporary relevance (ibid., p 1–2).

The present situation is a result of a number of historical issues through which, from a Sinhalese Buddhist point of view, there is a grievance to be rectified. As an example, during the period of British colonialism the influence of the sangha deteriorated:

> Under British subjugation monks headed the rebellions of 1818, 1834, and 1848. What the British soon became aware of was that a close identification and solidarity existed between the laity and the *sangha* and that *this unity between them had to be severed* if they were to gain control and rule peacefully. Thus a strategy of divide and rule was implemented to Christianize the country, during which elite Sinhalese families were indoctrinated to 'look down upon and despise Sinhalese culture ...'

(ibid., p 28)

This resulted in limiting the role of the *bhikkhus* to the margins of social influence and to a more reclusive life which reflected the model of a particular type of Christian monasticism (ibid., p 29). Thus, Buddhist nationalism in Sri Lanka is bound up with restoring and maintaining the historical right to Buddhist rule and the identification of any threat to this right. Within this the importance of the sangha in political affairs becomes self evident. The 1958 riots involving the Tamils were largely th result of denying them the use of their mother tongue in public life.

What Tambiah refers to as the 'restoration of Buddhism' in th 1960s and 1970s represents, in his view, an instrumental and selective use of Buddhism to underpin the Sinhalese nationalis cause, largely distanced from any central or foundationa Buddhist teachings (ibid., p 58ff). The Movement for th Protection of the Motherland in the 1980s emphasized Sinhales domination in which monks were actively politically engaged Tambiah writes that:

> An account of the transformation of Buddhism is gravely distorted and deficient if there is no account of the political direction taken by Buddhism in this century ... the larger truth about the sangha in this century is that it is differentiated on sectarian and regional bases and further fragmented by ordination lineages and property interests.

> (ibid., p 93)

By the late 1980s some monks were openly supporting violenc against Tamil rebels. Monks were actively recruited by th militant JVP party. The political motivation was to ensure S Lanka was a sovereign Buddhist and Sinhalese territory an some were implicated in violence to that end. They were critica of elder monks whom they accused of being 'trapped in world interests of property, rank, and temple building' (ibid., p 99). was also the case that younger monks were more fully draw from lower classes and more actively politically involved than a any time in the sangha's history. Indeed, Tambiah conclude their participation was indistinguishable from that of the la person (ibid., p 100). For the traditional Buddhist these change are worrying:

To many of us who live in the glow of the classical
Buddhist heritage, witnessing the increasing participation
of monks, especially young monks being educated in
monastic colleges and national universities, in violence,
whether directly or indirectly, is a disturbing experience.

(ibid., p 100)

Tambiah points out that turning to sanitized Pali texts does not
help. There is a tradition of monks opposing imperialism and
supporting working-class protest movements and repression in
the twentieth century, for example, in Burma, against its
repressive military regime, but, in his view, there is a large
question to be resolved about the contemporary role of
Buddhism:

as religion, civilization, and way of life ... There is an
inescapable dilemma here which surely must tug at the
conscience and moral sensibilities of all Buddhists. It
cannot be ignored; it has to be confronted, even if it
cannot satisfactorily be resolved.

(ibid., p 101)

Thus, the larger questions for Buddhism in the above and other
similar contemporary situations are how it survives as a migrant
religion belonging to an ethnic minority, and how it identifies its
relationship with nationalist ideologies and attitudes toward
ethnic minority discrimination, as with the Tamils, when it is the
indigenous majority religion.

Buddhists consequently have to scrutinize critically the
relationship between Buddhist texts and the tradition
developing in their socio-political contexts and determine how,
in the contemporary world, the community representing the
tradition takes a stance in relation to its socio-political
environment. From the point of view of the situations described
above, there is no point in either trying to reinvent Buddhism as
a pure but unassociated dharma or, concomitantly, trying to set
up Buddhist practice within a sanitized environment. The lotus
grows out of the samsaric mud. No mud – no lotus!

Both the examples given above relate to 'non-Western' groups of
Buddhist. What of the 'views from the West'? Here we can
identify some significantly different characteristics and, perhaps,
more helpful intimations of the impact of dharma.

Views from the West

Dharma practice and 'engaged Buddhism'

Stephen Batchelor has been an articulate spokesperson for envisioning a new understanding of dharma practice in the Western context. In identifying a degeneration in the understanding of the dharma in both East and West he offers a new way forward based on the collapse of religious–secular distinctions. For example, he writes:

> Just as contemporary agnosticism has tended to lose its confidence and lapse into scepticism, so Buddhism has tended to lose its critical edge and lapse into religiosity. What each has lost, however, the other may be able to restore. In encountering contemporary culture the dharma may recover its agnostic imperative, while secular agnosticism may recover its soul.

> (Stephen Batchelor, *Buddhism Without Beliefs:*
> *A Contemporary Guide to Awakening*,
> Bloomsbury, 1998, p 18)

Batchelor's view derives from a new impetus in Western thinking, a shunning of traditional and conventional religious forms and a search for more engaged and alternative ways of thinking about persistent and emergent environmental and social issues. These are linked to the concern in the West with ideas of individual freedom and autonomous action: the notion that each individual decides for him or herself as to what values stance each takes and how that influences lifestyle choices. On this matter Batchelor remarks:

> Dharma practice has become a creed ('Buddhism') much in the same way scientific method has degraded into the creed of 'Scientism'.

> (ibid., p 18)

But:

> While 'Buddhism' suggests another belief system 'dharma practice' suggests a course of action. The four ennobling truths are not propositions to believe; they are challenges to act ... The first truth challenges our habitual relationship to anguish.

> (ibid., p 7)

Further:

> At the heart of Buddhism's encounter with the contemporary world is the convergence of two visions of freedom. The Buddha's freedom from craving and anguish is converging with the individual's freedom to realize his or her capacity for personal and social fulfilment.
>
> (ibid., p 110)

Thus:

> ... a socially engaged vision of dharma practice recognizes that each practitioner is obliged by an ethics of empathy to respond to the anguish of a globalized, interdependent world.
>
> (ibid., p 112)

> Which, in turn, can be understood as bringing about the development of, 'A culture of awakening'.
>
> (ibid., p 113)

This individualized but collectivist view bringing the dharma to social action, or what has been called 'engaged Buddhism', owes much to the influence of the Vietnamese monk Thich Nhat Hanh, whose influence in the United States we considered in the previous chapter. During the Vietnam War he had been an activist drawing attention to the suffering of the population with the intention of 'moving the hearts of the oppressors' Stephen Batchelor, *The Awakening of the West: the Encounter of Buddhism and Western Culture*, Aquarian, 1994, p 354). His explanation of the self-immolation of Buddhist monks at that time was that they were 'a lotus in a sea of fire' (ibid., p 354). In 1973, at the end of the war, he was refused permission to return to Vietnam and moved to Fontvannes, near Paris, where he founded a rural community. Now this has moved to Plum Village in south-west France, near to Bordeaux. About 50 residents stay all year round, working to help Vietnamese refugees, political prisoners and tending the plum trees for income. For one month in the summer the community is open to the public, including children, and becomes a gathering place for Buddhist practitioners worldwide. From here Thich Nhat Hanh's presence and his writings have been an inspiration to Buddhists in the West to engage in Buddhist activism.

Such activism is described in terms of taking an anti-ideological stance, working on one's own inner development and attending to issues of both social and ecological concern. It also draws on non-Buddhist inspiration; for example, the writings of E.F. Schumacher, when focusing on ecological perspectives. Ken Jones' book, *Beyond Optimism: A Buddhist Political Ecology*, is an example of this. It takes an anti-ideological activist stance to shaping a green future based on the outer work of 'eco-social liberation' and the inner work of 'psycho-spiritual liberation', on the basis of Schumacher's conviction that:

> It is no longer possible to believe that any political or economic reform or scientific advance could solve the life and death problems of the industrial society. They lie too deep in the heart and soul of every one of us.

> (Ken Jones, *Beyond Optimism: A Buddhist Political Ecology*, Jon Carpenter, 1993, dedication)

Attacking the ideology of scientism, which states that 'there is an environmental crisis "out there" from which science alone can procure our salvation', Jones posits the need to recognize that 'there is an ecological crisis of which we are a part' (ibid. p 9) and that the 'cleverness' of scientism must be replaced by wisdom. Thus, quoting Schumacher again:

> The disease [affecting our civilization] having been caused by allowing cleverness to displace wisdom, no amount of clever research is likely to produce a cure. But where is wisdom? Where can it be found? Here we come to the crux of the matter: it can be read about in numerous publications, but it can be found only inside oneself. To be able to find it one has to liberate oneself from such masters as greed and envy.

> (ibid., p 9, in E.F. Schumacher, *Small is Beautiful*, Abacus Sphere, 1974, p 28)

The outer work of eco-social liberation Jones understands as best accomplished by avoiding extremes of the conflictual approach of radical greens and of the 'evolutionary approach' of consensualist greens. Empowerment of individuals and groups is the key to this alongside creating alternatives and changes in lifestyle. Thus the outer work must be accompanied by the inner (psycho-liberation). This amounts to working on yourself. Illustrative of this he quotes Thich Nhat Hanh:

Treat your anger [and all strong emotion] with the utmost respect and tenderness, because it is no other than yourself. Do not suppress it: simply be aware of it. Awareness is like the sun. When it shines on things they are transformed ... Mindfully dealing with anger is like taking the hand of a little brother.

> (ibid., p 181; from a talk given at a Buddhist Peace Fellowship Retreat in March 1983 at Tassajara Zen Mountain Centre, USA)

And the Thai Buddhist activist Sulak Sivaraksa:

Buddhism is an attempt to deal with what it sees as the disease of individualism. Buddhism is primarily a method of overcoming the limits of the individual self; consequently it entails a concern with the political and social dimensions.

> (ibid., p 178, in *A Buddhist Vision for Renewing Society*, Thai Watana Panich, 1981, p 162)

Relating these together Jones points to the development of organisational growth and collaboration of green movements which are distinctive but not conflictual in mentality: a shift to a higher consciousness that can claim political rewards, such as the election of a green Welsh nationalist in 1992, Cynog Dafis, with 'an uncompromisingly radical green programme' (ibid., p. 157). Pointers to other grassroots development such as initiatives in Kenya and Mexico also suggest hope, albeit fragile, since as Paul Elkins points out, 'most of the major global trends are still going in the wrong direction, some at an accelerating rate' (ibid., p 157, in Paul Elkins, *New World Order: Grassroots Movements for Social Change*, Routledge, 1992, p 114).

Elkins' observation seems significant. For activism to succeed it has to affect popular opinion radically, and attack the structures of capitalist politics and the global economy, not just particular issues or the effects of such a system at different times and in different places. It must also, therefore, be a movement that lives according to the ideal it promotes. Buddhist participation in such activism would seem to necessitate understanding the dharma to be spoken whenever wisdom is heard, whether couched in Buddhist terminology or not. What effect does this have on traditional understandings of Buddhism, its organization and the interpretations of the teachings?

Certainly, what constitutes a sangha becomes a pertinent question. The traditional monastic sangha, dependent for support on the laity, with the monks' and nuns' work being primarily that of offering an example and presence for the laity of the renunciant life dedicated to non-worldliness, fits awkwardly into the activist model – if at all.

Interpretation of the teachings suggesting that monastic renunciant lifestyle is the most important aspect of the Buddha's message and that daily individual and collective practice should reflect this certainly seems to require revision. Perhaps this is the most singular aspect of 'Westernized Buddhism' to have impacted on the tradition in the late twentieth and emergent twenty-first century. But it is not only Buddhist activism that has begun to question radically what it means to be part of a Buddhist community and what a Buddhist community's purpose is. Other strands in Western Buddhism have also questioned whether 'dharma' should in effect replace religious notions of 'Buddhism', and whether traditional forms of 'sangha' are out of touch with the times.

Feminist Buddhism

From a feminist perspective Rita Gross speaks of revalorizing Buddhism which:

> involves working with the categories and concepts of a traditional religion in the light of feminist values ... to revalorize is to have determined that, however sexist a religious tradition may be, it is not irreparably so. Revalorization is, in fact, doing that work of repairing the tradition, often bringing it much more into line with its own fundamental values and vision than was its patriarchal form.

> (Rita M. Gross, *Buddhism After Patriarchy: A Feminist History, Analysis and Reconstruction of Buddhism*, State University of New York Press, 1993, p 3)

Gross' project is doing much more than suggesting things have gone wrong because Buddhism hasn't modernized. Rather, she is determining a need to reconstruct the history of Buddhism as well, in order to rid it of its patriarchal manipulation. She notes:

> The single biggest difference between the practice of Buddhism in Asia and the practice of Buddhism in the West is the full and complete participation of women in Western Buddhism.

> (ibid., p 25)

Her point in reconstructing the history of Buddhism is so that 'we can "get it right" this time' (ibid., p 27). In particular, Gross focuses on the importance of sangha and the need to reconsider what a sangha should be like and what values it expresses and embodies. Patriarchal Buddhism produces patriarchal sanghas, which cannot appropriately represent or live out Buddhist values in community. We might say that in her view they are like dysfunctional families.

She advocates an 'androgynous view' in which Buddhism is reconceptualized. She emphasizes the need to address sangha, especially in relation to ordinary, everyday domestic life, much more directly as a *Buddhist* problem and area of neglect (ibid., p 258). Adequate communal support systems are an issue of importance for 'psychological comfort' and for overcoming 'inappropriate loneliness and lack of in-depth communication' (ibid., pp 262–3). Reconceptualization of sangha amounts to filling 'the profound and provocative category "*sangha*" with the feminist values of community, nurturance, communication, relationship, and friendship' (ibid., p 265). For this one must train, 'it is by no means "natural", especially for people trained in a masculinist culture' (ibid., p 267).

Her reconceptualization is radically anti-transcendentalist, revealed in her suspicion of the influences of theism indicating a lack of recognition of the tenet that: 'Now it is important to realize that to save ourselves by ourselves, it is necessary to create the social, communal, and companionate matrix of a society in which friendship and relationship are taken as categories of the utmost spiritual importance' (ibid., p 268). This view is emphasized with a critique of sangha seen as 'an alienated glorifier of loneliness' rather than a 'matrix of psychological comfort' (ibid., p 268).

There is also a critique of the dominance of monasticism in traditional Buddhism and neglect of lay society. She writes:

> The form of serious lay Buddhist practice and the transvaluation of values that comes with it will make more explicit that Buddhist monks do not have a monopoly on this level of spiritual development [luminous everyday awareness].

> (ibid., p 269)

The above possibility she identifies in the text of the *Therigatha*, poems written by early Buddhist nuns (ibid., p 274). She gives a new social and domestic meaning to the idea that enlightenment is found in the everydayness of life by rejecting the traditional distinction, or confusion, between 'real practice' and the tasks of daily life through reflecting on the experience of mothering and guilt over 'not practising' (ibid., p 277). She concludes that the purpose of Buddhism in the modern world must change:

> The final post-patriarchal question concerning spiritual discipline asks 'For what purpose?' ... In fact the whole orientation of practising a spiritual discipline to be prepared for death will probably not survive into post-patriarchal Buddhism. If a spiritual discipline promotes wholeness and balance, tranquillity and a deep peace, that will be sufficient ... Out of that grows the caring for community and for each other that is important for spiritual insight and well-being.

> (ibid., p 288)

If Gross and Batchelor are right in relation to their comments on the future of Buddhism as a religion then certainly we will see a significant shift in the way dharma is understood and practised and in the organization and character of the sangha. There is no doubt that the seeds of these interpretations were sown much earlier, at the beginning of and throughout the twentieth century, when Buddhism first impacted on the West. But at that time, through to the 1950s, there was an enchantment with Buddhism. It was an alternative to institutionalized spiritual ideas that held no fascination for generations seeking liberation from the established social and cultural order. Right through to the 1960s and 1970s there was still a romance associated with Buddhism, but especially Zen, that suggested an alternative lifestyle was possible which was not traditionally religious but something new. Rick Field's narrative history of Buddhism in America is instructive in this respect, especially in the section I paraphrase below.

In 1966 when Richard Baker started the project of the Tassajara Zen Mountain Centre, in the wilderness of the Los Padres National Forest in California, Robert Aitken wrote that: 'The development of the TZMC in a deep American forest marks the transition of expatriate Buddhism to a native religious discipline – the fulfilment of eighty years of Western Buddhist history.' It broke the rules and the mould of the traditional Zen monastery with men, women and married couples. The training was more individualistic and autonomous but it was a severe discipline to sit from 4 am to 10 pm in *zazen* – just sitting ... It was, romantically, an appeal to capture the original ethos and practice of Zen. But it was a place for periods of intensive training rather than monastic living. Returning to San Francisco the support was gone ... Zen centres needed to be in the inner city too (Rick Fields, *How the Swans Came to the Lake*, Shambhala (3rd edn.), 1992, pp 159–266).

The above image of Western Buddhists seeking the tranquillity of a mountain setting only to find themselves brought back to earth in the city does suggest, with hindsight, that the dharma and the sangha need to be situated where people actually live out their everyday lives. Taking this notion further what might be termed 'postmodern Zen', in which the individual appropriates Zen into his or her overall lifestyle, today perhaps most interestingly typified by that dark troubadour icon Leonard Cohen, now a Zen priest as well as a singer-songwriter, is an attractive idea but it bears the marks of Western individualism to such a degree that it is not embedded in any meaningful social reality. As Fields further observed concerning Zen in the 1960s:

> To a certain extent, the Zen Buddhists of the sixties presented a united front. But just beneath the smooth surface, none of it ever becoming public, there were stirrings of scandal, rivalries, hints of incompetence.
>
> (ibid., p 246)

So, there is no escaping the old samsaric problems by virtue of seeking to create an alternative lifestyle or community. It is necessary to ask not just 'What is the right dharma or sangha?' but 'What is the dharma or sangha *for*?' As a way of looking out from ourselves to the world. At the beginning of the twenty-first century the latter question seems to me the right one to ask. In the West, during its first-century infancy, perhaps there has been a tendency to be too beguiled by the first. We have no Buddha-eye view of the future but a useful starting point for reflecting on the above question is this statement by the Dalai Lama:

> Actually, I believe there is an important distinction to be made between religion and spirituality. Religion I take to be concerned with faith in the claims of salvation of one faith tradition or another, an aspect of which is acceptance of some form of metaphysical or supernatural reality, including perhaps an idea of heaven or *nirvana*. Connected with this are religious teachings or dogma, ritual, prayer, and so on. Spirituality I take to be concerned with those qualities of the human spirit – such as love and compassion, patience, tolerance, forgiveness,

contentment, a sense of responsibility, a sense of harmony – which bring happiness both to self and others. While ritual and prayer, along with questions of *nirvana* and salvation, are directly connected to religious faith, these inner qualities need not be, however.

(The Dalai Lama, *Ethics for the New Millennium*, Riverhead Books, 1999, p 22; also quoted in Thupten Jinpa, The Dalai Lama: Dimensions of Spirituality, in C. Erricker and J. Erricker (eds), *Contemporary Spiritualities: Religious and Social Contexts*, Continuum, 2001)

The import of this statement takes us back to the contemporary scenario outlined at the beginning of this chapter. It would seem that whether dharma does or does not continue to be cloaked in religious form, organization and convention is not the significant issue, but whether those qualities of the human spirit the Dalai Lama refers to continue to be manifest is. Whether 'Buddhism' or 'dharma practice' can make the world in the twenty-first century a better place than it was in the twentieth is a question for Buddhists as much as for anyone else. What forms of Buddhism contribute effectively to this goal remains to be seen, but below, in the final section of this chapter, we consider an example of how this question is being addressed.

Transmitting Buddhism to a new generation

The historical Buddha was open to the idea that the dharma could disappear from the samsaric world and yet manifest itself again later. This does not mean that the dharma would cease to exist, since the dharma is the truth of the way things really are, the reality obscured by delusion. What could be lost was the teaching. For Buddhists, therefore, the transmission of the dharma is vital to the health of the world and its development, even though the reality of the dharma (truth) is not dependent upon its transmission. Perhaps, by analogy, we could compare this to electricity. We speak of electricity being invented but what we really mean is that electricity was discovered. Just because we didn't know about it is not an indication that it didn't exist. Once discovered, however, it would be foolish to ignore it or omit to pass on our knowledge to the next generation.

The dharma has been passed on for the last 2,500 years in various ways, and its transmission has waxed and waned within the various cultures it has inhabited. Today, particularly in the West, the question of how the dharma can be effectively transmitted to the next generation is an important one because the traditional structures for doing so adopted in countries strongly influenced by Buddhism do not exist to the same degree in countries not so influenced. One possibility, in this respect, is the idea of Buddhist schools.

If you search the web it is difficult to find Buddhist schools. There are 'Buddhist' schools in Buddhist countries, for example Thailand, and a Buddhist school in a Tibetan Buddhist-oriented sub-culture in Dharamsala, India (**www.lowertvc.org**), which seeks to pass on Tibetan culture and values to a new generation that has become disenfranchised in that respect due to its exile. But if we consider how Buddhist transmission of the dharma is being passed down to the next generation in the West, Buddhist schools are thin on the ground. Only the Dharma School in Brighton, UK (**www.dharmaschool.co.uk**) and the Shambala School in Halifax, Nova Scotia, Canada (**www.shambalaschool.org**) are evident. The Shambala School advertises itself as an independent non-religious school that employs a creative integrated curriculum for the 3–17 age range and offers meditation and yoga for its older students. All other dharma schools operate as an equivalent of 'Sunday schools' or summer schools run by Buddhist temples or communities.

As to whether transmission of the dharma requires or is necessarily helped by opening schools within a state or mainstream system the argument could go either way. But if the dharma is considered to be an opportunity to enrich Western society rather than just a way of nurturing a next generation of Buddhists, then the idea of dharma schools in public sector education is worth considering. In doing so, I shall take the Dharma School, Brighton as a case study example.

The Dharma School, Brighton, UK

The idea of founding a Dharma School evolved from the family camps that have taken place at Amaravati Buddhist Monastery in Hertfordshire, England since the mid-1980s. The Summer Dharma Camps involved parents, children and members of the Forest Retreat Order Theravadan sangha and led, in 1989–90, to a group of parents exploring the possibility of a permanent Dharma School with the monks and nuns of the Order. This would be a school to which they would send their children instead of sending them to the local state primary school.

This resulted in a school opening on 9 September 1994 in the front room of a parent's house in Brighton, with four children enrolled. In 1995 The White House in Patcham, Brighton, a former nursery school, was purchased to accommodate increasing numbers of pupils. In 2007, the school had 82 pupils, its full capacity, spread across the age range of 3–11 years old.

Initial discussions as to the advisability of such a project and its purpose were rich in revealing what exactly a Buddhist-inspired education would entail and how it would be distinctive. Part of these discussions were recorded in a report of a conference on 'Buddhism and Education in the UK: A Dhammic Perspective' held at Sharpham House in Devon, UK, 7–9 June 1991. The subsequent report was called *The Elephant's Footprint: Buddhism and Education in the UK – The Dhamma School Project*. The participants at the conference consisted of four monastics from the Theravadin Forest Retreat Order, who were both bhikkhus (monks) and Buddhist nuns, plus ten other representatives who were either academics or teachers involved in mainstream or alternative education, or otherwise lay Buddhists. The vision behind the type of education that this conference and its report wished to promote is well expressed in the following extract:

> Two of the seventeen precepts of the Tiep Hien Order founded by the Vietnamese monk, the Venerable Thich Nhat Hanh, are relevant here:
>
> 1. Do not be idolatrous about or bound to any doctrine, theory or ideology, even Buddhist ones. All systems of thought are guiding means; they are not absolute truth.
>
> 2. Do not force others, including children, by any means whatsoever, to adopt your views, whether by authority, threat, money, propaganda or even education. However, through compassionate dialogue, help others renounce fanaticism and narrowness.
>
> (Peter Carey (ed.), 1992, *The Elephant's Footprint: Buddhism and Education in the UK – The Dhamma School Project*, p 21)

The report goes on to affirm the value of a Buddhist contribution to Western education but with an ambivalence as to how its contribution can be offered to young people.

It is widely recognized that Buddhism has something to offer the West. Its thought is subtle and pragmatic, not at all incompatible with much contemporary thinking; its values and practices, which are designed to develop peace of mind, compassion, care for living things and their environment, are particularly relevant to our time. The question arises as to what provision, if any, we should be making for the younger generation.

(Carey, 1992, p 4)

The decision to go ahead with The Dharma School was not lightly taken but the principles that underpinned its operation were clear. This was to be an education free of religious dogmatism, inclusive and democratic. In its development of young people it also emphasized their autonomy and 'skilful conduct in everyday life, especially silent observation (meditation), dialogue and enquiry' (Carey, 1992, p 5).

What is so intriguing is the way this mirrors the aims of the European Enlightenment project in its democratic and autonomous nature, yet adds those elements of Buddhist teachings and practice concerned with wisdom and compassion.

In practice, the progress of the Dharma School has encountered a number of obstacles, typical of those small schools offering an alternative educational model. For example, small alternative schools are often initially reliant on charismatic leadership and can falter when that leadership disappears; size can often result in a lack of resources; and being a non-state funded school requires that parents have to pay for their children to attend. Disposable income mitigates against inclusivity of intake. The Dharma School has faced all these challenges but survives with its original vision intact. Parents, children and teachers are in part Buddhist but others are not, though they empathise with the school's aims. There is no selection policy in this respect, either for staff appointments or places for pupils. In practice, the school provides a curriculum in accordance with the standards set in England and Wales, but its environment also provides for children in a more caring and responsive way than most schools could. In particular its daily pujas, allowing time for silence and reflection on values issues, along with its precepts for moral guidance and reflection, are its most significant feature derived from Buddhist practice. Evidence of their effectiveness and of that of the school's support for children's personal development generally is attested by the national inspection authority, the Office for Standards in Education (Ofsted) which, in its recent report, states that 'It promotes outstanding personal and social development, as well as securing spiritual and moral values' (Ofsted Inspection Report: Dharma School, 12–13 June 2007, p 2). This judgement could, of itself, be seen as evidence of the need for Buddhism to engage more fully with mainstream Western educational life in order to enhance the development of young people and, as a consequence, enrich Western society in the future.

In conclusion

This chapter has focused on the question of how Buddhism is meeting the challenges of, and seeking to influence, the modern world. It is useful, at this point, to remind ourselves that the Buddha described his teaching as the Middle Way. This suggests that it is a reconciliation of opposites. And yet, throughout this book, the diversity of Buddhism and its evolving profile have been obvious. Also, it has been clear that different forms of Buddhism are not necessarily reconcilable with one another. In the light of this you may find it a useful exercise to go back to the quotation ascribed to the Buddha at the beginning of Chapter 1 and read it while comparing it to the quotation from the Dalai Lama, on pages 215–16 above, and ask 'How do I put these two statements alongside each other?'

taking it further

Further reading

Introductory and general studies

Buddhism Without Beliefs: A Contemporary Guide to Awakening S. Batchelor, Bloomsbury, 1998. This book puts the case for understanding dharma in a non-religious fashion with relevance to the contemporary West.

The Awakening of the West: the Encounter of Buddhism and Western Culture S. Batchelor, Aquarian, 1994. A substantial but very accessible survey of the way in which the West first encountered Buddhism and the development from then on until the present day.

How the Swans Came to the Lake: A Narrative History of Buddhism in America R. Fields, Shambhala (3rd edn.), 1992. This is an excellent historical commentary on the development and diversity of Buddhism in the United States.

The Dhammapada Narada Thera, John Murray, 1972. This is one of a number of translations of this popular and important collection of some of the Buddha's sayings.

What the Buddha Taught W. Rahula, Wisdom Books, 1985. The latest reprint of an authoritative and readable introduction to the Buddha's fundamental teachings.

The Buddha M. Carrithers, Oxford University Press, 1983. A valuable account of the life of the Buddha and the development of his teaching.

The Buddhist Handbook J. Snelling, Rider, 1987. An introduction to the main schools of Buddhism, their teachings and practices.

An Introduction to Buddhism: Teachings, History and Practices P. Harvey, Cambridge University Press, 1990. A more detailed introduction to the tradition as a whole.

Being Nobody, Going Nowhere Ayya Khema, Wisdom Publications, 1987. A very useful and practical guide to Buddhist meditation by a Buddhist nun.

A Guide to the Buddhist Path Ven. Sangharakshita, Windhorse Publications, 1990. A collection of talks given by the author on aspects of Buddhist teaching and practice, from the perspective of the FWBO.

Zen Mind, Beginner's Mind Shunryu Suzuki, Weatherhill, 1982. A collection of influential talks on Zen meditation and practice by a respected Japanese master.

The Buddhist Directory The Buddhist Society, London. This directory is updated every few years. It gives information of Buddhist groups and centres in the UK and Ireland.

The World of Buddhism H. Bechert and R. Gombrich (eds), Thames and Hudson, 1984. A large-format, beautifully illustrated survey of Buddhism.

Buddhists in Britain Today D. Cush, Hodder & Stoughton, 1990. A very readable collection of interviews with British Buddhists.

Buddhism (*A Student's Approach to World Religions* series) D. Cush, Hodder & Stoughton, 1994. A substantial but readable introduction to Buddhism.

Buddhism P. Morgan, Batsford, 1987. A dictionary with explanations of key terms in Buddhism.

Buddhism: Beliefs and Practice Merv Fowler, Sussex Academic Press, 1999. A scholarly but accessible introduction covering the life of the historical Buddha, the historical development of Buddhism and the teachings of the different schools.

Food for the Heart: the Collected Techniques of Ajahn Chah Ajahn Chah, Wisdom Publications, 2002. A posthumous collection of the teachings of the founder of the Thai Forest Retreat Order.

The Power of Buddhism His Holiness the Dalai Lama and Jean-Claude Carriere, Doubleday, 1996. A collection of dialogues on contemporary issues from a Buddhist perspective, translated from the French edition.

The New Buddhism, David Brazier, PalgraveMacmillan, 2002. The author seeks to make Buddhism appropriate for modern life and offers a vision of how it can engage with suffering today and social concern. He is a prolific writer on psychology and Zen.

Ten Thousand Miles Without A Cloud, Sun Shuyun, HarperCollins, 2003. Sun Shuyun retraces the journey of Xuangzang, a seventh-century CE Chinese monk in his efforts to chart Indian Buddhist sites and bring the Yogacara scriptures to China.

An End to Suffering: the Buddha in the World, Panjak Mishra, Picador, 2005. Mishra weaves reflection on his own life and that of our modern world, especially India, in with meditations on the Buddha's message to provocative effect.

More specific studies

Theravada Buddhism: A Social History from Ancient Benares to Modern Colombo R. Gombrich, Routledge, 1988. A more detailed investigation of the development of this branch of Buddhism.

Mahayana Buddhism: the Doctrinal Foundations P. Williams, Routledge, 1989. A survey of the diversity and complexity of the Mahayana.

Ethics for the New Millennium His Holiness the Dalai Lama, Riverhead Books, 1999. A most significant book in which the Dalai Lama distinguishes between religion and ethics, on a Buddhist basis, and appeals against sectarianism.

Buddhism After Patriarchy: A Feminist History, Analysis, and Reconstruction of Buddhism R. M. Gross, State University of New York Press, 1993. An important text for understanding feminist arguments within contemporary Buddhism.

Beyond Optimism: A Buddhist Political Ecology K. Jones, Jon Carpenter Publishers, 1993. An ecological approach to Buddhist activism drawing on Buddhist and non-Buddhist influential figures.

Buddhism in America: the Social Organization of an Ethnic Religious Institution T. Kashima, Greenwood Press, 1977. A rare in-depth longitudinal study of 'migrant' Buddhism in the twentieth century.

Buddhism Betrayed? Religion, Politics and Violence in Sri Lanka S. J. Tambiah, University of Chicago Press, 1992. An important commentary on Buddhist nationalism in relation to traditional Buddhist understandings.

Zen Tradition and Transition: An Overview of Zen in the Modern World K. Kraft (ed.), Rider, 1992. A diverse collection of essays on Zen; not entirely what it says since some are historical, written in differing styles but of a high standard.

Transforming the Mind: Teachings on Generating Compassion His Holiness the Dalai Lama, Thorsens, 2000. This collection is about transformation and its basis in compassion, or altruism, and insight. A more technically Buddhist collection of teachings than the above.

Contemporary Spiritualities: Religious and Social Contexts C. Erricker and J. Erricker (eds), Continuum, 2001. This volume contains two chapters on Buddhism. One is on the Dalai Lama as a contemporary spiritual leader by his former chief interpreter, Thupten Jinpa. The other is a case study of the Thai Forest Retreat Order founded by Ajahn Chah, written by Clive Erricker.

Contemporary Buddhist Ethics Damien Kowen (ed.), Curzon, 2000. A range of essays on moral issues from Buddhist perspectives. It also explores the nature and development of Buddhist ethics.

Essence of the Heart Sutra His Holiness the Dalai Lama, Wisdom Publications, 2002. A commentary by the Dalai Lama on one of the classic, central texts of the Mahayana tradition.

The Tibet Guide Stephen Batchelor, Wisdom Publications, 1987. A travel guide to visiting Tibet, but it also has an excellent section on the history of Tibet and an introduction to Tibetan Buddhism.

Meditation and education

Buddhism in World Cultures: Comparative Perspectives Stephen Berkwitz (ed.), ABC Clio, 2006. An overview of Buddhism across cultures, showing how it has adapted to social and cultural change

Being Benevolence: the social ethics of engaged Buddhism Sallie B. King, University of Hawaii Press, 2006. An in-depth study of the writings on engaged Buddhists and their approaches to Buddhist social ethics, human rights and contemporary political situations.

Towards A Contemporary Understanding of Pure Land Buddhism: Creating a Shin Buddhist Theology in a Religiously Plural World Denis Hirota (ed.), State University of New York Press, 2000. A scholarly collection of writings on Pure Land Buddhism in the modern world.

Soka Gakkai Karel Dobbelaere, Signature Books, 2001. A short introduction to the Soka Gakkai movement by an established and scholarly writer.

Buddhism in America Richard Hughes, Columbia University Press, 2000. An exhaustive survey of the current situation of Buddhism in America, charting different groups and issues of change and adaptation.

Contemporary Tibet: Politics, Development and Society in a Disputed Region June Tenfel Dreyer and Barry Sautman, M. E. Sharpe, 2005. A comprehensive analysis of the Tibet question and the global, religious and political issues it raises.

A Buddhist Psychology Caroline Brazier, Constable and Robinson, 2003. A Buddhist approach to psychology from a practising psychotherapist and Buddhist, this offers a critique of psychotherapy from a Buddhist viewpoint.

British Buddhism Robert Bluck, Routledge, 2006. An up-to-date survey of Buddhism in Britain covering the seven largest Buddhist traditions in the United Kingdom. This is a valuable contribution to the study of contemporary Buddhism in the West and changes taking place in the Buddhist world.

The two following books are useful in introducing children to meditation techniques.

Teaching Meditation to Children David Fontana and Ingrid Slack, Element Books, 1997. This is a practical guide to the use and benefits of meditation technique. It gives practical examples of meditational activities with children and reports on their effects. An excellent handbook. Primarily aimed at parents but useful for anyone working with children.

Meditation in Schools: Calmer Classrooms Clive and Jane Erricker (eds), Continuum, 2001. This book is structured to give practical activities that can be used by teachers in relation to subject and cross-curricula learning. Also useful for parents and home educators.

Non-Buddhist studies of related interest

The Pimlico History of the Twentieth Century C. Pontin, Pimlico, 1999. A very thorough analysis of themes, issues and events in the twentieth century and the impact, in particular, of war and political and economic change on the conditions in which people have lived.

No Logo: Taking Aim at the Brand Bullies N. Klein, Flamingo, 2000. Klein exposes the greed and corporate control of the multinational companies, the exploitation they employ and the effect of this on both Western consciousness and Third World conditions.

Captive State: the Corporate Takeover of Britain G. Monbiot, Macmillan, 2000. Monbiot, in an analysis not dissimilar to Klein's, researches and presents the corporate power affecting political decisions and local communities in the British Isles.

Useful addresses

The addresses below provide information on specific centres related to branches of Buddhism in the United Kingdom. For information on centres elsewhere in the world consult the website addresses section. On the internet there are also location specific centres worldwide.

Amaravati Buddhist Monastery, Great Gaddesden, Hemel Hempstead, Hertfordshire HP1 3BZ.

Angulimala, The Buddhist Prison Chaplaincy Organisation, The Forest Hermitage, Lower Fulbrook, Warwick, Warwickshire CV35 8AS.

Buddhapadipa Temple, 14 Calone Road, Wimbledon, London SW19 5HJ.

Buddhist Hospice Trust, 5 Grayswood Point, Norley Vale, Roehampton, London SW15 4BT.

The Buddhist Society, 58 Ecclestone Square, London SW1V 1PH.

The Friends of the Western Buddhist Order, Lesingham House, Surlingham, Norwich NR14 7AL.

International Zen Association, UK, 91–93 Gloucester Road,

Bishopston, Bristol, Greater Bristol BS7 8AT.

Kagyu Samye Ling Tibetan Centre, Eskdalemuir, Langholm, Dumfriesshire, Scotland DG13 0QL.

Manjushri Mahayana Buddhist Centre, Conishead Priory, Priory Road, Ulverston, Cumbria LA12 9QQ.

Network of Engaged Buddhists (UK), Plas Plwca, Cwmrheidol, Aberystwyth, Dyfed SY23 3NB.

Network of Buddhist Organisations UK, The Old Courthouse, 43 Renfrew Road, Kennington, London SE11 4NA.

Pure Land Buddhist Foundation of Great Britain, 48 Laburnham Crescent, Kettering, Northamptonshire NN1 69PJ.

Sakyadita: International Association of Buddhist Women (UK), 16 Nun Street, Lancaster, Lancashire LA1 3PJ.

Throssel Hole Priory, Carrshield, Hexham, Northumberland NE47 8AL.

For further information on regional groups consult *The Buddhist Directory*, published by the Buddhist Society or *Religions in the UK: A Multi-Faith Directory*, Paul Weller (ed.), available from the University of Derby, Mickleover, Derby DE3 5GX, in association with the Inter-Faith Network for the United Kingdom, 5–7 Tavistock Place, London WC1H 9SN.

For a directory of Buddhist organizations in the USA, type 'Buddhist directory USA' into your search engine and this will give you a host of results, although there is not a single directory for the whole country.

Website addresses

Today, if you put 'Buddhist Centres' into a search engine it will give you 2,130,000 websites worldwide. When I wrote the previous edition there were only 4,700 websites worldwide. Some of these overlap, others are location specific; in total they cross the globe. No doubt this is, in part, due to the growth of Buddhism, but also due to the growth in the internet culture. Below are some useful starting points for exploring the network of Buddhist centres and publications on Buddhism from which you can proceed to more specific interests.

http://www.ciolek.com/WWWVL-Buddhism.html
This is the Buddhist Studies Virtual Library, which provides listings of information facilities in Buddhism and Buddhist studies.

http://www.aboutbuddhism.org
This is actually a site that approaches Buddhism from the New Kadampa perspective, with links to other sites.

http://www.buddhanet.net
This is an information network that provides various meditation techniques, teachings, event information and contact details. It has directories for different parts of the world.

http://www.meta.co.uk/retreats.asp
Provides a collection of retreat and meditation centres: Buddhist based and open.

http://www.dharmanet.org/infoweb.html
A Buddhist InfoWeb providing information on Buddhist organizations from different traditions.

http://www.nibbana.commeditatabn.htm
This is a Dhamma Publications website that advertises meditation and retreat centres.

http://jetairtours.com/buddhist.htm
This Jetair Tours site has information on tours of Buddhist sites in India.

http://www.wisdompubs.org
This is the website of Wisdom Publications, which allows you to browse its catalogue and order online.

glossary

Note: (P) and (S) refer to Pali and Sanskrit respectively.

Abhidamma (P), **Abhidharma** (S) Buddhist philosophical texts.

Amitabha Buddha of the Pure Land.

Anagarika Literally, 'wandering one', a truth seeker.

anapanasati Meditation on the breath.

anatta The doctrine of no-self.

anicca Change, impermanence.

Anuradhapura Ancient capital of Sri Lanka, and a place of pilgrimage.

arahant (Arhat) One who has achieved liberation.

Ashoka Buddhist Emperor of India.

Avalokiteshvara (Chenrezig) Bodhisattva of Compassion.

bardo The state between death and rebirth mentioned in the *Bardo Thodol* (*Tibetan Book of the Dead*).

bhavana Mental development or meditation.

bhikkhu (M), **bhikkhuni** (F) A monk or nun in the Theravadin tradition.

Bodh Gaya The place of the Buddha's Enlightenment.

bodhi Enlightenment.

Bodhidharma An Indian monk who took Buddhism to China in the sixth century CE.

bodhisattva A being with the essence of enlightenment.

Buddha Enlightened One.

chela Pupil of a guru.

Dalai Lama Head of Tibetan Buddhism; incarnation of the Bodhisattva Avalokiteshvara.

dana Literally, 'giving' or 'generosity'; the only meal of the day for Theravadin monks.

darsana A teaching or 'sermon'; discourse of the Buddha.

dependent origination The process of the cycle of samsaric existence, also called 'conditioned co-production'.

devas Gods.

dhamma (P), **dharma** (S) The teaching of the Buddha; the Truth or Law.

Dhammapada Popular collection of the Buddha's teachings.

Dharmachari Literally, 'dharma farer'; the title given to Order members of the FWBO.

Dharamsala The Indian Himalayan town where the Dalai Lama has his palace in exile.

dukkha Suffering, unsatisfactoriness, dis-ease; the First Noble Truth.

Guru Spiritual teacher or master.

Hui-Neng Sixth Patriarch of the Zen tradition.

Jatakas Tales of the Buddha's former lives.

kamma (P), **karma** (S) Literally means 'action'; the Law of Cause and Effect.

Kangyur Tibetan Scriptures.

karuna Compassion.

Kathina Literally means 'difficult' or 'frame'. The robe-giving ceremony in Theravada Buddhism.

koan A 'riddle' or technique used in Zen Buddhism.

kusala (P), **kausalya** (S) Skilfulness.

Lao Tzu Taoist teacher.

Losar Tibetan New Year.

Lotus Sutra, or **'Saddharmapundarika'** Literally, the 'Lotus of the True Law'; important Mahayana Scripture.

Lumbini The place of the Buddha's birth.

magga Literally, 'path'; refers to the Eightfold Path in Buddhism; the fourth Noble Truth.

Mahayana Literally, 'The Great Way'; one of the main branches of Buddhism.

mandala Literally means 'circle'; a design used for meditation in Mahayana Buddhism.

Manjushri Bodhisattva of Wisdom.

Mara Lord of Death.

Maya Illusion or creative play of the universe.

mendicant One who relies on others for his material and physical needs.

merit Reward for good deed; store of goodness.

metta Loving kindness.

Milinda King who features in the Theravada Scriptures in dialogue with the Buddhist monk, Nagasena.

mitra Literally, 'friend'; term used by the FWBO.

mondo Story used in Zen Buddhism.

Nagasena Buddhist monk.

nibbana (P), **nirvana** (S) Literally, 'to extinguish'; enlightenment.

nirodha The third Noble Truth; letting go of suffering.

Padmasambhava Tibetan saint.

Pali Language of the Theravada Scriptures, also thought to have been used by the Buddha.

paranibbana (P), **paranirvana** Passing into nirvana upon death.

prajna Wisdom.

precepts Rules of behaviour.

pretas Hungry ghosts.

puja Worship.

relics Holy objects; remains of the Buddha or a great Buddhist teacher.

refuge Refers to the Three Jewels as Refuges; that in which one can trust.

sadhu Holy man.

Sakyamuni Title given to the Buddha, literally, 'Sage of the Sakya clan'.

samanera Literally 'child of a Samana' (religious seeker); refers to a novice monk.

samatha Calm, inner peace; form of meditation technique.

samsara Cycle of existence.

samudaya The second Noble Truth; the origin of suffering.

sangha The Buddhist community or order.

shastras Commentaries on the Buddha's teachings.

Siddhatta Gotama (P), **Siddhartha Gautama** (S) Name of the historical Buddha.

sila Ethical Conduct; second part of the Eightfold Path.

sima Ordination area in Theravada Buddhism.

skandhas The five elements that constitute a person.

stupa Burial mound or building to house relics; also called a chorten or chedi.

Sukhavati The Pure Land.

sukkha Happiness, bliss or ease; the opposite of dukkha.

sunyata Voidness.

sutta (P), **sutra** (S) Literally means 'thread'; name for the Buddhist Scriptures.

tanha Thirst or craving.

Tantra Form of Tibetan Buddhist practice and name of a type of scripture.

Tao Literally, 'The Way'; a Chinese tradition that influenced Zen Buddhism.

Tara Female bodhisattva, 'Mother of Compassion'; there are two Taras, Green Tara and White Tara.

Tathagatha Literally, 'Thus Gone One'; title given to the Buddha.

Tengyur Name of the shastras in Tibetan Buddhism.

Theravada 'Way of the Elders'; branch of Buddhism.

Tsongkhapa Tibetan saint and teacher.

tulku The rebirth of a great teacher in Tibetan Buddhism, especially the Dalai Lama.

upaya Skill in means.

Uposatta Weekly days of observance based on the lunar cycle; full-moon days are the most important.

vihara Monastic residence.

vinaya Code of Monastic Discipline laid down by the Buddha.

vipassana Insight, form of meditation.

Wesak Theravada festival celebrating birth, enlightenment and death of the Buddha.

Zen Japanese form of Buddhism; from the Chinese 'ch'an' and Sanskrit 'dhyana', meaning meditation.

index

From Advanced Sudoku to Zulu, you'll find everything you need in the **teach yourself** range, in books, on CD and on DVD.

Visit **www.teachyourself.co.uk** for more details.

Advanced Sudoku and Kakuro	Beginner's French
Afrikaans	Beginner's German
Alexander Technique	Beginner's Greek
Algebra	Beginner's Greek Script
Ancient Greek	Beginner's Hindi
Applied Psychology	Beginner's Hindi Script
Arabic	Beginner's Italian
Arabic Conversation	Beginner's Japanese
Aromatherapy	Beginner's Japanese Script
Art History	Beginner's Latin
Astrology	Beginner's Mandarin Chinese
Astronomy	Beginner's Portuguese
AutoCAD 2004	Beginner's Russian
AutoCAD 2007	Beginner's Russian Script
Ayurveda	Beginner's Spanish
Baby Massage and Yoga	Beginner's Turkish
Baby Signing	Beginner's Urdu Script
Baby Sleep	Bengali
Bach Flower Remedies	Better Bridge
Backgammon	Better Chess
Ballroom Dancing	Better Driving
Basic Accounting	Better Handwriting
Basic Computer Skills	Biblical Hebrew
Basic Mathematics	Biology
Beauty	Birdwatching
Beekeeping	Blogging
Beginner's Arabic Script	Body Language
Beginner's Chinese Script	Book Keeping
Beginner's Dutch	Brazilian Portuguese

Bridge
British Citizenship Test, The
British Empire, The
British Monarchy from Henry VIII, The
Buddhism
Bulgarian
Bulgarian Conversation
Business French
Business Plans
Business Spanish
Business Studies
C++
Calculus
Calligraphy
Cantonese
Caravanning
Car Buying and Maintenance
Card Games
Catalan
Chess
Chi Kung
Chinese Medicine
Christianity
Classical Music
Coaching
Cold War, The
Collecting
Computing for the Over 50s
Consulting
Copywriting
Correct English
Counselling
Creative Writing
Cricket
Croatian
Crystal Healing
CVs
Czech
Danish
Decluttering
Desktop Publishing
Detox
Digital Home Movie Making
Digital Photography
Dog Training

Drawing
Dream Interpretation
Dutch
Dutch Conversation
Dutch Dictionary
Dutch Grammar
Eastern Philosophy
Electronics
English as a Foreign Language
English Grammar
English Grammar as a Foreign Language
Entrepreneurship
Estonian
Ethics
Excel 2003
Feng Shui
Film Making
Film Studies
Finance for Non-Financial Managers
Finnish
First World War, The
Fitness
Flash 8
Flash MX
Flexible Working
Flirting
Flower Arranging
Franchising
French
French Conversation
French Dictionary
French for Homebuyers
French Grammar
French Phrasebook
French Starter Kit
French Verbs
French Vocabulary
Freud
Gaelic
Gaelic Conversation
Gaelic Dictionary
Gardening
Genetics
Geology

Lithuanian
Magic
Mahjong
Malay
Managing Stress
Managing Your Own Career
Mandarin Chinese
Mandarin Chinese Conversation
Marketing
Marx
Massage
Mathematics
Meditation
Middle East Since 1945, The
Modern China
Modern Hebrew
Modern Persian
Mosaics
Music Theory
Mussolini's Italy
Nazi Germany
Negotiating
Nepali
New Testament Greek
NLP
Norwegian
Norwegian Conversation
Old English
One-Day French
One-Day French – the DVD
One-Day German
One-Day Greek
One-Day Italian
One-Day Polish
One-Day Portuguese
One-Day Spanish
One-Day Spanish – the DVD
One-Day Turkish
Origami
Owning a Cat
Owning a Horse
Panjabi
PC Networking for Small
  Businesses
Personal Safety and Self
  Defence

Philosophy
Philosophy of Mind
Philosophy of Religion
Phone French
Phone German
Phone Italian
Phone Japanese
Phone Mandarin Chinese
Phone Spanish
Photography
Photoshop
PHP with MySQL
Physics
Piano
Pilates
Planning Your Wedding
Polish
Polish Conversation
Politics
Portuguese
Portuguese Conversation
Portuguese for Homebuyers
Portuguese Grammar
Portuguese Phrasebook
Postmodernism
Pottery
PowerPoint 2003
PR
Project Management
Psychology
Quick Fix French Grammar
Quick Fix German Grammar
Quick Fix Italian Grammar
Quick Fix Spanish Grammar
Quick Fix: Access 2002
Quick Fix: Excel 2000
Quick Fix: Excel 2002
Quick Fix: HTML
Quick Fix: Windows XP
Quick Fix: Word
Quilting
Recruitment
Reflexology
Reiki
Relaxation
Retaining Staff

Romanian
Running Your Own Business
Russian
Russian Conversation
Russian Grammar
Sage Line 50
Sanskrit
Screenwriting
Second World War, The
Serbian
Setting Up a Small Business
Shorthand Pitman 2000
Sikhism
Singing
Slovene
Small Business Accounting
Small Business Health Check
Songwriting
Spanish
Spanish Conversation
Spanish Dictionary
Spanish for Homebuyers
Spanish Grammar
Spanish Phrasebook
Spanish Starter Kit
Spanish Verbs
Spanish Vocabulary
Speaking On Special Occasions
Speed Reading
Stalin's Russia
Stand Up Comedy
Statistics
Stop Smoking
Sudoku
Swahili
Swahili Dictionary
Swedish
Swedish Conversation
Tagalog
Tai Chi
Tantric Sex
Tap Dancing
Teaching English as a Foreign Language
Teams & Team Working
Thai

Thai Conversation
Theatre
Time Management
Tracing Your Family History
Training
Travel Writing
Trigonometry
Turkish
Turkish Conversation
Twentieth Century USA
Typing
Ukrainian
Understanding Tax for Small Businesses
Understanding Terrorism
Urdu
Vietnamese
Visual Basic
Volcanoes, Earthquakes and Tsunamis
Watercolour Painting
Weight Control through Diet & Exercise
Welsh
Welsh Conversation
Welsh Dictionary
Welsh Grammar
Wills & Probate
Windows XP
Wine Tasting
Winning at Job Interviews
Word 2003
World Faiths
Writing Crime Fiction
Writing for Children
Writing for Magazines
Writing a Novel
Writing a Play
Writing Poetry
Xhosa
Yiddish
Yoga
Your Wedding
Zen
Zulu

Christianity
john young

- Do you want to explore the core beliefs of Christianity?
- Would you like to learn more about Christ and his teachings?
- Are you interested in the challenges facing Christianity today?

Christianity is a comprehensive guide to the origins, history, beliefs and practices of this major world religion. Covering all the main elements of the Christian faith, from the teaching and impact of Jesus Christ and the Bible to modern movements within the Church and current ethical debates, this book is a fascinating and informative read.

John Young is a Canon Emeritus of York Minster and co-founder of *York Courses*. He has written several books on Christianity.

Discrimination in Housing
Law and Practice in the Management of Social Housing

Alyson Kilpatrick, Barrister

Lemos & Crane

Published in Great Britain 2000 by
Lemos & Crane
20 Pond Square
Highgate
London N6 6BA
Telephone: 020 8348 8263
Fax: 020 8347 5740
Email: admin@lemos.demon.co.uk

ISBN 1-898001-34-0

A CIP catalogue record for this book is available from the British
Library

Cover design by Blue Frog Ltd, London
Typeset by David Chapronière, London
Printed and bound by Redwood Books, Trowbridge

Contents

Table of Cases

Table of Statutes

Table of Statutory Instruments and EU Legislation

Statutory instruments

EU Legislation

Abbreviations

AIA	Asylum and Immigration Act 1996
BC	Borough Council
CC	County Council
CDA	Crime and Disorder Act 1998
CRE	Commission for Racial Equality
DDA	Disability Discrimination Act 1995
ECJ	European Court of Justice
ECHR	European Court of Human Rights
EEA	European Economic Area
EOC	Equal Opportunities Commission
EU	European Union
FBHO	Federation of Black Housing Organisations
GLC	Greater London Council
HA	Housing Act
HRA	Human Rights Act
LBC	London Borough Council
NOSP	notice seeking possession
PATH	Positive Action Training in Housing
RBC	Royal Borough Council
RRA	Race Relations Act 1976
SDA	Sex Discrimination Act 1975

Introduction

According to *The Chambers Dictionary*, to discriminate is 'to treat differently especially because of one's feelings or prejudices about a person's sex, race, religion'. This book is, however, concerned with the legal definition of discrimination, which does not encompass racism or prejudice *per se*. The law, as it relates to anti-discrimination, deals with peoples' actions, not with peoples' attitudes or motives.

The law is concerned with protecting the rights of legally defined individuals and groups. Specific protection has been afforded to named groups previously seen as disadvantaged, such as women and ethnic minorities. The law ensures that those belonging to a defined group have equal rights under the law and an equal opportunity of education, health care, welfare benefits and housing. Historically, unfair treatment was institutionalised and apparent. The common law did not afford adequate protection of the rights of the disadvantaged.

As a result of the civil rights movement, anti-discrimination law was enshrined in a number of 'codes' such as the Race Relations Act 1976, the Sex Discrimination Act 1975, and now the Disability Discrimination Act 1995.

Discrimination often results because of stereotyping. It is not uncommon for certain groups to be ascribed characteristics with assumptions being made according to those characteristics. Once those assumptions are acted upon and that group is thereby disadvantaged or treated less well than other groups, they are deprived of the right to equality of opportunity. It is that deprivation which forms the basis of discrimination.

Currently, almost 7.5 per cent of the total population of Great Britain (i.e. four million people) were born elsewhere in the world. That percentage is much higher, however, if those people from ethnic groups who were born in Great Britain are included. The population of London, for example, includes 30 per cent of people not born in Great Britain (see CRE survey 1998). It can be seen that Great Britain is becoming increasingly multi-cultural and that brings with it a diverse range of histories, cultures, beliefs and languages. It has also, unfortunately, brought tension, confrontation and mistrust.

There has been much discussion (and action) by interested bodies on discrimination in terms of employment; however, much less attention has been given to discrimination in the field of housing. Research has shown that ethnic minorities do suffer discrimination in housing, both in terms of access to housing and in the quality of housing which is allocated.

It is essential that all those providing or managing social housing are familiar with the anti-discrimination legislation. The law applies not only in relation to landlord and tenant situations, but to employer/employee relations, management of anti-social behaviour, access to and allocation of housing, the provision of services, and access to and availability of funding.

This book focuses on the law as it relates to discrimination in the field of housing. It discusses the legal framework of the legislation, the rights of those who are or may be discriminated against and the remedies available to them. The book is aimed at all those working in the field of social housing—managers, decision-makers, policy-makers, contractors and housing staff. It highlights the obligations imposed on them, gives guidance on how to avoid discriminating unlawfully and what to do if a complaint is made or legal proceedings instituted.

Local authorities have an obligation to eliminate unlawful racial discrimination, and promote equality of opportunity and good race relations by virtue of section 71 of the Race Relations Act 1976. The same duty is placed on the Housing Corporation by section 56 of the Housing Act 1988. This book discusses the extent (and limits) of those obligations and gives practical examples of their application.

There is now also the Human Rights Act 1998 to contend with, which has been viewed by many as the most significant human rights reform in the last half century. For the first time the 'positive right' to freedom from discrimination will be enshrined in domestic law. The Act intends to incorporate the European Convention on Human Rights into UK law with the effect that the Convention will apply to all public authorities which perform a public function. This book discusses the impact of the Human Rights Act and the Convention as it applies to those working in the field of social housing.

Part I
The Legislation

1.
Legal Framework

Primary legislation / European law / European
Convention on Human Rights

The law on discrimination as it relates to the provision and
management of social housing is contained primarily in three
Acts of Parliament: the Sex Discrimination Act 1975 (SDA),
the Race Relations Act 1976 (RRA), and the Disability Discrimination Act 1995 (DDA). There is also a number of provisions
contained in other Acts which impact on discrimination in
housing. Just as important to housing managers are the Codes
of Practice issued by the commissions set up to ensure compliance with the law on anti-discrimination.

Primary legislation

The SDA, RRA and DDA

All three Acts are structurally similar. They contain provisions
dealing with unlawful discrimination, what it amounts to,
examples of specific acts which are deemed to be discriminatory and the enforcement of the anti-discrimination regime.
The RRA and the SDA respectively provide for the constitution
of the Commission for Racial Equality (CRE) and the Equal
Opportunities Commission (EOC).

The courts have construed the similar provisions of the
SDA and the RRA in like manner. It is anticipated that the
DDA will also be construed in line with the other two Acts.

As a result, case-law arising under one Act is helpful in construing similar provisions in one of the other Acts. Where, however, the wording differs, it is construed differently. Reliance on case-law which derives under a similar but materially different provision could be misleading.

As the courts have dealt with an increasing number of cases of alleged discrimination, a pattern has emerged of purposive interpretation. This means the courts tend to give effect to the purpose or intention of Parliament in enacting the legislation rather than looking to the strict letter of the law. Concepts have developed and principles emerged from case-law which are not specifically mentioned in the Acts.

Codes of practice

Both the CRE and the EOC have the power to issue codes of practice (RRA, s. 47; SDA, s. 56A). The codes themselves are not statutory; therefore, failure to observe a code does not leave an individual or organisation open to legal or administrative proceedings. The codes are, however, admissible as evidence in court proceedings and the court will have regard to them (SDA, s. 56A(10); RRA, s. 47(10)). In any event, the codes are informative and give helpful guidance on compliance with the Acts. Compliance with the codes will go a long way to avoiding non-discrimination notices or legal proceedings.

The CRE's *Code of Practice in Rented Housing* (1991) provides useful guidance and makes recommendations which should be followed to ensure policies and practices are soundly based to avoid racial discrimination and promote equal opportunities. This Code applies where housing is rented, leasehold or occupied pursuant to a licence.

European law

The European Union (EU) is made up of a number of countries referred to as 'member states'. In each of the member states, domestic law has been affected by the European legislature in almost every field. Where European law exists it is capable of giving rise to rights and obligations for individuals and groups. These rights may be invoked and obligations enforced by court proceedings brought in the member states' domestic courts, as well as in the EU courts. In this way, European law is part and parcel of UK law and regard must be had to it.

UK courts must ensure judicial protection for the rights of individuals arising from European Community provisions. As a result, UK law has been considerably expanded. The law may be subject to further change to meet the EU's continuing demands. In so far as is relevant to this book, it is the protection of the rights of individuals (i.e. natural or legal persons) that are considered.

The EU institutions have power to make Regulations, issue Directives, take Decisions, make Recommendations or deliver Opinions.

EU legislation

The EU legislates by Regulations, Directives and Decisions, all of which state the reasoning on which they are based. The reasoning is contained in a preamble to the legislation and can be very helpful in understanding and interpreting the legislation. Only Regulations, Directives and Decisions are referred to here, and only in outline. For a fuller discussion of EU law and its application, readers are advised to refer to the specialist text books (e.g. Craig & DeBurca, *EC Law*; J. Steiner, *Enforcing EC Law*).

Regulations

A Regulation has general application. It is binding on and applicable to all member states. A Regulation takes immediate effect and applies in its own right; it does not require the member states to take any action themselves to implement it.

Directives

A Directive is only binding as to the result to be achieved by the member states to which it is addressed. In other words, it directs member states to achieve a certain result but leaves it to the national authorities to decide how to go about achieving that result. Accordingly, a Directive requires implementation.

Decisions

A Decision is binding in its own right on those to whom it is addressed. It is an individual act, targeted at a named addressee. A Decision may be issued to a member state, an organisation (public or private) or an individual.

European Principles

The European Court of Justice (ECJ) and the European Court of Human Rights (ECHR) have introduced a further source of law in the form of general principles developed through case-law. The general principles are mostly drawn from those applicable in the member states. The category of general principles is not exhaustive, but those adopted so far include:

- the right to equal treatment
- the right to the inviolability of the home
- proportionality
- certainty
- protection of legitimate expectations
- protection of procedural rights (e.g. to a fair hearing)
- the right to pursue complaints by judicial process.

Public authorities are required to act with these principles in mind. A local housing authority must, accordingly, be aware of, and pay regard to, the EU principles.

Enforcement

Directly effective legislation can be invoked and relied upon by individuals in their national court. It may be used to challenge or avoid the application of national laws which are inconsistent with EU laws.

European Convention on Human Rights

The European Convention on Human Rights (the Convention) is, effectively, a Code of Rights and Freedoms which must be secured to everyone within the Convention's jurisdiction. The United Kingdom is a signatory to the Convention but has not, as yet, incorporated it into national law. The effect of that is to reduce the impact of the Convention for individuals who seek to complain of infringement of their rights and freedoms. The national authorities are not compelled to ensure the Convention is enforced—in other words, an individual has not been able to go before a national court and rely simply on non-compliance with the Convention (see, however, the Human Rights Act 1998, below).

Rights and freedoms

The rights protected by the Convention and subsequent protocols include, so far as are directly relevant to the provision and management of social housing:

- the right to respect for private and family life, for correspondence and for the home
- the freedom of thought, conscience and religion
- the freedom of expression
- the freedom of assembly and association
- the right to an effective remedy
- the prohibition of discrimination
- protection of property.

Freedom from discrimination

UK law has intervened to control unlawful discrimination in a fairly limited way. It applies only to certain identified forms of discrimination (race, sex or disability), and then only for certain purposes (housing, provision of goods and services, employment, and education) (see Chaps 8, 9 and 11).

Article 14 of the Convention provides that the enjoyment of the rights and freedoms contained in the convention shall be secured for all without discrimination on any ground such as sex, race, colour, language, religion, political opinion, national or social origin, association with a national minority, property, birth or other status. Thus the categories of illegitimate grounds for discrimination are much broader than those specified by national law. However, the article is confined in its application by referring only to those rights contained in the Convention: therefore, if the Convention did not mention housing (which it does, albeit indirectly), article 14 would be of no assistance to an aggrieved individual. Over the years the ECHR has addressed this by holding that article 14 provides a remedy so long as the discrimination occurs in one of the general areas covered by the Convention.

Under the Convention, discrimination is unlawful if a distinction is drawn which has no objective and reasonable justification, similar therefore to the derogation discussed in relation to national law (see Chaps 3 and 5). For discrimination to be justified under the Convention it must have a legitimate aim and the means employed to achieve that aim must not be disproportional with that aim.

Article 14 may provide a remedy where none is available under national law: examples are racial or sexual discrimination authorised by statute or statutory instrument and therefore not susceptible to challenge under the SDA or RRA; and discrimination on grounds other than race or sex where national law provides no remedy (e.g. discrimination on grounds of sexual orientation—see further Chap. 5).

The Human Rights Act 1998

The European Convention will now, by virtue of the Human Rights Act (HRA) be given greater effect in UK law. At the time of writing, the HRA is due to become law in 2000. It will give a constitutional guarantee to certain freedoms contained in the Convention; accordingly, the Convention rights and freedoms will become directly enforceable in the national courts (for a detailed study see e.g. C. Baker, *Human Rights Act 1998: A Practitioner's Guide*).

Most relevant in the context of this book are articles 8 and 14. Article 8 requires that public bodies respect the 'home' and 'family life'. What Article 8 does not do, however, is provide a right *to* a home. Article 14 provides for the protection of the rights in the Convention without discrimination on any ground such as race, sex, colour and national or social origin. It is only rights covered by the Convention that come within article 14. There is no freestanding right to freedom from discrimination (see further e.g. Human Rights and the European Convention Brice Dickson).

Example

A person who was not placed on a waiting list for accommodation because he or she did not come within the class of persons to whom the housing organisation would allocate a property has not been discriminated against in respect of a Convention right.

2

Enforcement of the Legislation

Proceedings by individuals / Relief / The
Commissions for Racial Equality and Equal
Opportunities / Codes of practice

This chapter looks at the structure of the enforcement provisions of the RRA and the SDA. The Acts combine the right of individual access to legal remedies with the strategic functions of the CRE and the EOC, which have certain powers to take action in their own names.

Proceedings by individuals

If a person believes he or she has been discriminated against by another contrary to Part III of the Acts, he or she may bring proceedings in either a county court specially designated for the purpose by the Secretary of State or an employment tribunal (see further Chap. 12). Complaints arising in the course of employment are taken to an employment tribunal. All other complaints can be taken to a county court. There is a right of appeal from the county court to the Court of Appeal and to the Employment Appeal Tribunal from the employment tribunal.

Time limits

A claim in the county court must be filed within six months of the alleged discriminatory act occurring (SDA, s. 76(2); RRA, s. 68(2)). The point at which time starts to run against a claimant (i.e. when an act is said to occur) depends on the nature of the discriminatory act.

If the act complained of is a *deliberate omission* this occurs when a decision to deliberately omit is made (SDA, s. 76(6)(c); RRA, s. 68(3)(c)). For these purposes a person is assumed to have decided upon an omission when either:

(a) he or she acts in a way that is inconsistent with doing the act alleged to have been omitted; or

(b) the point has passed at which a person intending to do an act would reasonably have done it.

If an act is *continuing* (i.e. prolonged over a period of time) it is taken as having been committed at the end of the period. If the complaint arises from a term of a contract the act continues throughout the duration of the contract (SDA, s. 76(6); RRA, s. 68(7)).

If the court considers it just and equitable to do so, it may dispense with the time limit (SDA, s. 76(5); RRA, s. 68(6)).

Procedure

Both the RRA and the SDA provide the procedure to be adopted in court proceedings, as set out below.

Questions

If a person thinks he or she may have been discriminated against, before instituting proceedings he or she may make use of the questions procedure (SDA, s. 74; RRA, s. 65). The aggrieved puts questions to the person alleged to have discriminated (the respondent). The respondent then has the opportunity to reply. The aim of the questions procedure is to focus attention between the parties on what is really in issue.

The procedure also gives the respondent an opportunity to explain, for example, why conduct which on its face may appear discriminatory is in fact not discriminatory within the Act. A carefully prepared response may show the complaint to be groundless or based on a misunderstanding. Court proceedings may thus be avoided.

If the complaint is proceeded with, the questions and answers are admissible in evidence (SDA, s. 74(2); RRA, s. 65(2)). If the respondent deliberately omits to reply to the questions within a reasonable time, or the reply was evasive or unhelpfully ambiguous, the court or tribunal may draw whatever inference it feels appropriate, including an inference that the respondent committed an unlawful act (SDA, s. 74(2)(b); RRA, s. 65(2)(b)).

The questions procedure is subject to time limits which are prescribed by the Secretary of State. If proceedings have not been issued, questions must be served within the time limited for issuing proceedings (see p. 15 above). If a complaint has been brought to an employment tribunal, the period for serving questions is either:

- 21 days beginning on the date on which the complaint was presented, or
- if the 21-day period has expired and leave of the tribunal is required to serve questions, such time as is determined by the tribunal.

Where a claim has been brought in the county court, the leave of the court is required for service of questions, and the time for service is such as is determined by the court.

Burden and standard of proof: the hearing

The standard of proof (in both the county court and the employment tribunal) is the usual civil standard: the balance of probabilities (i.e. more likely than not). The burden of proof can, however, shift from complainant to respondent. Once a complainant establishes that, on the face of it, the respondent has committed an unlawful discriminatory act, it is for the respondent to prove that he or she did not. If the respondent can provide a reasonable explanation for why the conduct is not unlawful, the burden shifts back onto the complainant to ultimately prove his or her complaint.

Relief

If the court upholds the complaint it can make a declaration that the act complained of amounts to unlawful discrimination; give injunctive relief which can be mandatory or prohibitory (i.e. a person may be ordered to perform certain acts or refrain from committing further unlawful acts); make recommendations to the respondent; or award the complainant damages.

Damages

Compensation may be awarded for all loss or damage caused by the discrimination. Injury to feelings is included, as is loss of earnings. The award is, however, limited to that which is reasonably foreseeable as arising directly from the unlawful act of discrimination.

The Commissions for Racial Equality and Equal Opportunities

Both the RRA and the SDA established Commissions to enforce the legislation and promote equality of opportunity. The Commissions have general responsibility for advising the Government and have discretion, where there are special considerations, to assist individuals who feel aggrieved by alleged unlawful discrimination (SDA, s. 75; RRA, s. 66). Aside from taking a claim to an employment tribunal or to court, a person who believes he or she has been discriminated against may

take a complaint to the CRE or the EOC. The Commissions
are concerned (under SDA, s. 53; RRA, s. 43) with

1. assistance and representation for complainants in
   appropriate cases;
2. investigating practices and procedures in areas covered
   by the legislation, both informal and formal;
3. working towards the elimination of racial or sexual
   discrimination, including research into discrimination
   and monitoring the effectiveness of the legislation;
4. making recommendations; and
5. enforcement of the legislation.

The Commissions' powers of enforcement may be keenly felt
by any organisation which fails in its obligation not to
discriminate. The first step is often the 'formal investigation'.
If satisfied that the organisation under investigation has been
guilty of discriminatory conduct (within the Acts) a 'non-
discrimination notice' can be served (SDA, s. 67; RRA, s. 58).
The Commissions can also, in certain circumstances, assist
individuals to bring their own claims to court (see generally
pp. 14–17 above).

Formal investigation

A formal investigation can be undertaken for any purpose
connected with the Commissions' duties. Such an investigation must be undertaken if the Secretary of State so directs.
Investigations may be general or specific (SDA, ss. 57–61; RRA,
ss. 48–52).

A specific investigation (also called a 'belief' investigation) is conducted into the alleged discriminatory acts of
named individuals or organisations (SDA, s. 58(3A); RRA,
s. 49(4)). This often follows the lodging of a complaint by a
person who feels aggrieved by that act.

A general investigation may be initiated pursuant to
the Commissions' monitoring role. The Commissions will not
target a named individual or organisation necessarily but will
carry out investigations into particular *issues*. The CRE has in

the past conducted investigations into various local housing authorities to ensure compliance with the RRA.

The Commissions must draw up terms of reference for each and every formal investigation (which may be amended after commencement—e.g. from general to specific). Once the terms of reference are drawn up the Commissions must inform the 'target' of the investigation of their findings (SDA, s. 58; RRA, s. 49).

Notice

The requirement of notice varies depending on whether the investigation is general or specific.

A general investigation requires prior notice, called a 'general notice', which must be published at a time and in a manner that ensures those likely to be affected by it will see it (e.g. an advertisement in a local newspaper: SDA, s. 58; RRA, s. 49).

If the investigation is specific and names individuals or organisations, they must be informed clearly and individually of the reason for the investigation, and they must be given an opportunity to make representations (which may be with the assistance of a solicitor, counsel or other person) (SDA, s. 58; RRA, s. 49).

Disclosure

The Commissions may require the production of documents or other information (which could be required by the High Court under the Rules of the Supreme Court) and the attendance of any person at the investigation (SDA, s. 59; RRA, s. 50). A person required to produce information or attend must be first served with a notice. Such a notice may only be served where either it was authorised by the Secretary of State, or the terms of reference state that the named person or organisation may be guilty of discriminatory acts, practices, advertisements, instructions and pressure (for an explanation of these last two acts, see p. 31 below).

If a person served with a notice fails to comply, or the Commission believes he or she will not comply, the county court has jurisdiction to order the production of the information or that person's attendance. Breach of such an order is a summary offence.

The Commission may, at any time, make recommendations to the person under investigation or to the Secretary of State. Once the investigation is complete the Commission drafts a report containing its findings. The Secretary of State may order that the report is not published (SDA, ss. 60(2) and (3); RRA, ss. 51(2) and (3)).

Non-discrimination notices

If the Commission is satisfied breach of the relevant Act has occurred it may serve a non-discrimination notice (SDA, s. 67; RRA, s. 58). Before serving the notice the Commission must (under SDA, s. 67(5); RRA, s. 58(5)):

1. inform the person concerned that service of a non-discriminatory notice is contemplated, and on what grounds;
2. give the person concerned the opportunity to make representations (either orally or in writing) within no less than 28 days; and
3. take proper account of the representations.

If, having completed these preliminary steps, the Commission is still satisfied that a discriminatory act has been or is being committed, a non-discrimination notice may be served. The notice requires (under SDA, s. 67(2); RRA, s. 58(2)):

1. the cessation or non-repetition of any acts; and
2. the person concerned to notify the Commission (if compliance requires changes to practice) when those changes have been carried out and what was entailed.

The Commission may also require the production of documents or information to satisfy itself that the notice has been complied with (SDA, s. 67(7); RRA, s. 58(7)).

Non-discrimination notices which have become final are entered in a register which the Commissions are obliged to maintain (SDA, s. 70; RRA, s. 61). The register is open to inspection by members of the public.

Right of appeal

A person served with a non-discrimination notice has a right of appeal. This must be done within six weeks and the appeal is to the county court designated for the purpose (SDA, s. 68; RRA, s. 59). If the county court allows the appeal it may:

1. quash any requirement contained in the notice; or
2. substitute different requirements.

At the hearing of such an appeal the Court may consider the reasonableness of the requirements and the findings of fact giving rise to the notice. For this purpose the person served may call witnesses to give evidence and cross-examine the Commission's witnesses.

If the appellant either fails to appeal within six weeks or appeals unsuccessfully, the notice becomes final. The notice also becomes final if an appeal is withdrawn or abandoned.

Non-compliance with notice

Once a notice is received and has become final the recipient is liable, for the next five years, to the Commission issuing proceedings if the recipient persists in carrying out unlawful acts. Failure to comply with any requirement of a notice to furnish information to the Commission or any other person renders the recipient liable to enforcement procedures (SDA, s. 71; RRA, s. 62). The Commission can go to the court and ask for an order requiring the production of the information.

Codes of practice

Both Commissions have the power to issue codes of practice. The codes are not statutory; therefore, failure to observe a code does not leave a person or organisation open to legal or administrative proceedings. The codes are, however, admissible in evidence in court proceedings and regard will be had to them. In any event, the codes are informative and give helpful guidance on compliance with the Acts. Compliance with the codes will go a long way to avoiding non-discrimination notices and legal proceedings.

The CRE's *Code of Practice in Rented Housing* (1991) provides useful guidance and makes recommendations which should be followed to ensure policies and practices are soundly based to avoid racial discrimination and promote equal opportunities. The Code applies where housing is rented, leasehold or occupied pursuant to a licence.

Equal opportunities policies

The *Code of Practice in Rented Housing* recommends that social landlords adopt an equal opportunities policy which states a commitment to equal opportunities and which explains what will be done to achieve that purpose. All members of staff should be made aware of the contents of the Act, the Code and the policy. It is advised that such a policy should include:

1. a declaration that the RRA will be complied with and the Code implemented wherever possible;
2. an undertaking to keep tenants or prospective tenants informed of the policy's progress;
3. an allocation of responsibility to a specified person, group or committee for the implementation of the policy.

In order to fully implement the equal opportunities policy, housing organisations need to develop a clear action programme which includes opportunity for review of the policy, monitoring, and training of staff. An action plan must include effective procedures for combating racial harassment (see further at Chap. 11).

Part II

Types of and Procedures for Avoiding Discrimination

3.

Discrimination on Grounds of Race or Sex

Direct discrimination / Indirect discrimination

A high percentage of housing managers will have experience, either directly or indirectly, of allegations of unfair treatment on the ground of race or sex. Complaints may be from tenants, service users, staff or contractors, and may ultimately result in legal proceedings. If a complaint is made it must be assessed and acted upon quickly. The first thing that will need to be determined is whether the complaint could form the basis of legal action under the RRA or SDA. This chapter is concerned with the legal definition of discrimination, as prescribed by the Acts. Sex and race are dealt with together in this chapter.

Direct discrimination

According to the Acts, direct discrimination occurs (under SDA, s. 1; RRA, s. 1) when:
1. a person is treated less favourably
2. on the grounds of sex, race or (in the context of employment) marital status
3. than another person is, or may be, treated in comparable circumstances.

Less favourable treatment

To *treat* a person less favourably *because of* his or her sex, race, colour, nationality or national or ethnic origin is unlawful. Prejudice in itself is not unlawful (unless that prejudice is acted upon or shared with others which may amount to the crime of enticement to racial hatred under the Public Order Act 1986—see further p. 120 below).

> ### Example
>
> Mr Bottomley (a housing officer) was aggrieved because women housing officers, though contractually working to the same hours as men, were permitted to leave their office on a large and dangerous estate ten minutes earlier than male colleagues so that they may avoid being stranded at the bus stop with some men on the estate who had been harassing women as they were waiting for their bus. Mr Bottomley complained that he was being treated less favourably because of his sex. This is unlikely to be found to be unlawful. An employer is entitled to take account of the natural differences between men and women. In this example there was a genuine and justifiable reason for treating the women officers differently.

In *Peake v Automotive Products Ltd* (1978) the Court of Appeal held that it was not discrimination to treat womankind with courtesy and chivalry. In the course of the judgment Lord Denning MR remarked that there was 'ample scope for the operation of the [Sex Discrimination] Act without trespassing on sensible administrative arrangements'.

If, however, a person is directly discriminated against solely because of his or her race or sex, motive is irrelevant. Administrative practice cannot be relied upon to deny the benefit of a service to a person because of their sex or race. Once less favourable treatment is proved, and race or sex is the sole or significant factor, direct discrimination is made out. It does not matter that the real motive behind the differentiation was not prejudice of a racial or sexual nature if there was factual differentiation on either ground. Accordingly, it matters not that the individual or group accused of discriminating believed they were acting in good faith and with the best of intentions.

Once a complainant has established that, on the face of it, he or she has been treated less favourably, it is for the person or group accused to show that the less favourable treatment was not by reason of sex, race or ethnic origin. The burden therefore shifts to the alleged discriminator to show good reason for treating the complainant differently. In other words, unlawful discrimination may be *inferred* from a course of conduct unless it is proved otherwise.

> **Example**
>
> Between 1985 and 1997 a local authority housing department allocated 70 per cent of its void properties to white families with two or three children despite receiving equal numbers of applications from same size black families. Unless the authority can prove that the pattern of allocation was reflective of factors other than race, unlawful discrimination will be inferred. To assist complainants in the process of establishing inference from facts or a course of conduct, they are entitled to such statistical evidence as is available (e.g. figures which show percentage allocation of properties, time spent on housing waiting lists etc.).

It is very difficult to prove a negative, which is why record-keeping and monitoring are essential. These are discussed in detail in Chap. 7.

On grounds of race or sex

Sex

The SDA prohibits discrimination on grounds of sex (i.e. gender). It applies equally to men and women. It does not apply to discrimination on grounds of sexuality or sexual orientation (see further Chap. 5).

Race

The RRA prohibits discrimination on racial grounds. By section 3 of RRA 'racial grounds' means colour, race, nationality or ethnic or national origin. A racial group is a group of persons defined by reference to one of those factors. Black, white, Jewish, Irish and Somali people and gypsies and Sikhs have all been held to constitute racial groups.

The term 'ethnic' is construed relatively widely in a broad cultural and historic sense. It is not used in a biological or even strictly racial sense. The RRA applies to members of a group defined by reference to ethnic origins. 'Ethnic origins' in the context of this provision means a group which is:

> 'a segment of the population distinguished from others by a sufficient combination of shared customs, beliefs, traditions and characteristics derived from a common or presumed common past, even if not drawn from what in biological terms was a common racial stock, in that it was that combination which gave them an historically determined social identity in their own eyes and in those outside the group.'

See *Mandla v Dowell Lee* (1983) where it was held that Sikhs had 'ethnic origins'.

In *Commission for Racial Equality v Dutton* (1989) the Court of Appeal held that gypsies were capable of being a separate racial group because, despite their long presence in England and the fact that they were no longer 'derived from common racial stock, they had not merged wholly with the population but remained an identifiable group defined by reference to their "ethnic origins"'. See further p. 36 below.

Comparable relevant circumstances

To determine whether an individual or group has been discriminated against it is necessary to make a comparison between different groups. In other words, it must be established whether one group is treated differently to another group in the same (or not materially different) circumstances, once issues of race or sex are omitted. Relevant circumstances are those that actually apply, not those which would apply in an ideal world.

✻   The test is an objective one: would the complainant have received the same treatment, on the same terms, regardless of his or her sex or race? (See e.g. *James v Eastleigh BC* (1990).)

Examples

A housing association provides a special free house cleaning service for those tenants who are pensioners. Women qualify for the service at the age of 60 and men at the age of 65. A man of 62, for example, could use the service but would have to pay for it. Mrs Jones, who is 61, has the benefit of the free service, but her neighbour, Mr Smith, also 61, pays £10.00 per week.

In this example the association has discriminated against Mr Smith on grounds of sex. Had he been a woman he would have had his flat cleaned by the local authority for free.

Mr Modgil, an Indian housing officer, complains that his promotion prospects have been reduced as he has not been sent on a certain training course even though all of his less experienced white colleagues had attended the course. Unless his employer can justify the failure to afford him the opportunity of attending the course by reasons other than race, Mr Modgil has been directly discriminated against.

Discrimination by association

Race   Section 1 of RRA prohibits discrimination on 'racial grounds'. The section is therefore wide enough to include less favourable treatment perpetrated on someone because of the colour, race, nationality or ethnic origin of someone with whom he or she is associated. The RRA covers all cases of discrimination on racial grounds regardless of whether the racial characteristics in question were those of the complainant or of some other person. The only question in each case is whether the unfavourable treatment is caused by racial consideration (see e.g. *Showboat Entertainment Centre v Owens* (1984)).

> ### Examples
>
> Mrs Smith, a white applicant for housing, is put to the bottom of a waiting list because her partner is Asian. She has been discriminated against by the social landlord.
>
> Mr Jones, a white housing officer in charge of allocations, who refused to carry out a racially discriminatory policy excluding young black men from the housing waiting list, was dismissed. Mr Jones has been discriminated against because of the race of third persons (i.e. those he was instructed to exclude from the waiting list).

Sex   The SDA only protects those who claim unlawful discrimination because of their own unfavourable treatment. Accordingly, there can be no complaint under the Act of discrimination by association.

Victimisation

If someone brings proceedings, gives evidence in relation to proceedings, makes an allegation of discrimination, or threatens to make such an allegation in reliance on the anti-discrimination legislation, it is unlawful to treat him or her less favourably because of it (SDA, s. 4; RRA, s. 2). To do so amounts to victimisation of that person. In other words, such a person is 'protected' in so far as he or she may choose to rely on the Acts, or assist another to rely on them. The treatment applied by the alleged discriminator is compared with the treatment he or she has or would apply to persons who have not done the relevant protected act.

It is particularly important that people who threaten to invoke the legislation are brought within its protection as many avoid complaining of discrimination, believing it will simply make matters worse. It is common in the field of employment law for an unsuccessful job applicant to allege that the prospective employer discriminated against him or her owing to a complaint of discrimination having been made against a previous employer. This applies equally to persons who apply for housing. If a landlord refuses to house an applicant because of rumours that he or she has invoked the legislation, this would amount to victimisation and be unlawful.

For an allegation of victimisation to be made out, the complainant must show that the accused's conduct in treating him or her less favourably was directly related to the very fact an act has been done pursuant to the RRA or the SDA. Unlike other forms of discriminatory conduct, victimisation requires an element of intent. In other words, the complainant must prove that the accused acted consciously intending to treat the complainant less favourably *because* the legislation had been invoked.

A person complaining of victimisation must be able to establish that he or she has been less favourably treated because of reliance on the Acts. Therefore it must be shown that the alleged discriminator, in his or her treatment of the complainant, was influenced by the earlier reliance on the Acts or the involvement in legal proceedings. If there is evidence that the complainant would have been treated in the same way whether or not they proposed action under the Acts, the complaint will fail (see e.g. *Aziz v Trinity Street Taxis* (1988)).

Pressure or instruction to discriminate

It is unlawful for a person to *instruct* or attempt to *put pressure on* another person to do an act which contravenes the Acts (SDA, s. 39; RRA, s. 30). Such pressure need not be applied directly: it is unlawful if it is applied in such a way that the other person is likely to learn about it. It includes words or conduct which cause or are likely to cause an infringement of the Acts by another (see e.g. *Commission for Racial Equality v Imperial Society of Teachers of Dancing* (1983)).

> **Examples**
>
> A housing manager when discussing allocation of accommodation with his staff expresses a preference for housing white families.
>
> Tenants living on a small estate apply pressure by presenting a petition to their neighbourhood housing officer to prevent vacant flats being allocated to Somalian refugees.

Similarly, it is unlawful *to act on* a discriminatory instruction or to respond to pressure.

> **Example**
>
> In the example above, the social landlord gives in to the pressure of the tenants and allocates a flat to a white family in preference to a Somalian family.

Harassment and unlawful eviction

Harassment on grounds of race or sex is not expressly referred to in the Acts. Those being harassed for reasons of race or sex are not, however, left unprotected. If the complainant can establish that the reason for the harassment is racial or sexual, he or she can show less favourable treatment under the Acts. If the person is harassed for a different reason (e.g. solely to persuade them to quit the premises to enable the landlord to sell), this does not form the basis of an action under the Acts.

A landlord who evicts a tenant because he or she has relied, or threatened reliance, on either the RRA or the SDA is guilty of unlawful victimisation within the legislation (SDA, s. 30(2)(b); RRA, s. 21(2)(b)). For example, if a tenant makes a complaint of racial discrimination which results in abusive or threatening conduct on the landlord's part to encourage that tenant to quit the premises, he or she is guilty of victimisation. If the tenant actually leaves the premises in consequence of the conduct, this also amounts to unlawful eviction.

As stated at p. 31 above, the complainant must prove that reliance on the legislation had *caused* the abuse. Proving the essential element of causation makes it very difficult to establish victimisation; evidence of any ulterior motive may well defeat the complaint.

Protection from Eviction Act 1977

Section 1 of this Act makes it an offence for any person (not just the owner or landlord) to harass a residential occupier to induce him or her to give up occupation or to refrain from pursuing any remedy or relying on any right. The protection afforded by the Act covers, amongst others:
- contractual tenants
- licensees
- lodgers
- service occupiers
- former service occupiers whose contract of service has expired
- statutory tenants under the Rent Act.

The offence of harassment may be committed by an individual, an organisation, a company and/or its directors, managers or any other person purporting to act in the capacity of officer of the company. See further Chap. 11.

Indirect discrimination

This is the imposition of a requirement or condition to the provision of jobs, services or goods which, although applying equally to all people, adversely affects (or is less easily met by) persons of a particular sex or racial group and cannot be justified on any other legitimate grounds. In other words, it involves the way things are done and the rules, regulations and procedures which may seem quite fair because they apply to everyone. On closer inspection the *effect* of those rules and regulations may be to bar people from certain groups from taking advantage of opportunities or benefits. Indirect discrimination may be a covert form of discrimination and is often more difficult to detect.

It is often not appreciated by those responsible for imposing requirements or conditions that some may be less able to comply by reason of their sex or race. It is, however, no less invidious than direct discrimination. Indirect discrimination requires no mental element or motive (*R v Commission for Racial Equality, ex p Westminster City Council* (1984)).

The test

A complainant must establish (under SDA, s. 1; RRA, s. 1) that:
1. there is a condition or requirement which is compulsory for everyone (i.e. it is a precondition);
2. a considerably smaller proportion of a group can comply with the condition or requirement than the proportion of people from other groups;
3. there is no valid reason for the condition or requirement;
4. by reason of the condition or requirement there is a detriment to those who cannot so easily comply.

Requirement or condition

The first hurdle to be surmounted by a complainant is proof of the imposition of a 'requirement or condition'. The expression is capable of including any obligation, whether full- or part-time. Where a specific or express requirement is provided for there is little difficulty for a complainant in proving the necessary imposition. Where, however, there is nothing expressed as such, a complainant may have to argue that a requirement or condition was implied (e.g. owing to the inclusion of an obligation in, say, a tenancy agreement which deters applicants of a particular racial group from applying).

It must also be shown that the requirement or condition is a prerequisite to obtaining a benefit. The prerequisite must be mandatory and operate as a complete bar which prevented the applicant complying with it at the relevant time (i.e. the time when an application was or would have been made).

> **Example**
>
> A local authority states that only applicants who have resided in Great Britain for ten years prior to their application for local authority accommodation will be considered for properties with gardens. Here, persons who have immigrated from another country are unable to comply and are therefore deprived of the opportunity of obtaining accommodation with a garden.

Considerably smaller proportion

There is no statutory definition of 'considerably smaller proportion'—it is a question of fact and degree in each case. Often, complainants will rely on statistical evidence. A complainant is entitled to discovery of statistical data (e.g. recording the number of applicants on a housing waiting list and the ethnic breakdown of successful and unsuccessful applicants). Inferences may well be drawn from such data. The law places a burden on housing managers to monitor their own practices and policies, so it is important that social landlords keep proper records, not least because these statistics will reveal to housing managers any potential discrepancies.

> **Example**
>
> Liverpool City Council was alleged to have discriminated against black people on its housing waiting list because black nominees were given poorer quality accommodation and the allocation targets for new-build properties had operated to the detriment of black nominees. The council applied a requirement or condition that, to be rehoused in new property, a person seeking rehousing had to be in the medical or decants access channels. The council used the same system in its nomination to housing association new-build. As a matter of fact, black applicants were under-

> represented in the medical and decants access chan-
> nels, and so black applicants had more difficulty
> complying with the criteria and suffered a detriment
> as a result.
>
> Following a formal investigation, the CRE con-
> cluded that the council had unlawfully indirectly dis-
> criminated against black applicants in the way it set
> targets for the allocation of new-build properties and
> had directly discriminated against them in that black
> applicants nominated to housing associations were
> treated less favourably on racial grounds in relation to
> the quality of accommodation they obtained.

Able to comply

Being 'able to comply' does not mean being *physically capable*.
What is relevant is whether a person can reasonably comply
taking into account custom, cultural conditions and disability
directly linked to race, sex or marital status.

> ### Case report
>
> Mr Dutton was a licensee of a public house and dis-
> played a 'No travellers' sign on the door, following an
> incident with some people who were living in caravans
> nearby. The CRE brought an action against him on
> the basis that the sign was referring to gypsies who
> were a group coming within section 1 of RRA. The
> Court of Appeal held that gypsies are a racial group
> within section 1 and that while the term 'traveller' is
> not necessarily synonymous with 'gypsy' it was clear
> that the proportion of gypsies who could comply with
> the condition was substantially smaller than the
> proportion of non-gypsies. *Commission for Racial
> Equality v Dutton* (1989)

Housing managers may not appreciate that discriminatory practices are occurring, often because they come
about because of inherent and unrecognised prejudice or value
judgements, and sometimes purely because of convenience
or the impact of 'neutral policies'.

> **Examples**
>
> A housing co-operative operates an allocation system which depends on vacancies being filled by friends of members. This may be attractive in its simplicity but may amount to indirect discrimination if the members are predominantly from one racial group.
>
> A housing department operates a scheme whereby current tenants' sons and daughters are given re-housing priority even though they have no other right to such tenancies. If current tenants are predominantly from one racial group, other racial groups are less able to comply and therefore the rule may be unlawful.

Also, when considering whether a person comes within the housing provider's own policy (e.g. whether another could reasonably be expected to reside with a homeless applicant for the purposes of Part VII of the Housing Act 1996), it should be borne in mind that different racial groups have different cultures and traditions.

Justification

The legislation provides the 'defence' of justification. To rely on the defence the accused must establish that the requirement or condition was justified on some basis *other than* sex or race. In considering whether the defence of justification is made out, a court will look at the circumstances of each particular case and apply an objective test.

Note that 'justifiable does not equate with 'necessary', in spite of recent attempts to extend the meaning of the word. Justifiable is given its ordinary and natural meaning and has been said to refer to 'adequate grounds' which would be acceptable to 'right-thinking people as sound and tolerable reasons' (*Ojutiku and Oburoni v Manpower Services Commission* (1982)). An example of a sound and tolerable reason would be one such as public health and safety. It is certainly not tolerable to impose a requirement or condition which operates to the detriment of one section of society simply because the majority of the population say they prefer it (e.g. as is often said about male police officers).

In *Steel v Union of Post Office Workers* (1978) the Employment Appeal Tribunal outlined the factors relevant to the consideration of indirect discrimination. It was held that, in order to show a requirement or condition was one which was justifiable, regardless of (in this case) the sex of the person to whom it applied, a heavy onus rested on the alleged discriminator to prove the case was a genuine one where it could be said that the requirement or condition was necessary. In reaching its decision a tribunal should take account of all the circumstances of the case. It should examine the discriminatory effect of the requirement or condition if it were allowed to continue. It is then required to weigh the need for the requirement or condition against that effect. In distinguishing between a necessary requirement or condition and one which is merely convenient, it is relevant to consider whether other non-discriminatory methods of achieving the object could be found.

An objective balance needs to be struck between the discriminatory effect of the requirement or condition and the reasonable needs of the person applying it (*Hampson v Department of Education and Science* (1990)).

Housing managers considering the lawfulness of a requirement contained in, for example, a tenancy agreement or allocations policy should ask themselves:

1. Has the discriminatory effect been considered?
2. How serious is it?
3. Is there a less discriminatory way of achieving the same purpose?
4. Most importantly, would a right-thinking person consider it to be fair and reasonable?

Detriment

A complainant must also establish that he or she has personally suffered some detriment because of the requirement or condition. Detriment is not confined to financial or property loss, and includes injury to feelings. Only a person who has actually suffered can bring a claim. It cannot be used for the benefit of a particular group.

> ### Examples
>
> A social landlord operates a policy whereby applicants who have been resident in Great Britain for more than the previous five years get more points for the purposes of advancing up the waiting list. While this applies to every applicant equally, it can be seen that there would be fewer Asian families who could comply than white families, simply because fewer can establish the long residence requirement. This could be unlawful indirect discrimination.
>
> A local authority operates a policy of housing persons of particular racial groups on particular estates regardless of their needs or preferences. This often arises because of racial stereotyping and an assumption that people will be more comfortable with others of the same racial group. This is discriminatory and unlawful.
>
> A housing association operates a policy that, to be accepted for housing, the applicant must be a decant case from local authority accommodation where the decant cases are nearly all white. This would be indirectly discriminatory and unlawful.

Religious discrimination

[handwritten annotation: Should be applied because as a racial factor it denominates peosome people in society]

It is not unlawful in Great Britain to discriminate on grounds of religion (although note that in Northern Ireland it is unlawful to discriminate on grounds of religion in employment). 'Racial grounds' within the RRA does not include religion; however, in certain circumstances Jews and Sikhs have been found by the courts to be racial groups within the Act.

It is suggested that religious discrimination *in effect* amounts to indirect discrimination against a particular racial group. To discriminate against Hindus, for example, could be indirect discrimination against Indians.

> **Example**
>
> Mrs Malik (a Pakistani woman of Muslim faith) was required to wear a skirt as part of her uniform. She objected as to do so would have been contrary to her Muslim faith. The Manchester Industrial Tribunal held that to require her to wear a skirt was to indirectly discriminate against her on grounds of race. *Farhath Malik v British Home Stores* (1980)

Other unlawful acts

Parts IV of RRA and of SDA extend the provisions discussed above to other unlawful acts which, although not in themselves unlawful, are designed to produce or might result in unlawful discrimination. Only the CRE and EOC may enforce these provisions. Both may institute legal proceedings on their own behalf against perpetrators (see Chap. 2).

Discriminatory practices

It is unlawful to apply, or to operate a provision which would call for the application of, a condition or requirement which results or which is likely to result in an act of indirect discrimination (SDA, s. 37; RRA, s. 28). A classic example of such a practice is the imposition of a condition or requirement to the obtaining of a benefit which is so effective a deterrent to persons of a particular sex or racial group that none actually apply and none are refused.

Any act which is designed to have a discriminatory effect, even though not *of itself* discriminatory, will contravene the Acts.

> **Example**
>
> A landlord may have a reputation for only placing men in sheltered accommodation. Nothing is done to dispel that rumour and women choose not to apply.

Discriminatory advertisements

It is unlawful for a person to publish or cause to be published an advertisement which indicates, or might reasonably be understood to indicate, an intention by a person to do any act which is, or might be, unlawful under the Act (SDA, s. 38; RRA, s. 29).

> *Example*
>
> A social landlord advertises housing vacancies to women only.

It is not unlawful, however, to publish an advertisement which indicates an intention to do an act of discrimination if the act itself falls within one of the exceptions contained in either Act (e.g. genuine occupational qualifications).

> *Example*
>
> A special needs housing association which caters for single Asian women advertises for an Asian woman for the post of residential warden.

4.
Disability

Meaning of 'disability' / Discrimination / Positive
discrimination / Ensuring compliance

The DDA brings in new measures to prevent discrimination
against disabled people in key areas. It aims to do for disability
discrimination what the RRA did for racial discrimination.
The Act applies to employment, the provision of goods and
services and to the selling, letting or management of premises.
Any provider of services which are generally available to the
public is caught by the Act, whether operating in the public,
private or voluntary sector. It is irrelevant that the service may
be provided free of charge. The Act does not make unlawful
anything done in order to comply with other legislation (i.e.
acts done under statutory authority—see pp. 83–85 below).

Services not generally provided to the public (e.g. to
members of a private club) are not covered by the Act.

The Code of Practice *Rights of Access: Goods, Facilities,
Services and Premises* (July 1996), prepared by the National
Disability Council, describes and explains the duties imposed
on those falling within the categories listed. The Code itself
imposes no legal obligation but may be relied upon in legal
proceedings. Courts must take the Code into account where
relevant.

Compliance with the Code will help to avoid litigation
arising under the DDA.

Meaning of 'disability'

'Disability' for the purpose of the Act is physical or mental impairment which has an effect which is:
- significant (not trivial),
- adverse, and
- long term (lasting or expected to last for at least 12 months)

on that person's ability to perform normal day-to-day activities and chores (DDA, s. 1).

'Mental impairment' means recognised mental illness (Sched. 1, para. 1(1)). It covers a wide range of impairments relating to mental functioning, including recognised learning disabilities. Alcoholism, drug addiction and certain personality disorders are expressly *excluded* from the definition. 'Schizophrenic disorders' are included. Physical or mental impairment includes a sensory impairment, such as deafness and blindness.

'Normal day-to-day activities' are those which are carried out by most people on a fairly regular and frequent basis (Sched. 1, para. 4).

A personality disorder is a tendency to act in an unusual or anti-social way which is not dependent on or related to a clinically recognised illness (e.g. exhibitionism, hyperactivity and aggression). Such traits often influence a landlord in letting premises, since other residents must also be considered; however, it can be extremely difficult as a layperson to distinguish between illness which is protected by the Act and a personality trait which is not.

'Long-term adverse effect' requires that the disability must have lasted, or be likely to last, 12 months (Sched. 1, para. 2(1)). Persons who have been disabled within the meaning of the Act but who have now recovered are included.

For further guidance see *Matters to be taken into account in determining questions relating to the definition of disability* (1996), issued by the Secretary of State for Education and Employment.

Discrimination

Section 24 of DDA provides discrimination is unlawful if:
1. for a reason which relates to the disabled person's disability,
2. he or she is treated less favourably than others to whom that reason does not or would not apply, and
3. it cannot be shown that the treatment in question is justified.

'Less favourable treatment' is considered in Chapter 3.

> ### Example
>
> A landlord assumes that disabled tenants are unable to safely use the communal laundry facilities and tries to make it a term of the tenancy that they cannot use the common facilities unsupervised. Unless the landlord can justify this prohibition for 'proper' reasons (see pp. 47–48 below) the tenant is unlawfully discriminated against *because of* the disability.

It is not necessary to prove that others *were* treated more favourably than the disabled person so long as they *would have been* treated more favourably (i.e. in the example above, able-bodied tenants would have been permitted free use of the common facilities).

Provision and management of housing

The Act makes it unlawful for anyone who sells, lets or manages property to discriminate against disabled persons by reason of their disability (ss. 22–24). It therefore applies to local authorities, housing associations, private sector landlords, estate agencies, letting agencies and developers. The Act follows closely the RRA and SDA.

Services

It is unlawful under sections 19–21 for a service provider to:

1. refuse to provide a service which is, or would be, provided to members of the public;
2. deliberately not provide a service which is, or would be, provided, to members of the public; or
3. provide a service the standard of or the manner in which it is provided is less favourable to the disabled person.

Reasonable adjustments

By virtue of the *Disability Discrimination Code of Practice on Rights of Access, Goods, Facilities, Services and Premises*, service providers are required to make reasonable adjustments for disabled people so that they can use the service. The duty applies when access to a service is impossible or unreasonably difficult. The duty is introduced in two stages. The first stage applies from 1 October 1999; the second will not be brought into force until 2004.

From 1 October 1999, service providers are additionally required to:
1. make reasonable adjustments to policies, procedures or practices which exclude disabled people;
2. provide auxiliary aids and services to enable, or make it easier for, someone to use the service; and
3. where there is a physical feature which is a barrier to providing the service to a disabled person, find a reasonable alternative method of delivering the service.

Examples
- Guide dogs should be exempted from any policy prohibiting dogs from entry to a registered social landlord's housing office.
- Terms and conditions of tenancy can be provided on cassette for visually impaired people.
- If the local housing office is inaccessible to wheelchair users, housing officers could arrange to visit at home or provide an alternative address for interviews.

When providing an auxiliary aid, service providers are not required to do anything which would result in making a permanent alteration to, or which would have a permanent effect on, the physical fabric of premises, fixtures, fittings, furniture or equipment.

Premises (s. 22)

Disposal

It is unlawful for any person disposing of premises to discriminate:

1. in the terms on which the disposal is offered;
2. by refusing to dispose of premises;
3. in the way a disabled person is treated in relation to others on a waiting list for accommodation.

'Disposing of premises' includes the sale and letting of both land and buildings.

It is unlawful to refuse to sell or let premises to a disabled person. If, for example, a landlord were to take account of a person's disability in assessing the likelihood of him or her keeping up with rent payments and thereby refuses to let the premises to him or her, the landlord is acting unlawfully. Further, the terms on which premises are sold or let must not be discriminatory. For example, it is unlawful to require a mentally ill tenant to pay a damage deposit if a tenant who was not mentally ill would not.

A landlord is not permitted to withhold consent to the disposal of premises on grounds of disability. This applies to requests for consent to assign, sublet or part with possession of the premises (s. 22(4)). It applies to tenancies created before and after the coming into force of the DDA.

If a social landlord has a waiting list for accommodation, it is unlawful to discriminate against the disabled in operating that list (e.g. by placing disabled applicants automatically at the bottom of the list). Conversely, as it is not unlawful to discriminate in favour of the disabled: it is permissible (under the DDA) to place all disabled applicants ahead of others on the list. This is, however, always subject to statutory duties under the housing legislation (see further at Chap. 9).

Management

It is unlawful for any person managing premises to discriminate:
1. in the manner in which a disabled person is to make use of facilities or benefits;
2. by refusing or deliberately not allowing the disabled person to make use of facilities or benefits; or
3. by eviction or subjection to any other detriment.

Disabled persons must have equal access to and use of benefits and facilities (save where to do so would put the disabled person or others in danger—see below regarding justification). This includes access to shared recreational facilities, shared cooking or bathroom facilities and laundry facilities.

As under the RRA, to evict an occupier, or indulge in a course of conduct designed to make the occupier quit premises because of their disability is victimisation under the Act and unlawful.

Is less favourable treatment justified?

The circumstances in which less favourable treatment is justified are limited. Section 24(3) expressly provides that less favourable treatment can be justified in four situations:
1. It is necessary for the avoidance of danger to the health or safety of any person (which may include the health and safety of the disabled person).
2. It is reasonable owing to the disabled person being incapable of entering into an enforceable agreement, or giving informed consent.
3. For a case falling within 1. above, if it is necessary to enable the disabled person, or any occupier of other premises which form part of the building, to make use of a facility or benefit.

4. For a case falling within 2. above, if it is necessary to enable other occupiers of premises forming part of the building to make use of the facility or benefit.

The above is subject to the important proviso that the treatment must be *reasonably* and *genuinely* believed to be necessary. It must be remembered that discrimination is unlawful regardless of intention. It may be thought that the disabled person is actually being helped, but if he or she is treated less favourably then he or she has been discriminated against unlawfully. Similarly, the provision of a service cannot be refused because another provider caters better for the disabled person's needs.

For example, if a disabled person applies for housing with a housing association, and otherwise qualifies for housing, the association cannot (save where one of the four exceptions can be proved) refuse to house that applicant because another association caters specially for disabled persons.

Health and safety

Spurious health and safety reasons will not suffice. It is common for landlords to refuse to let premises above the ground floor of a block of flats to wheelchair-bound applicants. Fire regulations are often relied upon as the justification. This should not be assumed without proper investigation: it is for the manager of the block together with the appropriate fire authority to reach an informed decision.

In the 1980s, when many landlords were ignorant about HIV and AIDS, they refused to let to persons suffering the disease, for the purported protection of the other residents. This is now caught by the Act and is unlawful.

Unable to contract

The Act does not require a landlord or provider of services to enter into contractual relations with a person who, because of such severe mental impairment, is unable to understand the contract terms or to provide an informed consent (s. 24(3)(b)).

If an applicant cannot, for example, understand the concept of rent, the landlord can reasonably refuse to offer him or her a tenancy. Care must be exercised when assessing a person's ability or inability to understand transactions. It is the particular transaction at issue which is relevant. Unless there is clear evidence to the contrary, a person must be assumed to be capable, not the other way around.

Necessary to provide benefit or facility

It may be justifiable to restrict access to or use of benefits or facilities associated with premises if this is *necessary* to allow access to others or to the disabled person (s. 24(3)(d)). Thus, a mentally ill tenant who persistently destroys the flower beds may be refused access to a shared recreational area.

Greater expense

As a general rule, it is unlawful to charge a disabled person more for a service because of his or her disability. However, where additional costs are incurred in providing a special service to cater for that person's particular needs, the added cost may be passed on.

Alteration and adaptation

There is no obligation under the DDA to alter or adapt any premises to make them suitable for disabled persons. It is not unlawful, for example, to refuse to let premises in a high-rise block to a disabled person confined to a wheelchair, provided there is a reasonably held belief that that person would be unable to safely negotiate the stairs. When considering the extent of a disabled person's ability to use facilities, regard must be had to what the disabled person believes he or she can manage. Discrimination can stem from lack of awareness about disability or the making of assumptions. For example, many housing managers assume that all persons in wheel-chairs will be unsafe in premises which are not specially adapted. This is certainly not the case. The first question must always be what the applicant regards as his or her require-ments, not what an able-bodied housing officer assumes will be required. The golden rule must be to ask the disabled person before any decisions are taken.

Employers, trade organisations and service providers do have a duty to make reasonable alterations or adjustments to premises to ensure the aims of the Act are not thwarted. Tenants may apply for consent to alter premises to provide for the special needs of a disabled occupant. Where the premises are leasehold and the lease provides for alteration subject to consent (DDA, s. 16, as amended by the Disability Discrimination (Sub-leases and Sub-tenancies) Regulations 1996, that consent to such alterations must not be unreasonably refused.

Unreasonable refusal is presumed if the landlord fails to respond to the request within 21 days and the alteration or adaption is such that is permitted under the terms of the lease subject only to consent. It is, however, reasonable to withhold consent if that consent is dependent upon the landlord obtaining the consent of some other person or body (e.g. the freeholder), who withholds their consent, or attaches con-ditions to the consent. If it is a condition of the freeholder that the landlord pays a sum of money which cannot be recouped from the tenant, that condition means the landlord's refusal is held to be reasonable. See generally the Disability Dis-crimination (Services and Premises) Regulations 1996.

It is not unlawful for a landlord to attach certain con-ditions to the giving of consent. The regulations provide that a landlord may require the tenant to:
1. obtain any necessary planning permission or consent;
2. submit plans for the works to the landlord for his or her approval;
3. make the works available for inspection, during and after completion;

4. reimburse him or her for costs reasonably incurred in connection with the giving of consent;
5. reasonably reinstate the premises upon expiry of the lease.

Victimisation

It is unlawful to victimise or treat less favourably any person, whether disabled or not, who has:
1. instituted legal proceedings under the DDA;
2. given evidence or information for the purpose of such proceedings;
3. acted in any other way in reliance on the DDA;
4. made a complaint that the DDA has been infringed.

This also applies to a person who intends to take any of the actions listed above.

Encouraging or assisting in unlawful discrimination

It is just as unlawful to lend assistance to anyone discriminating against a disabled person. One exception to this is where the assistance is given in reliance on a statement that the action is not within the Act and it is reasonable to rely on that statement.

> ### Example
>
> A caretaker is approached by a disabled tenant complaining that the central heating is not working. The housing manager instructs the caretaker not to fix the heating as it will simply be broken again within minutes as the tenant abuses the system. The caretaker questions this but is told that the DDA permits less favourable treatment where a disabled person has deliberately caused damage to premises.
>
> In such a situation it is arguable that the caretaker is protected by the Act, but the housing manager has acted unlawfully and is not protected.

Vicarious liability

An employer is liable for the actions or inaction of his or her employees while acting in the course of their employment, even if he or she is unaware or disapproving of the employee's actions. The only real defence to such a charge is that the employer took all steps that were reasonably practicable to prevent his or her employees from discriminating against disabled persons. This is another good reason for the education and training of all housing managers and staff.

Similarly, if an agent infringes the DDA the principal may also be held to have unlawfully discriminated, so long as the agent was acting with either express or implied authority. Authority may be given both before and after the commission of the unlawful act.

Positive discrimination

It is not unlawful to treat disabled persons more favourably than others. It is permissible, therefore, to discriminate in favour of disabled persons.

Ensuring compliance

To ensure the Act and Code of Practice are complied with, both in spirit and form, the following is a suggested checklist for social landlords:
1. *Information and education*   It must be explained to officers, managers and staff that it is unlawful to discriminate. The DDA and Code of Practice should be available for consultation.
2. *Formulation of policy*   It is wise to have a written policy referable to the Act and Code which is communicated to all staff.
3. *Training*   The National Council for the Disabled advises training in disability awareness.

4. Monitoring To satisfy oneself that the policy is achieving its objective, records should be kept and monitoring regularly carried out.

5. Complaints procedure Having an appropriate complaints mechanism is essential to the operation of a proper procedure.

Everyone involved in the provision and management of housing and services should be made aware that it is unlawful to discriminate against disabled persons.

Unlawful contract terms

Any term in an agreement, including a lease, is void if its effect is to:

1. require someone to do something which would be unlawful under Part III (services and premises) of the Act;
2. exclude or limit the application of Part III; or
3. prevent a claim being brought under that Part.

> **Example**
>
> A tenancy agreement contains a term precluding a tenant from parting with possession of part of the premises to someone who is mentally ill. That term is unenforceable.

Conclusion

The DDA has introduced a new code of protection for the disabled. It applies to all those working in the field of social housing. The Act largely replicates the RRA and the SDA, yet it introduces new concepts and obligations which relate to the particular disadvantages of those who are disabled. Further, unlike under the RRA and the SDA, it is not unlawful to discriminate in favour of a disabled person. The Act requires some landlords to alter or adapt accommodation to make it more suitable for the disabled. There are, however, qualifications to that obligation.

5.
Sexual Orientation
Relevant issues / European law

The SDA prohibits discrimination on grounds of sex (i.e. gender). It applies equally to men and women. It does not, however, apply to discrimination on grounds of sexual orientation. Yet European law (see Chap. 1) is expanding in such a way that it is expected to protect some forms of discrimination on grounds of sexual orientation. For example, in *R v Secretary of State for Defence, ex p Perkins* (1997) the judge remarked that there was a real prospect of the European Court of Justice extending the protection of the Equal Treatment Directive to cover discrimination on grounds of sexual orientation.

The national courts are, however, becoming more inventive in seeking new ways to protect individuals from discrimination while waiting for Parliament to progress change.

> ### Case report
>
> Mr Smith, a gay man, was the subject of a complaint to his employer by a fellow, female employee. He denied the allegation, explaining that it was motivated by malice and that the complainant had used abusive language referring to his sexual orientation. His employer dismissed him for gross misconduct.
>
> Mr Smith argued that he had been subjected to unlawful sex discrimination in that, first, the female complainant's allegations would not have been made against a woman and, secondly, in dismissing him instead of the female complainant he had been treated

less favourably than her. His case was taken up to the Court of Appeal which held that, although discrimination on the grounds of sexual orientation did not fall within the SDA, discrimination against a male homosexual based on his homosexuality could be discrimination against him as a man. In relation to his complaint about the treatment he received from the female colleague, the comparator was a homosexual woman. *Smith v Gardner Merchant Ltd* (1999)

Relevant issues

As national law, and thus far European law, has failed to protect those who are discriminated against on grounds of sexual orientation, there is very little which can be directly referred to. The courts have not been much concerned with the issue as complainants cannot go before the court and rely on a right to be treated equally regardless of their orientation. The issue has, however, notably arisen in the housing context in relation to the rights of succession.

Succession rights

The right to succeed to a tenancy is afforded to those (and only those) who can bring themselves within the statutory framework of one of the relevant Housing Acts. For secure tenants the right is limited to: a deceased tenant's spouse; members of the deceased tenant's family; and a person who lived with the deceased tenant as his or her husband or wife (see further C. Hunter, *Tenants Rights* (Arden's Housing Library, 1995)).

Many lesbians and gay men who lived with a tenant have attempted to avoid being removed from the accommodation following the tenant's death by arguing that they are qualified to succeed as they lived with the tenant as husband or wife, or should be viewed as a member of the deceased's family. The interpretation of this phrase has exercised the mind of many a judge over the years. So far, the outcome has always been that a same sex partner is not capable of coming within the definition of 'member of the family' or of 'living as husband or wife'.

Case report

The lesbian survivor of a council tenant claimed that she was a member of the deceased tenant's family. The court held that the statutory right to succeed was given only to those who expressly fell within the provision of the statute. It was decided that the statutory provision did not contemplate same sex partners as being within the categories of persons entitled to succeed. This case was referred to the European Commission on Human Rights on the basis that article 8 of the European Convention on Human Rights (which protects an individual's right to respect for private and family life) conflicted with the succession provisions contained in the national law, which was thereby rendered unlawful and unenforceable. The Commission, however, agreed with the national court and held that the protection of same sex partners in the context of succession rights did not fall within the scope of article 8 and accordingly the national provisions were not unlawful. *Harrogate BC v Simpson* (1984)

Since *Simpson* was decided there have been further attempts to persuade the courts that the statutory provision should be construed widely.

Case report

Mr Fitzpatrick was the homosexual partner of a Rent Act protected tenant with whom he had lived for many years. On the death of the tenant, he applied to have the tenancy transferred to him. The housing association refused and the Mr Fitzpatrick sought a declaration that he had succeeded to the tenancy, as he was either the tenant's spouse or a member of his family for the purposes of the Rent Act 1977. He argued that 'spouse' should be interpreted, taking account of the current climate, as including two persons of the same sex intimately linked in a relationship which was not merely transient but which had all the ingredients of a marriage. Alternatively, the relationship he had with the tenant was sufficiently intimate that he should be regarded as having been living with him as a member of his family.

He was unsuccessful at all stages until reaching the House of Lords, which decided that at least in the context of the Rent Act 'spouse' meant legally a husband or wife. On the other hand, the word 'family' is used in a number of different senses. Over the years the courts have held that the word is to be applied flexibly and is not confined to legally binding relationships. The hallmarks of the relationship are that there should be a degree of mutual interdependence, of the sharing of lives, of caring and love, of commitment and support. In considering who was a member of a deceased tenant's family, the court had to have regard to changes in attitudes to same sex relationships: if the person claiming to be entitled to succeed established, as a matter of fact, the necessary indicia of the relationship, then as a matter of law there was no reason why a same sex partner could not succeed under the Rent Act. *Fitzpatrick v Sterling Housing Association Ltd* (1997)

While the above case is confined to Rent Act tenancies and is not of general application to secure or assured tenancies, it is interesting to note that the definition of 'member of the family' has been expanded because of the progressive shift in public perception. It is anticipated, however, that a parliamentary amendment will be required before the same will be applied universally.

Some local authorities have attempted to get round this anomaly by specifically providing in their tenancy agreement for same sex partners to succeed if a heterosexual partner would succeed. There has been much debate, however, over whether this is outside the scope of local authority powers and unenforceable. Under Part VI of the Housing Act 1996, such a policy is only possible if the local authority makes express provision for same sex partners in their allocations policy (see further at Chap. 10).

AIDS and HIV

While AIDS and HIV are not confined to homosexuals, it is they who have, over the years, felt the full force of public ignorance and fear of the diseases. This has manifested itself in cases of discrimination against individuals who have acquired AIDS or HIV in relation to the provision of housing, goods and services.

Special considerations for sufferers

People with AIDS and HIV infection are vulnerable to debilitating illnesses. That risk is exacerbated by poor living conditions. They require self-contained, warm, centrally heated accommodation which is clean and dry if they are to minimise their risk of contracting infections. Therefore, if an applicant for housing (or rehousing) has contracted HIV this becomes relevant to the quality of accommodation which can be considered to be suitable for him or her.

> **Example**
>
> A single man with AIDS loses accommodation in the private sector and applies (as a homeless person) to a local authority for housing under Part VII of the Housing Act 1996. The local authority decides he is in priority need and entitled to the full housing duty. The accommodation he is offered, however, is a room in a hostel with shared facilities and is in a state of disrepair. This is not suitable for him and the local authority has failed to discharge its duty towards him. (See further Chap. 10.)

For those with symptomatic HIV infection or with AIDS it is essential that good quality accommodation is found for them. Also, many people living with AIDS have to reduce their working hours (and some give up work altogether), so the rent at which accommodation is offered is a relevant consideration.

Harassment

Society's attitude to the disease is changing, although many who suffer are still harassed because of their condition, or because of the misguided assumption made by some that the person is necessarily homosexual and therefore on grounds of sexual orientation.

European law

The Treaty of Amsterdam, which the present Government has committed to, aims to protect individuals from discrimination on grounds of sexual orientation. It is therefore anticipated that, in the future, discrimination on grounds of sexual orientation will be expressly prohibited.

In *Grant v South-West Trains Ltd* (1998), which was heard by the European Court of Justice, it was found that it was not unlawful discrimination for an employer to deprive the same sex partner of an employee a benefit which was received by heterosexual partners. The court stated:

> While the European Parliament had indeed declared that it deplored all forms of discrimination based on a person's sexual orientation, the Community had not as yet adopted rules providing for such ...

It is therefore clear that until special express provision is made, the law will continue to fail to protect adequately individuals who are discriminated against by reason of their sexual orientation.

6.

General Public Duties

Local authority obligations / The Housing
Corporation / Tenants' associations / Discrimination
in the private sector / Positive action

The RRA imposes a duty on all local authorities, Housing
Action Trusts, the Housing Corporation, Scottish Homes, and
Housing for Wales to make appropriate arrangements with a
view to securing that their functions are carried out with proper regard to the need to eliminate discrimination and promote
equality of opportunity. The Local Government Acts 1966 and
1988 also impose certain obligations on local authorities.

Local authority obligations

Race Relations Act 1976

Local authorities may have an enormous influence on the
quality of equal opportunities in their districts. They also have
a direct legal duty to do so. Section 71 of RRA provides that
local authorities must:

> … make appropriate arrangements with a view to
> securing that their various functions are carried out
> with due regard to the need:
> (a) to eliminate unlawful racial discrimination; and
> (b) to promote equality of opportunity, and good
> race relations, between persons of different racial
> groups.

In fulfilling this 'general statutory duty' local authorities still have to comply with the other provisions of the Act.

Obligation to promote equality of opportunity and racial harmony

For a local authority properly to comply with this obligation, it must be fully aware of the housing needs of people within its district and the effect of its housing policies upon persons of different race or ethnic origin. Every authority should, with section 71 in mind, carry out regular reviews of its policies and be prepared to modify or rewrite policy if judged necessary. Clear criteria should be laid down for allocating or granting access to housing which do not discriminate against or disadvantage certain groups.

Often, housing is not equally accessed because of lack of knowledge of availability of social housing. This may arise because of language difficulties. Housing organisations are advised by the CRE Code of Practice to adopt specific measures for particular groups to overcome communication difficulties. Relevant information materials, application forms and tenancy agreements can be translated into the different languages which reflect the make-up of the area.

It is also advisable to train staff and officers who are responsible for monitoring and record-keeping to be alert to signs of discrimination. They should be made aware of the geographical breakdown within the authority's district and how this may correspond to ethnic origin.

Obligation to eliminate unlawful discrimination

Local authorities are obliged to use this statutory duty to eliminate unlawful discrimination not only within their own walls but within their districts. The duty may be prayed in aid for sanctioning individuals and organisations who discriminate (e.g. a works contractor engaged to renovate houses on an estate who refuses to consider black people for labouring jobs may be removed from the approved list). Authorities may also incorporate terms into contracts which require the other contracting party to be race or gender friendly.

It must be remembered, however, that an authority considering tenders from private companies is forbidden (by Local Government Act 1988, s. 17) from taking account of 'non-commercial' matters, which would include political stance. Authorities may continue to ask questions such as whether the organisation complies with the RRA and SDA.

Local Government Act 1966

Section 11 provides a mechanism for all local authorities to establish posts to address the needs of people from ethnic minorities.

Local Government Act 1988

This sets out a framework within which local authorities can ensure that companies and other bodies applying for inclusion in select or approved lists, bidding for contracts and working under contract take reasonably necessary steps to comply with the RRA and the CRE codes.

Local authority contractors

Since the Local Government Act 1988 became law, the scheme of local authority purchasing and contracting has undergone dramatic change. Local authorities are required to put specific activities such as housing management, repairs and legal services out to tender. This had an adverse effect on equal opportunities policies which had been developed and monitored in-house. Local authorities had to consider how to ensure continued good practice in employment by their contractors.

The Act precluded authorities from considering 'non-commercial matters' when selecting contractors. This means authorities cannot, for example, take account of a contractor's politics when considering the award of contracts. There is an important exception, however, when it comes to the promotion of racial equality. The Act gives authorities scope to pursue their duties under the RRA.

Many authorities now pursue their equal opportunities policies *through* their contracts. Contractors can be required to include in their contracts an obligation to comply with the RRA, the SDA and the DDA and the codes of practice.

At the time of writing it is expected that the requirement for competitive tendering will be repealed in 2000 and replaced by a concept of 'best value' (which may involve some testing). This is likely to make it easier to pursue better discrimination policies in connection with employment and contracts.

The Housing Corporation

The Corporation, which was established in 1964, oversaw the operation of housing associations which were eligible for public funding. Such associations were registered with the Corporation where the Corporation was satisfied there was a requirement for another association. If a new housing association intended to target minorities who were otherwise not adequately catered for, this was a factor the Corporation took into account. The Corporation, additionally, is charged with maintaining a register of all social landlords, including those formerly registered as housing associations. The Corporation has power to supervise, regulate and intervene in social landlords' activities. It has control and management of funding for social landlords which were previously controlled by local government. It also issues guidance in the form of Housing Corporation Circulars.

The Corporation has issued guidance to housing associations determining priority of those on its waiting list. Housing associations must have regard to the Corporation's procedural requirements. One of those requirements is publication of the allocation policy, which covers eligibility and determination of priority. Priority should be given to those most in need and take account of four basic criteria:

- existing (and future) housing conditions;
- the applicant's ability to cope with those conditions;
- the length of time the applicant has already had to cope with those conditions;
- other options which may be available to the applicant.

The policy should also describe allocation of accommodation by size and type and how requests for transfers are dealt with.

As with other landlords, housing associations must not unlawfully discriminate on the basis of race, sex or disability. The Corporation's *Tenants' Guarantee* (reproduced in the Corporation's *Performance Standards*) requires wider considerations to be taken into account in the selection of tenants:

> Registered housing associations will be required to comply with the code of practice on race relations in the field of housing ... Associations should also conform with best practice to avoid any kind of discrimination and to promote equality of opportunity both in access to accommodation and the provision of services to all members of the community who may be disadvantaged by race, sex or disability.

The Corporation also requires that, for the purpose of access to sheltered accommodation, there must be a common qualifying age for men and women.

The Corporation advises that if associations discover, as a result of their ethnic monitoring, that fewer people from ethnic minorities are taking up tenancies than would be expected given the make-up of the local population, they should take positive action to redress the imbalance.

Tenants' associations

A tenants' association is a formally constituted group of tenants on, for example, an estate who meet to consider local housing issues. The RRA makes it unlawful for tenants' associations to discriminate against anyone on grounds of sex or race. Membership and the benefits arising from it must be open to all. Local authorities, housing associations and other social landlords have a responsibility to ensure their tenants' associations are acting within the law. There has been a shift towards tenants' involvement in management in recent years.

The *Council Tenants' Charter* in 1992 advised local authorities to foster tenants' associations and the Corporation mirrored this in its *Performance Criteria*. Compulsory competitive tendering has now been extended to housing management and the result has been that tenants' associations have become powerful bodies in the context of managing social housing. The replacement of competitive tendering by best value (see p. 63 above) is unlikely to affect this. Most local authorities use tenants' associations to consult with tenants. Fewer housing associations do this, but it is on the increase.

Tenants' associations have a key role to play in the campaign for racial equality and against racial violence. Social landlords can make good use of tenants' associations in the implementation of their monitoring policies and to advertise racial equality policies. They can also play an important role in the management of racial harassment. Tenants' associations are often at the forefront when it comes to victim support, giving evidence in court proceedings and by taking a firm stand against any members who may have been involved.

It remains the case, however, that ethnic minorities are under-represented in tenants' associations, even in areas with a high percentage of ethnic minority tenants. This is less marked, however, in those associations where the local authority or housing association has shown a commitment to racial equality and has a clear and well-drafted policy. Local authorities and housing associations have both a moral and a legal responsibility to promote racial equality, including within its own tenants' associations.

There are many things that can be done *vis-à-vis* the associations to improve on equality performance. The local authority or registered social landlord can make it a requirement that the association commits to a racial equality policy before being officially recognised. (For example, the London Borough of Southwark introduced a requirement that tenants' associations adopted a constitution which included equal opportunity clauses. If the association refused, the council refused to recognise them, and helped set up others.) The association can be given advice and assistance on compliance with the RRA and the Code. Ethnic records can be kept and the association monitored against these records. Local authority and registered social landlord policy on tenant participation and consultation can include a commitment to racial equality and stress the importance of the association representing the concerns of *all* tenants. New tenants should be told about the tenants' association and encouraged to participate.

Discrimination in the private sector

The CRE has uncovered widespread discrimination within the private rented sector by accommodation agencies, private sector landlords, hoteliers and hostel managers etc. While individuals are able to challenge discriminatory acts and the CRE has power to take action against private individuals, they largely react to incidents as and when they are reported. Local authorities and housing associations are well placed to encourage better practice in the private sector in the way it deals with those who discriminate. As central Government continues to promote the private rented sector as an alternative to social housing, and more social landlords become involved in using private sector accommodation to fulfil their own duties, they can make a positive contribution to racial equality in their areas by, for example, refusing to deal with discriminatory individuals or organisations and nominating tenants to, or placing them with, landlords who have a good record on race relations.

Positive action

Discrimination on grounds of sex, race and disability is unlawful if it cannot be justified on objective and reasonable grounds. Generally, this is so whether or not the discriminatory practice favours a particular group which many believe requires special assistance. For example, to adopt a policy of promoting only female housing managers is detrimental and therefore discriminatory against male candidates for promotion. Likewise, a housing association which prefers to focus its resources on single white men rather than single black women unlawfully discriminates against black women.

It has been recognised, however, that in the interests of promoting equal opportunity and the elimination of invidious discrimination, a regime of 'positive action' may be adopted. The justification for positive action is the need to redress the imbalance in certain groups.

By virtue of the DDA it is permissible to discriminate in favour of disabled people. Positive action on sexual grounds is permitted *only* in the field of employment (see Chap. 12). Positive action on racial grounds is only permitted in relation to the provision of welfare and education for the special needs of racial groups.

Housing provision exclusive to particular racial groups

Generally speaking, a housing provider cannot provide housing exclusively for one racial group unless it is within the 'special needs' provision (see below). There are, however, two exceptions under the RRA:

1. *Section 26* An association of persons (whether corporate or unincorporate) which has at least 25 members and whose membership is regulated by a constitution may, so long as it is the main object of the association, restrict the benefits of membership to persons of a particular racial group, defined other than by reference

to colour. (Note that organisations with less than 25 members are not covered by the legislation at all (see Chap. 1).)

2. *Section 34* Charitable bodies may confer benefits on a particular class of persons, defined other than by reference to colour. The enabling provision of the Act must be set out in the association's charitable instrument (e.g. the articles of association).

Example

A housing co-operative wishes to provide housing for West Indian people only. This is lawful so long as those to be accommodated are also to be members of the association.

Special needs

Section 35 of RRA states:

> Nothing in Parts II to IV shall render unlawful any act done in affording persons of a particular racial group access to facilities or services to meet the special needs of persons of that group in regard to their education, training or welfare, or any ancillary benefits.

Welfare

The provision of housing can only come within the term 'welfare'. For the exception to apply, however, it must be shown that the *group* targeted is *disadvantaged* in its living conditions. It is repeatedly shown that various racial minorities suffer discrimination in housing in terms of both quality and tenure. If the provision of services or benefits is actually directed to meeting a group's special needs, then positive action is lawful.

Section 35 permits the prioritisation of the special needs of a particular racial group in respect of welfare, training and education. Accordingly, an applicant for services or benefits who is a member of an identified racial group may be preferred over another applicant if those services or benefits are designed to meet the special needs of the group. This provision is not for the purpose of redressing the effects of past discrimination; it is not necessary that the special needs have arisen *because of* racial discrimination.

'Special needs' are regarded as needs that 'are either different in kind from, or are the same as but particularly greater than, those of the rest of the population' (see *Positive Action and Racial Equality in Housing* (CRE)). The special need does not have to be exclusive to a particular group; it is sufficient if that group experiences the need to a greater extent than others.

Section 35 has been relied upon in the past to set up specialist housing schemes for, amongst others, black elderly people, black single homeless and Indian women subject to domestic violence. It may also be relied upon in the context of employment of persons from a particular racial group to provide access to facilities or benefits.

> ### Examples
>
> An RSL provides sheltered housing for single women. There is a significant number of Asian single women in its district who are under-represented in the general sheltered housing scheme. The association could create a post for an Asian woman specifically to provide access to the facility, for example by way of publicity, advice and support for those women.
>
> A local authority is concerned that the large community of Bangladeshi people is not accessing local authority housing. Section 35 permits the authority to devise a special poster campaign to inform Bangladeshis of their rights and encourage them to make applications.

Section 35 is exempt from the advertising provisions of the RRA. Accordingly, a housing organisation set up pursuant to section 35 can advertise itself as, for example, a black housing association and offer its service solely to black people.

Any housing organisation, before seeking to hide behind section 35, must first clearly identify the special need

intended to be met. The CRE recommends that any organisation setting up a special needs scheme should:
1. identify and define the needs to be met which are recognised by the local community as requiring special attention;
2. regularly review the scheme to check if the special need still exists; and
3. ensure that the need is a genuine need and not merely a preference of a particular racial group.

Targets v quotas

A target (in the context of measuring equality) is no more than an identifiable goal to work towards. It is very different from a quota, which is unlawful. A target should not be expressed in terms of minima or maxima. It is there merely to provide a focus for the future. A target is, most importantly, a yardstick by which to measure the success or failure of equal opportunities policies. In the provision of housing, targets can be valuable indicators of equality.

Positive action and equal opportunities policies

Positive action is not a short cut to the removal of discrimination. In isolation, positive action is of little benefit and can be counterproductive. Combined with an effective equal opportunities policy, however, the results can be dramatic.

Black housing organisations

The black housing association movement developed in response to perceived racial discrimination within housing. Because of changes brought about by the Housing Association Act 1974, however, many associations were starved of funding and either folded or were subsumed by larger mainstream associations.

In 1987 the Housing Corporation announced its black and ethnic minority strategy of setting targets for black and ethnic minority housing associations, and for the number of homes they built or managed. It was highly successful. By 1996 approximately 50 black and ethnic minority housing associations and co-operatives had been set up, managing more than 17,000 homes—positive action which was both lawful and effective.

7.
Monitoring

Setting up a system / Ethnic categories / Collection of data / Monitoring data / Equal opportunities training

For a social landlord to comply with its responsibilities it is essential that the extent of the problem is identified. As long ago as 1969 the Cullingworth Committee reported:

> ... records must be kept and used to establish how many coloured people [*sic*] were applying for council houses, how many were getting them, and what type and quality of house they were obtaining.

Yet it was not until quite recently that housing providers appreciated the importance of monitoring. In 1984 the CRE published a report of its formal investigation into the London Borough of Hackney. The report was preceded by a non-discrimination notice, the main directive of which was about keeping ethnic records and their subsequent monitoring. In 1985 the Housing Corporation issued a circular which required housing associations to follow advice on monitoring from the NFHA (now the National Housing Federation). The CRE's *Code of Practice in Rented Housing* (1991) also stressed the importance of implementing ethnic monitoring systems and recommended that all housing organisations formulated their own system. It is important to remember that failure to implement recommendations contained in a Code may be considered a material factor in subsequent court proceedings.

This chapter gives practical guidance on monitoring steps which can be taken first to discover the extent of the problem within organisations, and secondly to bring about a decline in complaints of discrimination and to prevent further litigation arising from alleged discriminatory acts.

Setting up a system

Social landlords should first consult their tenants and applicants with the aim of establishing trust. It is important that people who are to be monitored are aware of the reason for the record-keeping, the purpose it will serve and what classification system will be used. They must also feel confident that the records remain confidential. It should not be possible to recognise anyone from the data: monitoring reports should deal with numbers, not faces. The CRE recommends that individuals be able to classify themselves by deciding which ethnic category they belong to.

Once records are collected it is as important that the records are monitored at regular intervals. It is suggested that the monitoring exercise be carried out at least once a year and ideally every few months. If the monitoring reveals that discrimination is occurring the housing provider needs to respond. This should involve a review of practices and procedures, communication and discussion with housing officers and staff, and finally implementing changes to deal with the problem.

Ethnic categories

The assignment of categories according to ethnicity to describe people has always been contentious. Each housing provider should decide for itself which categories to use, based on local knowledge. The ethnic categories adopted, however, should always relate to the primary objective of monitoring—the identification of those who may be discriminated against. If there is a specific category which represents a not insignificant proportion of tenants or applicants, this should be expressly included (e.g. in Tower Hamlets there is a large community of Bangladeshi people on the waiting list or homeless, and in Hackney there is a large number of Orthodox Jews). Before categories are finalised, therefore, it is essential to consult with local people and organisations.

The CRE recommends following the census classification with its mix of colour, ethnic and national categories: White; Black Caribbean; Black African; Black Other; Indian; Pakistani; Bangladeshi; Chinese; Other (please specify). People should be free to identify themselves and choose which category they feel most comfortable with.

Collection of data

Information can be collected initially by careful use of application forms. Local organisations such as housing advice centres can provide invaluable assistance in collecting the data (e.g. by providing access to its own records).

Monitoring data

Once all the information is collected it needs to be analysed. To avoid the system of monitoring becoming a purely statistical exercise, the results must be interpreted and measured against performance targets. The London Boroughs of Hackney and Lambeth were among the first social landlords to develop targets for lettings of residential accommodation. Whether or not targets are met is a useful indication of performance. Targets are *not* the same as quotas, and do not amount to positive discrimination. For further guidance see *Accounting for Equality: A Handbook on Ethnic Monitoring in Housing* (CRE, 1991).

Why monitor?

Without clear records it is virtually impossible to assess realistically whether people are being discriminated against. Before making any realistic assessment of a problem managers must be aware of its extent. Once procedures are put in hand to tackle it, it is important to judge whether they are effective. Monitoring is a good way of providing the information required for both purposes and shows an active and genuine intention to curb discrimination within an organisation. It should be seen as another management tool, approached in a low-key manner, avoiding any discussions about moral codes.

Equal opportunities training

The adoption of an equal opportunities training programme is to be encouraged in all organisations, even those that believe they do not have a problem of discrimination. As employers can be vicariously liable for the acts of employees it is essential that each and every member of staff is aware of the rules and is trained to comply with the legislation and the codes of practice. Staff need to be sensitive to different people's cultural beliefs and practices and must avoid making any assumptions based on stereotypes. They must also be taught to recognise discrimination when it arises both in themselves and others and to appreciate how the use of language can be offensive to some or misinterpreted. A routine programme of education which is ongoing can be of enormous help and ultimately illuminating.

8.
Monitoring and the Asylum and Immigration Act 1996

Who is liable? / Asylum and Immigration Act v Race Relations Act / Is the AIA retroactive?

The Asylum and Immigration Act 1996 (AIA) applies in relation only to employment. Section 8 makes it an offence for an employer to take on as an employee a person (defined as being over 16 years) who is subject to immigration control, unless he or she is specified by the AIA and regulations as being entitled to be employed. A person subject to immigration control is one who, under the Immigration Act 1971, requires leave to enter or remain in the UK. The AIA does not affect anyone who started work before 27 January 1997. Nor does it apply to the employment of:

- British citizens
- Irish citizens
- Commonwealth citizens with the right of abode in the UK
- citizens of any country in the European Economic Area and members of their family.

An employer may rely on the defence (contained in s. 8) that before he or she employed the person a document was produced which appeared to be one described by the regulations and which appeared to relate to the prospective employee. The employer must also have kept or copied the document.

Note that should it be proved that the employer, in spite of the production of the document, knew the person could not be lawfully employed, he or she falls foul of section 8.

Who is liable?

The AIA specifies that it is the employer who is liable. Where the employer is a corporate body (e.g. a local authority), any person who is responsible for overall management (and with whose consent or acquiescence the person was employed) could be prosecuted under the AIA. Also, managers could be prosecuted for failing to take steps to ensure the AIA was complied with. The manager must be involved in *overall management* to be caught by the AIA. A member of staff employed for the purpose of recruitment (e.g. a personnel officer) is not subject to prosecution.

Asylum and Immigration Act v Race Relations Act

On first reading it may appear that to comply with the AIA employers would necessarily infringe the RRA. This is not so. The AIA does not require employers to make inquiries before offering employment. Unless the employer actually knows the prospective employee cannot be lawfully employed, he or she merely needs to see (and keep or copy) one of the documents listed in the Appendix to the AIA. Aside from this there is no need to enquire into immigration status. Indeed, to do so could amount to unlawful racial discrimination.

Is the AIA retroactive?

The AIA does not operate retroactively. Accordingly, an employer need not take any action in relation to an employee who was employed before 27 January 1997. This is so even if the employee is being transferred to another post. Note that employees transferred under the Transfer of Undertakings (Protection of Employment) Rgulations 1981 (commonly referred to as TUPE) are treated as existing employees and are, therefore, outside the scope of the AIA. The TUPE Regulations safeguard existing employees' rights where the employer proposes to transfer the business or organisation.

9.

Housing Services

Provision of goods, facilities and services / Disposal
and management of premises

Provision of goods, facilities and services

It is unlawful under the SDA, RRA and DDA for anyone concerned with the provision of goods, facilities or services to
the public or a section of the public to discriminate by refusing
or deliberately omitting to provide them, by providing them
in differing quality, or by providing them in a different manner
or on different terms. It does not matter that there is no charge.
Housing services under the DDA are covered separately in
Chap. 4. This chapter deals solely with discrimination in the
provision of housing services under the RRA and the SDA.
    The Acts apply to, amongst other things:
1. access to and use of any place which members of, or a
   section of, the public are permitted to enter;
2. accommodation in an hotel, boarding-house or other
   similar establishment;
3. facilities by way of loans, credit, finance and grants;
4. facilities for education and recreation; and
5. services of any profession or trade, or any local or public
   authority.

Access to and use of public places

Public places must be accessible to all members of the public,
irrespective of sex or race. This includes access to communal

facilities on an estate such as recreation areas, laundries and meeting rooms.

Hotels and boarding-houses

These include all establishments which typically offer the services of board and lodging (e.g. bed-and-breakfast or hostel establishments used for housing the homeless). Specialist hostels which, for example, provide accommodation for special classes of person such as the disabled or the elderly may restrict themselves to people who fall within that class. They may not, however, avoid the provisions by excluding, for example, disabled people who are black.

Loans, credit, finance and grants

A person or organisation may not refuse to provide credit to a person or group by reason of sex or race. Similarly, grants must be available to all who qualify. Qualification cannot take account of sex or race. Local authorities and housing associations must take care when considering applications for financial assistance that the effect of their policies is not indirectly discriminatory.

> **Example**
>
> A local authority only approves grant funding for improvements to properties within certain geographical areas. Those areas are made up largely of owner occupiers who have purchased under the right to buy. As the majority of right-to-buy applicants are white this could be indirectly discriminatory against ethnic minority tenants.

Sections 29 of SDA and 20 of RRA do not apply where the transaction is purely private and personal in nature. Otherwise, the Acts do apply to local authorities, housing associations, private sector landlords, estate agencies, letting agencies and developers.

Disposal and management of premises

Disposal

It is unlawful for a person who has power to dispose of premises to discriminate in:

1. the terms on which he or she offers the premises for disposal;
2. rejecting or accepting applications for the premises; or
3. his or her treatment of individuals in relation to lists of people in need of that kind of premises.

'Disposal of premises' includes the sale and letting of land, houses and buildings. The definition includes non-residential accommodation such as offices and shops. It is unlawful to refuse to sell or let premises to a person because of his or her sex, race or ethnic origin. If, for example, a landlord were to take account of a person's sex in assessing the likelihood of his or her keeping up with rent payments and thereby refuses to let the premises, the landlord is acting unlawfully.

Furthermore, the *terms* on which premises are sold or let must not be discriminatory. For example, it would be unlawful to require a single male tenant to pay a damage deposit if a single woman would not, or a woman tenant to provide a rent guarantor if a male tenant would not. The physical condition of a property is included as a term of the letting, so, for example, it would be unlawful for local authorities only to allocate hard-to-let properties to black families.

> ### Examples
>
> A housing association offers to redecorate, free of charge, those premises into which a current tenant is being transferred. The same service is not offered to those transferring from temporary accommodation. This could indirectly discriminate against black families who make up a higher proportion of those living in temporary accommodation.
>
> In 1983 the London Borough of Southwark decided to rehouse a group of residents of one estate into a new

development (of much better quality accommodation) just completed. Of the tenants on that estate 95 per cent were white, and those being rehoused were almost exclusively white. The general population of Southwark included 26 per cent ethnic minorities. The new-build estate represented 50 per cent of the new-build properties in Southwark. The CRE investigated Southwark's rehousing scheme and found that the effect of the agreement to rehouse the residents of one particular estate in this way was to deny other persons the opportunity of being offered a new property. Since a considerable number of these other people were black, the policy was unlawfully discriminatory. (See *Out of Order: A Report of a Formal Investigation into the London Borough of Southwark* (CRE, 1990).)

Where a tenant requires consent to dispose of premises, a landlord is not permitted to withhold consent to their disposal on grounds of sex or race. This applies to requests for consent to assign, sublet or part with possession of the premises (SDA, s. 31; RRA, s. 24). Therefore, it is unlawful for a landlord to refuse consent to sublet because, say, the intended subtenant is black.

The terms on which consent is given must also apply equally to all applications regardless of sex or race. The above applies to tenancies created before and after the coming into force of the Acts, but not to small premises.

Management

It is unlawful for any person managing premises to discriminate:

1. in the manner in which a person is to make use of facilities or benefits;
2. by refusing or deliberately not allowing a person to make use of facilities or benefits; or
3. by eviction or subjection to any other detriment.

> **Example**
>
> Indian families are precluded from cooking curries in the communal kitchen as other occupiers complain of the smell. This is discriminatory in that the Indian family is not afforded the same access to and use of cooking facilities.

Planning functions

Section 55 of the Housing and Planning Act 1986 amended the RRA to make it unlawful for a planning authority to discriminate against a person in carrying out their planning functions (RRA, s. 19A). Those functions are described by reference to the planning legislation, which include:
- applications for planning permission
- preparation of development plans
- enforcement of planning controls.

Exceptions

Discrimination is not unlawful where a person:
1. with power to dispose of premises also owns an estate or interest in them and occupies them (provided he or she does not use an estate agent or other professional for the purpose of disposing of or advertising them);
2. providing accommodation, or a near relative of his or hers, lives and intends to continue to live on the premises, and shares accommodation (other than storage accommodation or means of access) with other persons living there, who are not members of his or her household, and the premises are small.

Acts done under statutory authority

An act which amounts to unlawful discrimination may nevertheless be outside the scope of the Acts if it is done pursuant to, for example, an Act of Parliament or statutory instrument. The Acts provide a general exception to acts done under 'statutory authority' (SDA, s. 51(1); RRA, s. 41(1)). 'Statutory authority' is derived from:

1. any enactment or order in council; or
2. any instrument made under any enactment by a Minister of the Crown; or
3. any condition or requirement imposed by a Minister of the Crown by virtue of any enactment.

The provisions of SDA and RRA contain important differences, however, in relation to the extent of the defence. Under the SDA the defence applies only in relation to acts done pursuant to acts or instruments passed before the SDA (i.e. before 12 November 1975). The RRA provision, however, applies to all enactments, instruments, and orders in council, whether enacted before or after the commencement of the RRA.

Extent of the defence

Acts of a statutory body or authority which are protected by sections 51 of SDA and 41 of RRA are not confined solely to acts *required* to be done because of an express obligation contained in a statute. Conversely, the protection does not extend to all acts simply because the statutory body has *power* to do them. It depends on the application of the particular statute to the particular act in question. For example, an act which is done in performance of a specific duty (e.g. a local authority's duty to house a homeless person who qualifies under the Housing Act 1996) is done in pursuance of the Housing Act and is therefore protected.

Example

A woman of Hong Kong Chinese origin who qualified as a teacher in Hong Kong came to England hoping to continue her teaching career. However, she was refused the necessary accreditation to teach in English schools on the grounds that her training in Hong Kong was not comparable to that of English teachers whose qualifications were subject to approval by the Secretary of State. The Court of Appeal, in dismissing her claim, considered whether the defence of statutory authority covered the circumstances of this case and held that the regulations required the Secretary of State to either approve or disapprove an applicant's teacher training course. Accordingly, whichever decision he made would be made 'in pursuance of' those regulations and was not unlawful. *Hampson v Department of Education and Science* (1990)

10.
Housing Allocation and Homelessness

Eligibility / Homelessness and intentionality / Discharge / Local authorities / Housing associations / The allocation process / Segregation

The law of allocations is generally outside the scope of this book. Below, however, are some issues which may raise questions relating to treatment of persons from different backgrounds and races, where discrimination may be more likely to arise. For further discussion see, for example, Arden & Hunter, *Homelessness and Allocations* (5th edn) and H. Pawson *et al*, *The Allocation of Social Housing* (Arden's Housing Library, 2000). This chapter deals first with local authorities in relation to homelessness and allocation, and then with registered social landlords and their selection of tenants.

Eligibility

Part VII of HA 1996 introduced a statutory concept of eligibility for housing assistance. To be eligible, a person must not be excluded by the Act. The Act prescribes certain categories of person who are ineligible to receive the benefit of any function (under Part VII) which relates to accommodation or assistance in obtaining accommodation (HA 1996, s. 183(2)). Ineligible persons may, however, receive advice and assistance from an advisory service (s. 183(3)).

Persons from abroad

Persons from abroad are, generally, ineligible for housing. They are divided into groups depending on whether they are subject to immigration control.

Those subject to immigration control

The main group of disqualified persons are those subject to immigration control. A person is subject to immigration control, under section 13(2) of AIA, if he or she is a person requiring leave (under the Immigration Act 1971) to enter or remain in the UK. This applies whether or not leave has been given. According to the 1971 Act, everyone other than British citizens and specified commonwealth citizens with the right of abode requires leave to enter. (See below with regard to European Economic Area nationals.)

Certain persons subject to immigration control have been *re-included* by the Homelessness Regulations 1996:

1. refugees;
2. asylum seekers making a claim on arrival;
3. asylum seekers making a claim after arrival where the Secretary of State has made a declaration;
4. asylum seekers making a claim before 4 February 1996 who were entitled to housing benefit when claiming;
5. persons who have been granted exceptional leave to enter or remain, not subject to maintenance and accommodation conditions;
6. persons with current leave to enter or remain, not subject to any limitation or condition and who are habitually resident in the common travel area;
7. persons who are nationals of a state which is a signatory to the European Convention on Social and Medical Assistance or the Council of Europe Social Charter who are habitually resident in the common travel area; and
8. persons who are on an income-based Jobseekers' Allowance or in receipt of Income Support.

Those not subject to immigration control

There are persons from abroad who are not subject to immigration control (e.g. European Economic Area nationals). EEA nationals and their families are entitled to enter subject only to producing an identity card or passport proving membership of an EEA country.

The Secretary of State has declared certain other groups to be ineligible for housing assistance; these groups comprise:

1. those habitually resident within the common travel area who are, generally, eligible save for any requirement to leave the United Kingdom imposed by the Secretary of State (e.g. for reasons of national security); and
2. those not habitually resident within the common travel area who are, generally, ineligible save for re-inclusion by the Secretary of State (e.g. European Community 'workers').

'Habitual residence' is a question of fact and law and must be determined in light of all the circumstances of an individual case (see the DoE/DoH *Code of Guidance on the Housing Act 1996*). The main factors to be taken into account are:

- employment stability (e.g. permanent job v casual work)
- the nature of occupation (e.g. civil servant v seasonal worker)
- family ties and interests
- the reason for coming to the UK
- the length and continuity of residence elsewhere
- the claimant's intentions.

The House of Lords considered the meaning of 'habitual residence' in the context of entitlement to social security benefits in *Nessa v Chief Adjudication Officer* (1999). The court decided that a person who arrived in the United Kingdom with the intention of settling there did not become habitually resident from the moment of arrival, but that in order to qualify for assistance the applicant had to have taken up residence and lived in the United Kingdom for a period which showed that his or her residence was in fact 'habitual'.

In *Swaddling v Adjudication Officer* (1999), however, the European Court of Justice applied a different test, which had a Community-wide meaning. It stated that in determining whether the habitual residence requirement had been satisfied, account should be taken of the following:

- the applicant's family situation;
- the reasons which had led him or her to move;
- the length and continuity of his or her residence;
- whether he or she was in stable employment; and
- his or her intention as it appeared in all the circumstances.

The length of residence, though, could not be regarded as an intrinsic element of the concept of residence.

If the authority decides the claimant is not habitually resident the claimant may request a review of that decision, which could then be the subject of an appeal to the county court (see HA 1996, ss. 202–204).

European Community workers

Article 48 of the Treaty of Rome confers on all workers the right to move freely between all EC member states. The basic right is added to by Regulations (EC Regulation 1612/68). The right to move freely includes the right to take up an activity as an employed person within the territory of another member state. A worker is entitled to the rights and benefits accorded to national workers in terms of housing. The worker must have available to him or her, and to his or her family, housing which is of a kind considered 'normal for national workers in the region' where he or she is employed. Accordingly, EC workers were expressly re-included as eligible persons for the purposes of Part VII of HA 1996.

A 'worker' is a person who performs services for another, under his or her direction, for a certain period of time in return for remuneration. It includes part-time employment.

Former workers who entered the territory of another member state as a worker have the right to remain provided:

1. they have reached retirement age, having worked for the previous 12 months and resided in that state for more than three years; or
2. they have ceased to work owing to permanent incapacity and had resided in that state for at least two years (if the incapacity arises from an accident at work or occupational disease, the two-year requirement is disapplied); or
3. those who take up employment in another member state but remain resident have three years' continuous employment in the state in which they reside.

Once a worker obtains a residence permit it may not be withdrawn. See further Council Directive No. 68/360/EEC.

Rights and benefits

The rights and benefits to which the worker is entitled include housing benefit if he or she complies with the relevant criteria, and any other right or benefit afforded to nationals. Once a worker becomes habitually resident he or she will also then become entitled to housing assistance.

Dependants of persons from abroad

Under section 185(4) of HA 1996 persons from abroad who are ineligible under the section are disregarded when deciding what duty is owed to someone else who is an eligible person. For example, if a person from abroad lives with an eligible person, that does not deprive the eligible person of his or her eligible status (i.e. he or she remains eligible under HA 1996). This also means, however, that an applicant with no priority need cannot acquire priority through a dependant who is ineligible.

Example

A single man in good health who is eligible for assistance but is not in priority need is not owed the full

> housing duty. His dependent partner, who is entitled
> to reside with him, is in priority need and would there-
> fore be entitled to assistance if eligible. The eligible
> man cannot rely on his partner's priority need because
> she is ineligible for assistance under the HA 1996.

Furthermore, questions involving suitability of accommodation are also decided without reference to the needs of an ineligible person, even if dependent on the eligible person.

Likewise, an eligible applicant who is in priority need but has no local connection cannot rely on residence in the area with the ineligible person for the purpose of establishing a local connection.

Asylum-seekers

A person from abroad may also be an asylum-seeker. If not ineligible for assistance under section 185 of HA 1996, his or her entitlement may nonetheless be restricted by virtue of section 186(1), which provides:

> An asylum-seeker, or a dependant of an asylum-seeker who is not by virtue of section 185 a person from abroad who is ineligible for housing assistance, is not eligible for assistance under this Part if he has any accommodation in the United Kingdom, however temporary, available for his occupation.

It is essential to determine which section applies. It depends on whether the applicant made the claim for asylum at the point of entry, rather than after entry, and whether the claim has been refused. If the claim has been refused it makes no difference that the decision is subject to appeal.

Information

Authorities are entitled, when considering applications for assistance, to make enquiries of the immigration authorities and of the Secretary of State. They may also (without breaching confidence) supply the immigration authorities with information they have gathered. In fact, *R v Westminster City Council, ex p Castelli and Tristan-Garcia* (1996) held that the local housing authority was under a duty to report suspected illegal immigrants. (See further Arden & Hunter, *Homelessness and Allocations* (5th edn).)

Homelessness and intentionality

When is an applicant homeless?

A person is homeless if he or she has no accommodation which is available for his or her occupation and which it is reasonable for him or her to continue to occupy. If the applicant has accommodation anywhere in the world which otherwise satisfies the test he or she is not homeless within HA 1996 and authorities have no duty to house him or her.

'Available for occupation' means available to the applicant together with any person who normally resides with him or her as a member of his or her family, or any other person who might reasonably be expected to do so, for example carers, foster children and housekeepers (HA 1996, s. 176). A member of the family who normally resides with the applicant need not do so reasonably (e.g. a daughter may reside with the applicant even if she would not normally expect to reside with him or her). If another person wishes to join the applicant it must be shown that it would be reasonable for that person to expect to live with the applicant. While that is a matter for the housing authority to decide, it is open to challenge on ordinary principles of public law (e.g. irrationality—see J. Manning, *Judicial Review Proceedings* (1st edn)).

Housing officers considering such issues must be aware of cultural differences which may impact on reasonableness; for example, some cultures attach great importance to the cohesion of the family unit, including in-laws, who may adopt specific and important roles within the family.

'Reasonable to continue' to occupy must be looked at in light of all the surrounding circumstances. It is not reasonable to continue to occupy accommodation if it is probable that it will lead to violence or threats of violence likely to be carried out against the applicant or a person who resides (or might be expected to reside) with him or her, from a person with whom the applicant or such other person is associated (HA 1996, s. 177(1)). A neighbour is not included in the term 'person associated'. If an occupier, however, is subject to racial harassment or abuse by neighbours it may not be reasonable for him or her to continue to occupy that accommodation (see DoE/DoH *Code of Guidance on the Housing Act 1996*).

The physical conditions of the accommodation which is currently occupied must also be considered. Depending on the circumstances, it may be relevant to consider religious requirements such as male and female sharing arrangements. For example, to some people it is unacceptable because of strict religious rules for male and female children of the same sex, over a certain age, to share sleeping accommodation. This may make it unreasonable for one family to remain in accommodation where it would not be unreasonable for other families. It is the particular circumstances of the applicant and his or her family that are relevant.

> ### Example
>
> A woman who lived in Ghana in the matrimonial home came to England following the breakdown of her marriage. The authority considered it would have been reasonable for her to remain in the matrimonial home. In England a former spouse has certain rights of occupation. The authority had been given no information about Ghanaian domestic law which suggested the position was any different there. Note, however, that the authority, if presented with information that the applicant had no rights to remain, should have considered what alternatives were open to her under Ghanaian law.

Intentional homelessness

Even if an applicant is homeless and in priority need, he or she is entitled to housing if he or she has deliberately done or failed to do something the direct consequence of which has made him or her homeless. It is the applicant's conduct that is relevant. The applicant's intentionality also taints the application of another member of that household if that person acquiesced in the conduct. This may arise if a husband has been intentionally homeless and his wife makes a separate application. Whether or not she acquiesced is a matter for the authority.

The authority, however, must take account of all relevant circumstances, which may include cultural mores. For example, in some societies women are subservient to their husbands and are not invited or expected to take any active part in decision-making. Many women simply follow their husbands with no knowledge of the basis for his decisions. In such circumstances the authority should consider whether that particular woman could be said to have been party to the decision to quit accommodation. Assumptions should not be made without further investigation. In *R v Tower Hamlets LBC, ex p Khatun* (1995), however, a similar argument failed on behalf of a Bangladeshi wife who was held to have been content to leave decisions to her husband and had assisted in implementing those decisions. It is a matter of degree.

Discharge

Applications

Part VII of HA 1996 imposes various duties on local authorities to *inter alia*:

- conduct enquiries into an application for assistance;
- reach a decision on that application and notify it to the applicant; and
- secure that accommodation is made available to a person to whom a duty is owed.

Every application for assistance made by a person who may be homeless must be adjudicated fairly and without discrimination.

Enquiries

On receiving an application which, on its face, gives the authority reason to believe that the applicant is either homeless or threatened with homelessness, it must conduct enquiries (HA 1996, s. 184(1)). Those enquiries must be sufficient to satisfy the authority of whether the applicant is eligible for assistance. If the authority is so satisfied, it must also make enquiries to establish if a duty is owed to that applicant and, if so, what duty. It is for the authority to decide how the necessary enquiries should be made, who should interview, and which questions should be asked. It is essential that housing officers and managers are aware of the potential to make certain assumptions about people because of their race, colour etc. This is particularly true when investigating an applicant's eligibility (see p. 86 above). Questions should be asked sensitively and with an open mind. If there is any possibility of misunderstanding, the applicant must be allowed to clarify.

In conducting its enquiries the authority must act in a caring and sympathetic way (paragraph 11.12 of the DoE/DoH *Code of Guidance on the Housing Act 1996*, Parts VI and VII). The officer responsible should always be aware of potential inconsistencies arising owing to language difficulties. Access to competent interpreters should be ensured (para. 11.3 of the DoE/DoH Code). In particular, an authority must be aware of the different languages spoken within its area and make provision for them.

Securing accommodation

The ways in which an authority discharges its duty to secure available accommodation depend on a number of factors, the most important of which is the applicant's status. The provisions governing discharge are set out in Part VII of HA 1996. They are not repeated here. The provisions of the anti-discrimination legislation are relevant to the manner in which the authority seeks to discharge its duty.

> ### *Example*
>
> In 1988 the CRE published a report on homelessness and discrimination in Tower Hamlets LBC. The report followed a CRE investigation into alleged discrimination against Bangladeshis. The investigation was prompted by the growing problem of homelessness among the Bangladeshi community in Tower Hamlets and the authority's apparent inability or reluctance to deal with the problem (Inquiry into homelessness and discrimination). The investigation related to four main areas of housing provision:
>
> 1.   The treatment of council tenants forced to leave their homes because of fire, flood or other emergency.
>
> 2.   The treatment of homeless families and the allocation of poor quality temporary accommodation to Bangladeshi families.
>
> 3.   The treatment of applicants on the housing waiting list whose dependants were waiting overseas to be reunited.
>
> 4.   The disproportionate allocation of Bangladeshi applicants to worst quality housing estates.
>
> At the end of its investigation the CRE found the authority to have unlawfully discriminated against a number of individuals on grounds of race. One of its findings related to the length of time a Bangladeshi family spent in temporary accommodation pending a permanent offer being made following a fire at the family's council flat. It was found that the family had to wait significantly longer for a permanent offer than other families, without justification.
>
> The CRE also found that the authority indirectly discriminated against Bangladeshi families on grounds of race in its treatment of separated families in need of accommodation. The authority had a policy of awarding extra points to families separated owing to lack of accommodation which was available for them to share. This policy was not applied, however, to

families where some members were separated over-
seas. The CRE's concern arose from the fact that a
large proportion of Bangladeshi men had lived and
worked in Tower Hamlets while supporting their
families back in Bangladesh. When such a man applied for housing to enable his family to join him the
authority placed his application on a non-active waiting list which received no consideration until the family
had actually arrived in the country. Since most men
occupied single bedsits or rooms the family's arrival
necessarily resulted in homelessness. If, however, the
family had been separated in the UK the application
was given immediate priority points according to the
whole family's housing needs.

Local authority allocation of accommodation

Local authorities hold the vast majority of their stock under
Part II of the HA 1985. Under this Act the only constraint on
the allocation of housing was section 22, which required local
authorities to give preference to specified groups (e.g. the
homeless). Some viewed this mandatory prioritisation of
particular groups to be unfair. The HA 1996 sought to redress
the perceived imbalance by the introduction of Part VI, which
applies both to the allocation of local authority stock and to
nominations to other landlords, and provides quite tight rules
for the allocation of housing stock. Local authorities do,
however, retain a certain degree of discretion in making their
allocation decisions. So long as Part VI is complied with, a
local authority may allocate housing in such manner as it
considers appropriate.

'Allocation' is the selection of a person to become a
secure tenant or licensee. Allocation includes the nomination
of a person to be the secure tenant or licensee of, for example,
a housing action trust, and an assured tenant of a housing
association. There are exempt categories specified by sections
160 and 161 of HA 1996.

Qualifying persons

An allocation can only be made to a 'qualifying person' (HA 1996, s. 161). Some persons are expressly disqualified, such as those subject to immigration control (s. 161(2)), or not subject to immigration control but not habitually resident in the common travel area and who do not fall within the category of EC workers, and cannot be granted a tenancy or licence (see p. 87 above). In this way certain groups must be discriminated against as a matter of national law and are not protected by the RRA.

The Secretary of State may prescribe those persons who are qualifying persons (HA 1996, s. 161(3)). Those classes can be found in the various Regulations (e.g. Allocation of Housing Regulations 1996). Local authorities may also decide what classes of person are qualifying persons (s. 161(4)).

> ### Example
>
> A local authority housing officer believes that immigrants from Pakistan who had been living in sub-standard accommodation in Pakistan would be more comfortable in hard-to-let dilapidated properties than white applicants moving from within England. This is discriminatory and unlawful.

Are residential requirements ever lawful?

One form of qualifying condition for housing may be a residence requirement. Housing authorities often argue that a residence requirement as a precondition to allocation is essential if they are to fulfil their obligations to persons in need of accommodation within their area. Ethnic minorities are, as a matter of fact, less able to comply with such requirements. Whether those requirements can be objectively justified depends on their purpose and effect. In particular, consideration is given to whether the aim of the requirement is a reasonable, fair and objective one and whether there is an alternative, less discriminatory way of achieving the same purpose.

Housing associations: selection of tenants

Housing associations are primarily voluntary in nature. Unlike local authorities, they are not under any direct statutory obligation to provide any particular housing. An obligation to meet housing need, however, flows from registration with the Housing Corporation for the receipt of grant funding. Registration may limit the permissible objects of the association to prescribed housing (e.g. special needs, black housing).

The HA 1996 introduced provisions regulating the allocation of housing by local authorities, a high percentage of which is by way of nomination to housing associations. The housing association movement has become a major player in the provision of social housing and is well placed to exert a positive influence on the promotion of racial and sexual equality.

Housing associations are also responsible for selecting their own tenants. Associations maintain housing waiting lists in much the same way as (and sometimes in common with) local authorities. Entry onto the list is governed by policy, usually to do with housing need. The decision to accept or reject someone may be taken by an individual without much opportunity to challenge the decision.

Once accepted onto the list there is then a second stage whereby each applicant is prioritised, often based on specific needs criteria. When determining priority, social landlords must have regard to the Housing Corporation's procedural requirements, one of which is publication of the allocation policy which covers eligibility and determination of priority. Priority should be given to those most in need and take account of four basic criteria: existing (and future) housing conditions; the applicant's ability to cope with those conditions; the length of time the applicant has already had to cope with those conditions; and other options which may be available to the applicant. The policy should also describe allocation of accommodation by size and type and how requests for transfers are dealt with.

As with other landlords, housing associations must not unlawfully discriminate on the basis of race or sex. The Housing Corporation's *Performance Standards* require wider considerations to be taken into account in the selection of tenants:

> Registered housing associations will be required to comply with the code of practice on race relations in the field of housing ... Associations should also conform with best practice to avoid any kind of discrimination and to promote equality of opportunity both in access to accommodation and the provision of services to all members of the community who may be disadvantaged by race, sex or disability.

The Corporation also requires that, for the purpose of access to sheltered accommodation, there must be a common qualifying age for men and women.

The Corporation advises that if associations discover as a result of their ethnic monitoring that fewer people from ethnic minorities are taking up tenancies than would be expected, given the make-up of the local population, they should take positive action to redress the imbalance.

The allocation process

This is perhaps the most important function of any housing organisation. It is this process which governs access to housing. Everyone appreciates that demand for some housing far outweighs supply and decisions have to be made at various stages about who should be allocated this scarce resource. Because of the very nature of the allocation process, those making decisions are subject to criticism of partiality and favouritism. Housing managers must be aware at each and every stage of their obligations under the legislation and ensure, as best they can, that they are not found to be in contravention of the RRA, the SDA, the DDA and the related codes of practice.

Those who are eligible for assistance must first be made aware of the options open to them. Housing organisations

provide information on their services and advertise themselves in different ways. Some organisations advertise through
the local press and care must be exercised that such advertisements are not discriminatory (see p. 41 above). It should be
remembered that many people who would be eligible for housing assistance do not speak English. If advertisements and
information are provided solely in English, or solely in English
language newspapers, the organisation is failing to reach a
large proportion of potential tenants and is possibly perpetu-
ating the exclusion of some racial groups from social housing.

Some organisations, especially housing co-operatives
and housing associations, rely on word of mouth. This can
produce discriminatory results if those passing on the information to others are predominantly of one racial or sexual group.

Enquiries

At the initial enquiry stage an applicant may be interviewed
or asked to fill in a standard application form. The outcome
of this enquiry is important in determining an applicant's
chances of obtaining housing. The way in which these
enquiries are carried out can have discriminatory effects.

> **Example**
>
> A housing association requires everyone to fill in a
> standard form. Those applicants who categorise them-
> selves as Pakistanis are then called for an interview
> and subject to further questioning. Other applicants
> are not interviewed in this way. To distinguish between
> groups on grounds of race in the way in which they
> are considered for housing is discriminatory and
> unlawful.

Assessment

The preliminary enquiries are then assessed. Some organisations adopt a rigid points system depending on level of need.
Others may adopt a less formal approach which take account

of less objective factors such as ability to cope with present housing conditions. Both systems have potential for discriminating, particularly if factors which are open to discretionary interpretation are taken into account.

> ### Example
>
> A housing officer visits a Bangladeshi family at home in their current private sector accommodation. The family complains of overcrowding. Using objective criteria the family would be awarded 20 points for the overcrowding. The housing officer, however, takes account of general living standards in Bangladesh and concludes that Bangladeshi immigrants do not suffer the same effects as people born in Great Britain because 'they are used to it'. This assessment is based on stereotyping and assumptions, and is unlawful discrimination.

Waiting lists

Most social landlords organise allocations by means of a waiting list. The way the list operates may be discriminatory in effect and housing managers must be aware of potential difficulties. People can be housed directly from the waiting list into the landlord's own property or, if the landlord is a local authority, may be nominated to another RSL.

   If a social landlord has a waiting list for accommodation, it is unlawful to discriminate against any person because of their sex, race, ethnic origin or disability in operating that list (e.g. by placing certain racial groups automatically at the bottom of the list). The time spent on a waiting list is determined by a number of factors which themselves depend on the policy of the housing organisation operating the list. A common way of operating a list is to afford applicants a degree of relative priority depending on the assessment of their particular needs. Applicants may be given points according to their priority and thereby accelerate up the list faster than other applicants. The points scheme necessarily involves an element of subjective assessment, but must operate fairly and must not discriminate either directly or indirectly against anyone because of their sex, race, colour or ethnic origin. Waiting lists are dealt with in more detail at Chapter 3 above.

> **Example**
>
> A social landlord awards 20 priority points to single mothers but only 5 priority points to single fathers. Single fathers are necessarily further down the waiting list and have to wait a longer period of time before being accommodated. This is discriminatory and unlawful.

Discrimination can arise not only in the way in which a landlord allocates its own housing, but also in the way nominations are made. The power of a local authority to nominate is a facilitation of access to benefits, facilities or services within the RRA provided by housing associations (the actual providers of the services etc.). An example of this is the unlawful, indirect discrimination by Liverpool City Council against black people on its waiting list in relation to allocation of new-build properties (see pp. 35–36 above).

Allocating particular premises

Once an applicant is accepted for housing he or she must then be found a suitable vacant property. Again, decisions about suitability of accommodation must be made according to criteria which do not permit stereotyping or assumptions to be made according to racial or sexual characteristics. It is also unlawful to refuse to accommodate a family in housing which was available and suitable for them because of pressure applied by other residents in the area.

> **Examples**
>
> Housing officers interviewing applicants for housing assume all Indian applicants would wish to live on

estates having Indians as the majority of residents. As a result the applicant is not considered for housing available on a mostly white estate. This is discriminatory and unlawful.

A housing association managed a number of hostels for refugees. A complaint was made that the association was not housing people of Afro-Caribbean origin in a particular hostel because the residents (who at that time happened to be Vietnamese) 'did not like coloured people'. The association had unlawfully discriminated against Afro-Caribbean people.

Quality of housing

It is unlawful to discriminate on racial or sexual grounds in the relative quality of the accommodation that is provided. This is particularly relevant to those social landlords with a large housing stock and a wide range of properties available to it.

Example

A local authority awards points to every applicant applying for housing. Those who currently occupy local authority accommodation are given priority points for transfer and are therefore more likely to be transferred to the better quality accommodation. Homeless applicants receive fewer points and are allocated the hard-to-let properties. This is indirectly discriminatory if, for example, those currently occupying local authority accommodation are predominantly white and those homeless applicants on the waiting list are predominantly black. Note that if this can be justified for reasons other than race then it may be lawful.

Preferences

Most housing providers give applicants some opportunity to choose the type of property which they want or the area in which they live. If the housing organisation only gives this choice, or information about the options available, to certain groups (e.g. those who have resided in the area for a number of years) this could amount to unlawful discrimination.

Number of offers made

Many housing organisations have a policy of making a limited number of offers to any one applicant (e.g. applicants applying for a transfer from one local authority house to another may be made five offers of transfer, yet new applicants are made one offer only). This is indirectly discriminatory if those applying for accommodation are predominantly black, while those applying for transfers are predominantly white.

Segregation

According to section 1(2) of RRA, to segregate one person (or group of persons) from others on racial grounds is to treat that person less favourably than others, and is unlawful. To permit people to form their own groups does not, however, amount to segregation and is therefore not unlawful.

11.
Dealing with Harassment

What is harassment? / Dealing with incidents of harassment / Action against perpetrators / Criminal sanctions / Procedural model for dealing with harassment

A 'deliberate omission' can amount to an act of unlawful discrimination (SDA, s. 82(1); RRA, s. 78(1)). Accordingly, a complaint may be made against a landlord who deliberately fails to take action on a claim of harassment because of the complainant's sex or race. For example, if a landlord receives a complaint that one family is harassing another in breach of their tenancy agreement because of their race or colour, and the landlord fails to take any action because of shared prejudice or fear of upsetting a group of like-minded tenants, the landlord is acting unlawfully.

The *way* in which a housing organisation deals with complaints of harassment may also be discriminatory. For example, a landlord who reacts to reports of racial harassment by moving the victims against their choice to poorer quality accommodation, leaving the perpetrators where they are, is treating people differently on grounds of race in resolving the harassment.

This chapter discusses the variety of options available for dealing with perpetrators, the formulation of harassment policy, and the practical aspects of dealing with complaints of harassment. Social landlords have many possible courses of action open to them, such as taking possession proceedings (against the perpetrator on the ground of nuisance and annoyance to neighbours), mediation, injunctions and criminal prosecution. See further C. Hunter and K. Bretherton, *Antisocial Behaviour* (Arden's Housing Library, 1998).

The general public duties imposed on local authorities and housing associations to combat racial harassment and discrimination are discussed in Chap. 6.

What is harassment?

'Harassment' is not expressly recognised in the principal Acts, but victims of racial and sexual harassment are afforded some protection.

Sexual harassment

'Harassment' is not in the SDA, but in *Wileman v Minilec Engineering* (1988), the court held that it was 'legal shorthand for an activity which is easily recognisable as subjecting [a person] to any other detriment' under the SDA to amount to 'less favourable treatment' under the SDA. To establish a claim based on sexual harassment, it must be shown that the man or woman is disadvantaged because of his or her sex in a way in which someone of the other sex would not be so vulnerable.

Physical contact or verbal abuse which is of a sexual nature comes within the definition of unfavourable treatment. Injury to feelings is sufficient detriment for the purposes of the Act.

Racial harassment

A person who is subjected to a detriment, being abusive and offensive behaviour, which places them under a disadvantage because of their race, colour or ethnic origin, is racially harassed. It is essential when considering the definition of racial harassment that account is taken of how the victim views the harassment. A racial motive can often be hidden from the impassive observer.

The CRE has issued a *Code of Statutory Guidance* which should be complied with by local authorities and housing associations. The Code emphasises the need for social landlords to ensure they have a policy for reacting to racial harassment and to take action whenever it is appropriate. Further, local authorities, by virtue of section 71 of RRA, have a statutory duty to take steps to deal with racial harassment effectively. It is, therefore, essential that all social landlords and housing managers ensure they have a comprehensive policy and strategy for dealing with complaints (see further below).

Motive

It can be difficult to distinguish between harassment which amounts to discrimination and which is unlawful because it is as a result of sexual or racial prejudice, and harassment which arises independently of such prejudice.

> **Example**
>
> A landlord who harasses his or her tenant to make him or her give up their premises (the intention being to sell the property) has not unlawfully discriminated against the tenant.

Dealing with incidents of harassment

Harassment in and around the home continues to cause concern to social landlords and housing managers. This is a most serious problem as it affects a person's feeling of personal security and undermines the victim's sense of safety and well-being. It is a fundamental right of every person to peacefully enjoy his or her own home and its environs and particularly to feel secure and protected within his or her four walls.

Policy

Social landlords formulating policy for dealing with racial harassment should consult the CRE and EOC guidelines. The key elements which should be covered in a policy include:

- defining harassment in a meaningful way that is easily understood
- provision of support for those experiencing harassment
- an effective strategy of dealing with perpetrators
- liaison with other agencies and groups
- preventative action
- monitoring.

Information and support

Many victims of harassment do not make complaints. This can be for a number of reasons. It is essential, therefore, that tenants are informed of the landlord's harassment policy. They must be made to feel that a complaint will be sensitively received and taken seriously. The publication of the policy document in different languages is essential, as is the advertisement of persons and agencies who are available to victims. Tenants must be educated and encouraged to use the complaints procedure and staff trained to pass on complaints to the appropriate person or agency.

Often, evidence of harassment comes to light when a tenant makes an application for a transfer. Sometimes this is not expressed to be the cause of the request; rather, it is attributed to neighbour nuisance or simply a desire to leave the area. Housing managers who receive such requests must be alert to indirect or oblique evidence of harassment. It has been said that tenants wishing a transfer make spurious complaints of harassment in order to prioritise their application. In fact, the statistical evidence suggests the position is rather the opposite—that racial harassment tends to be under-reported.

Anyone who does make a complaint must be given support, reassurance and kept informed of progress and whatever subsequent steps the landlord or manager proposes to take. A victim of harassment may feel ostracised and isolated. It is the duty of housing managers to include him or her in the decision-making process and keep him or her updated.

Investigation

Every complaint, whether reported by the victim, indirectly through neighbours, the police or other agencies, must be thoroughly investigated. It is good practice to follow the same procedure regardless of the source of the information. There should be a common starting point with all complaints channelled through an appropriate named officer. That officer must decide, after an initial investigation, whether using the harassment policy is the appropriate course. To assist officers in this determination, examples of harassment should be included in the policy document and, ideally, members of staff would receive training in identifying racial harassment.

The victim should be interviewed as soon as possible to build up a picture of the harassment as he or she sees it. At this stage it is important that the victim is assumed to be telling the truth. It is all too easy to appear sceptical or judgemental about the likelihood of the alleged harassment.

The investigating officer should then compile a report for consideration by senior officers or managers who may then make a recommendation. Throughout the procedure, monitoring must continue. It is often worth approaching the perpetrator direct as this can be sufficient to put an end to the harassment. If not, then housing officers must decide what action to take.

Action

Once satisfied that a tenant is experiencing harassment, the social landlord should take action either by itself or together with the police. A harassment victim should not normally be left to take his or her own action.

Before formal action is taken, a warning letter should be sent to the alleged perpetrator inviting him or her to respond to the allegations and provide assurances that such behaviour will not continue. If this does not work, formal legal action can be considered. Legal remedies are considered in more detail below.

Liaison with the Commissions

The CRE and EOC are very keen to assist housing organisations to better manage cases of harassment and may intervene with tenants who are perpetrating harassment.

> **Example**
>
> Racial harassment and violence was common on an estate in Tower Hamlets. There were reports of hostile 'reception committees' and physical attacks on Asians. In one incident, a house which had been viewed by an Asian family (who were being rehoused as a result of racial harassment) was vandalised. The GLC referred to the Commission the fact that various tenants had petitioned the council and threatened to carry on the racial attacks if more Asian families were accommodated there. The CRE took the tenants to court and obtained undertakings from them that they would desist from applying pressure to the council. Breach of such an undertaking may result in imprisonment.

Action against perpetrators

Most people agree that action should be taken against perpetrators of racial or sexual harassment. People are less united, however, about what should be done with them. Some incidents of harassment involve attacks which amount to criminal offences. In those situations the best organisation to deal with it is the police, yet they have been subject to some criticism in the past over their reluctance to become involved. Local authorities also have obligations to victims of harassment, yet they have also been criticised for failing to adopt effective policies on harassment. Local authorities, however, were not until recently equipped to deal effectively with perpetrators. The HA 1996 has gone some way to providing them with a coherent scheme for tackling harassment. The scheme is set out in the following paragraphs.

Possession proceedings

Social landlords may take possession proceedings against perpetrators of harassment where warning letters have not worked and the evidence is sufficiently clear. Local authorities and housing associations may take proceedings for possession on the ground of breach of tenancy agreement if there is a clause forbidding nuisance or harassment, or may rely on Ground 2 of Schedule 2 to HA 1985, as amended by HA 1996 (if the tenant is secure), or Ground 14 of Schedule 2 to HA 1988 (if the tenant is assured). The wording of both grounds is identical and are considered together.

If a tenant or a person living in *or visiting* the premises is guilty of conduct causing or likely to cause a nuisance or annoyance to anyone living in, visiting or otherwise engaging in any lawful activity in the locality, this forms the basis of a ground of possession against the tenant. The enlargement of these grounds to include visitors is of great assistance to social landlords managing estates. Housing officers formerly experienced difficulties obtaining possession against secure tenants where that particular tenant was not causing a nuisance him- or herself, but his or her premises were a meeting point or focus for others who did cause a nuisance. Possession can now be sought where their present or past conduct has caused a nuisance or is *likely to* cause a nuisance. This means that third parties who witness a nuisance being caused to others may be relied upon to give evidence in proving the claim for possession. It is notoriously difficult to persuade harassment victims to give evidence in court against the perpetrator. It is no longer essential that the victim give evidence of actual nuisance or annoyance; instead, a housing officer or estate manager, for example, may give evidence of conduct likely to cause a nuisance to reasonable people.

Another important extension to these grounds is that the nuisance need not be caused to someone who lives in the relevant area, but may include persons carrying out some lawful activity (e.g. doing repair works). The relevant area is now the locality as opposed to the neighbourhood. Accordingly, this ground may be used against a tenant living on a large estate who is harassing another tenant living in a different part of the estate. It may be, for example, that a family is harassed while walking through the estate from the bus stop. In such a situation Grounds 2 (secure tenants) and 14 (assured tenants) may be used against the perpetrator of the harassment.

Nuisance and annoyance have been held to include racial and sexual harassment, as has the generation of excessive noise.

> ### Case reports
>
> Mrs Bistram was a local authority tenant who was accused of noise nuisance and of using vile and abusive language in respect of race and sexual orientation. Possession proceedings were instituted under the old Ground 2. When the matter got to trial, the only complaint relied upon was that of abusive language. In the county court the judge refused to make an order for possession as he was not satisfied it would be reasonable to do so. He commented that bad language was very much a part of society and a common experience in certain areas. The local authority appealed to the Court of Appeal; the appeal was allowed. It was held that a court should, when considering reasonableness, take into account the local authority duty to all of its tenants living on the estate, the effect of the conduct on those tenants and the likelihood of the conduct continuing. The use of local knowledge, unbacked by evidence, was to be discouraged. *Woking BC v Bistram* (1995)

> Ms Simmonds lived in local authority accommodation with her 13-year-old son. Her son regularly used racist language to other tenants which caused them offence. Ms Simmonds herself was not abusive and gave evidence that she found her son difficult to control. The court, however, was satisfied that a possession order should be made against her on the ground of nuisance and annoyance to neighbours. It was further held that the ground extended to those living with the tenant. *Kensington & Chelsea RBC v Simmonds* (1997)

Notice seeking possession

Possession proceedings against secure and assured tenants are begun by the service of a notice seeking possession (NOSP) which must be in the prescribed form, must specify the ground relied upon and give particulars of that ground. If the tenancy is periodic rather than for a fixed term, the notice must specify a date after which proceedings for possession can be begun, which cannot be earlier than the tenancy could have been brought to an end by service of a notice to quit (e.g. a weekly tenant must be given four weeks' notice—see A. Dymond, *Presenting Possession Proceedings* (Arden's Housing Library, 1996)). If Ground 2 of HA 1985 is specified, the NOSP must state that proceedings may be commenced immediately and specify a date on which the tenant is to give up possession. If Ground 14 (HA 1988) is specified, the NOSP must state that proceedings will be begun no earlier than the date of service of the notice.

Accordingly, Grounds 2 and 14 provide an expedited procedure for the obtaining of possession which can be used against anti-social tenants including the perpetrators of racial or sexual harassment.

Service of an NOSP may be dispensed with where the court considers it just and equitable to do so (HA 1985, s. 83(1)(b); HA 1988, s. 8(1)(b)). The power to dispense must be exercised judicially. The Court of Appeal in *Kelsey Housing*

Association v King (1996) (considering the like provision in HA 1988) commented that the discretion was unlikely to be exercised unless the tenant has in some way become aware of the intended proceedings. It was further remarked, however, that it may be appropriate to dispense with a notice in circumstances such that the tenant has been guilty of conduct which was so grave as to invite proceedings for possession. In other words, he or she behaved in such a way that the issue of proceedings would have been expected.

Injunctions with power of arrest (HA 1996)

Local authorities

Chapter III of HA 1996 introduced a regime to deal with the cause and effect of anti-social conduct, however it might reveal itself. Section 152 provides local authorities with the statutory framework for injunctive relief. This provision was welcomed by local authorities which had since the mid-1990s been using injunctive proceedings to control gangs on estates. An authority had to be creative in its use of, for example, tenancy agreements, powers contained in the Local Government Act 1972 or Part II of HA 1985 and duties under the RRA. None of these provisions were intended for this purpose and authorities encountered many problems in seeking to rely on them. Injunctions not covered by HA 1996 are discussed in more detail in Hunter & Bretherton, *Anti-social Behaviour* (Arden's Housing Library, 1998).

Section 152 introduces a tailor-made express power to deal with anti-social behaviour (both within specific premises or a locality) and provides where:

1. a person has used or threatened to use violence against a person residing in, visiting or otherwise engaging in a lawful activity in residential premises to which the section applies, and

2. there is a significant risk of harm to that person, or to a person of a similar description if the injunction is not granted,

the court has power to grant an injunction to prevent a person:

(a) engaging in any conduct causing, or likely to cause, a nuisance or annoyance to a person residing in, visiting or otherwise engaging in a lawful activity; or

(b) using or threatening to use residential premises for immoral or illegal purposes; or

(c) entering residential premises or being found in their locality.

'Residential premises' includes dwelling-houses held under secure or introductory tenancies from a local authority or accommodation provided by an authority under the homelessness provisions. 'Person of a similar description' includes, for example, persons from a particular ethnic group. 'Harm' in relation to an adult means ill-treatment or the impairment of physical or mental health; in relation to a child, it also includes impairment of development.

An injunction may be granted *ex parte* (i.e. without informing the perpetrator if it is just and convenient to do so). *Ex parte* proceedings should only be used where genuinely necessary. It is common to apply to the court *ex parte* if the service of court documents relating to the injunction would provoke the very thing that the injunction seeks to deter. If an injunction is obtained in this way, the person against whom the injunction is directed will be given the opportunity to come back to court and answer the charges or explain why an injunction is inappropriate.

Local authorities may use this new power to control the behaviour of tenants and their visitors on estates where there have been problems of a racial or sexual nature. Power of arrest may be attached to these injunctions.

Assisting individuals

A local authority is a creature of statute, which means that in order for it to take any action there must be explicit or implicit statutory authority. Local authorities are not specifically authorised to assist individuals by initiating legal proceedings on their behalf. Under section 111 of the Local Government Act 1972, however, a local authority may 'do anything ... which is calculated to facilitate, or is conducive or incidental to the discharge of their functions'.

By section 21 of HA 1985, local authorities have a general power to manage their housing stock. Accordingly, assisting an individual victim of harassment is calculated to facilitate this management function.

Other social landlords

Housing authorities, housing action trusts, RSLs and charitable housing trusts may also apply for injunctions (including *ex parte* and interlocutory) with power of arrest attached *so long as* they are acting in their capacity as landlord (HA 1996, s. 153). This section, however, only applies to breach or anticipated breach of the *terms* of the tenancy. The proceedings must be against a tenant (including joint tenants) who is a secure, introductory or assured tenant, or who has been provided with accommodation pursuant to the homelessness provisions. The breach or anticipated breach of tenancy includes:

1. engaging or threatening to engage in conduct which causes or is likely to cause a nuisance or annoyance to a person residing, visiting or otherwise engaging in a lawful activity in the locality;
2. using or threatening to use the premises for immoral or illegal purposes;
3. allowing a subtenant or lodger of his or hers or any other person residing (whether temporarily or otherwise) on the premises or visiting them to act in a prescribed way.

The court must also be satisfied that:

4. the tenant or other person mentioned above has used or threatened violence against a person residing, visit-

ing or otherwise engaging in a lawful activity in the locality; and

5. there is a significant risk of harm to that person or a person of a similar description *if* the injunction is not granted.

Examples

A West Indian family has been moved onto an estate made up largely of other West Indian families. This family is friendly with a Somalian family of refugees who live on another estate out of the borough. The Somalian family is subjected to verbal abuse, threats of violence and intimidation whenever they walk through part of the estate to visit their West Indian friends in another part of the estate. The daughter has been caused particular anxiety and is fearful about visiting her friends. The local authority could apply for an injunction restraining the perpetrators from continuing with such conduct and from entering into the locality of the West Indian family's premises.

A housing association is responsible for a large estate of new-build houses. Housing on the estate has been allocated to transfer applicants and persons from the waiting list. The estate is racially mixed, but one tenant is a member of a racist group and holds meetings at his home. At these meetings the group members discuss public demonstrations, disruption and resistance to persons from ethnic minorities. Included is a campaign of threats of violence to discourage prospective ethnic minority tenants from coming onto the estate. The association can apply for an injunction restraining the tenant from continuing with the threats of violence to *anyone* either living on, or viewing premises for the purpose of moving onto, the estate. Power of arrest may be attached. An injunction will not be granted to restrain the tenant from having his racist friends in the premises *per se*, nor from discussing matters of a racist nature.

Rehousing

Where other forms of action are proving inadequate or taking too long, rehousing is an option which social landlords may wish to consider. In such circumstances it is usually the victim who moves. While this may be undesirable for a number of reasons (it may be seen as victory for the perpetrator if his or her intention was to remove black families from the area), it is sometimes essential for the victim's protection. Many tenants are so desperate to move away that they will accept properties that are less than suitable. This must not be exploited. If suitable alternative accommodation cannot be found quickly enough the unsuitable property can be offered, but only as a temporary address.

Reletting

If one black family is moved owing to racial harassment a social landlord will obviously be reluctant to relet the property to another black family. A landlord cannot refuse to relet to such a family, as this in itself is unlawful discrimination, but before the property is let the prospective tenant should be informed of the history of harassment and given the option to refuse the offer. A local authority would be entitled to, and in the writer's opinion should, waive its 'one offer' policy in such circumstances.

Criminal sanctions

Physical attacks

Attacks on the person are covered by the Offences Against the Person Act 1861. Offences range from common assault to grievous bodily harm. Common assault includes jostling, pushing and throwing stones through a window knowing someone is on the other side. The police may be contacted when incidents of such kinds are reported to housing managers; however, they have been reluctant to involve themselves in what some think are 'trivial' matters. Housing organisations can intervene on the victim's behalf and liaise with the police and encourage them to take these incidents seriously.

Racially abusive language and racial hatred

The Public Order Act 1986 makes it an offence to use threatening, abusive or insulting words or behaviour, or display any writing, sign or other visible representation which is threatening, abusive or insulting with the intent to stir up racial hatred or, in circumstances whereby hatred may be stirred up, cause a person harassment, alarm or distress. The offence may be committed in public or in private, but if in private the offence only operates if the words can be heard outside the premises in which they are spoken.

Generally, prosecution of offenders is a matter for the police and the Crown Prosecution Service. Local authorities may, however, also take action pursuant to section 222 of the Local Government Act 1972 by taking out injunctions against perpetrators. This has been used in the past to ban individuals from specified areas.

Crime and Disorder Act 1998

This new Act (CDA) was introduced primarily to overcome the difficulty of obtaining injunctions against non-tenants. The CDA creates further offences of racial harassment. In particular, the offence of racially aggravated harassment is to be designated an arrestable offence. Under the CDA, a local authority (note that the remedy is not available to registered social landlords) may apply for an 'anti-social behaviour order' (CDA, s. 1(1)) against anyone aged 10 years or over. The pre-conditions for grant of such an order are that:

1. the person has acted in an anti-social manner, defined as 'in a manner that caused or was likely to cause alarm or distress';

2. the alarm or distress must have been caused to one or more persons who are not members of the same household as the person against whom the order is made; and

3. the order is necessary to protect persons in the authority's area from further anti-social acts or conduct.

If an order is obtained and the person against whom it is made breaches the terms of the order, the breach itself constitutes a criminal offence. It is clear from what is said above (at p. 115) in relation to other injunctions against anti-social behaviour that racial harassment would amount to conduct likely to cause alarm or distress.

Procedural model for dealing with harassment

The following is a suggested procedural model for dealing with complaints of harassment. This model is a practical guide to implementing the recommendations outlined above.

1. *Report of incident* This should be taken seriously and investigated as soon as possible. An incident form needs to be filled in and a record kept of the victim's details. Ideally, there should be easy access to interpreters.

2. *Repairs* If damage has been caused to property or graffiti has been daubed, this should be dealt with quickly. Clearly, if premises are left insecure as a result of the damage they should be immediately made secure or the occupants put in temporary accommodation.

3. *Police report* If a criminal offence has been committed, the police should be informed straightaway. This should only be done, however, if the victim consents. Any contact with the police should be recorded.

4. *Liaison with other agencies* There are many other agencies which can help, such as for victim support (see 6. below).

5. *Investigation*   Following the initial interview further investigations should be carried out speedily. Details should be taken of potential witnesses and of previous incidents, which may have gone unreported at the time. It is common for victims to know exactly who the perpetrators are.

6. *Victim support*   Many victims are afraid to report incidents. If they are not sympathetically dealt with when they do report incidents, it will deter other victims from coming forward. The reporter must be taken seriously and questioned sensitively. He or she may be put in touch with other agencies.

7. *Action plan*   This should set out the housing organisation's policy and practice on receipt of complaints of harassment and should lay down clear lines of responsibility. The action plan should be followed.

12.
Discrimination in Employment of Housing Staff

Employment / Recruitment / Positive action /
Harassment / Proceedings by individuals

Social landlords have to employ staff to carry out their powers
and duties. Achieving equal opportunity in housing is
inextricably linked with equal opportunity in employment.
As an employer, the social landlord must be aware of the law
relating to fair recruitment, selection and dismissal. The law
protects individuals in the context of their employment from
discrimination on grounds of sex, race, colour, ethnic origin,
nationality, marital status and disability. British law does not
yet protect those who may be discriminated against on
grounds of sexual orientation, although the European Convention of Human Rights does protect such individuals and
it seems increasingly likely that Britain will be forced to come
into line (see further Chaps 1 and 5).

Discrimination in the context of employment includes
access to employment, terms and conditions, and remuneration. It must be remembered that the law considers the
discriminatory effects or results of action or inaction, not the
intentions behind it.

This chapter describes how the RRA and the SDA deal
with discrimination in the employment field. Discrimination
on grounds of disability is dealt with in Chapter 4.

Employment

'Employment' means 'under a contract of service or of apprenticeship or a contract personally to execute any work or labour' (SDA, s. 82; RRA, s. 78). This includes the self-employed who contract to do work personally.

Contract workers

It is unlawful (under SDA, s. 7; RRA, s. 9) for the principal contracting party to discriminate against the other party's contract workers on grounds of race or sex by:
* refusing to let those workers do the work
* in the terms on which those workers are allowed to do the work
* by the way those workers are afforded access to benefits
* treating those workers unfavourably in any other way.

Religion

It is not unlawful to discriminate on grounds of religious belief except where membership of a religious group denotes sharing a common national or ethnic origin (e.g. Hindus). In certain circumstances, discrimination against Jews, Sikhs and Muslims is unlawful (see further at Chap. 3).

Sex

It is unlawful to discriminate against a man or a woman on the ground of his or her sex.

Marital status

The SDA makes it unlawful in the employment field for a person to discriminate against another because of his or her marital status. If, for example, an employer refuses to consider married women for a job because of the belief that they are bound to take time off because of pregnancy, this is unlawful.

Similarly, a housing organisation which refuses to consider unmarried mothers for employment because of their marital status is guilty of unlawful discrimination. The EOC has statutory power to investigate complaints and enforce the SDA.

> ### Case study
>
> Ms Horsey had been employed by various local authorities since leaving college. She took a further period of time off to study. In the meantime she had married. She applied to a local authority for a job as a social worker. It was a requirement of that job that she attend further courses (paid for by the authority) after which she be tied into her job for a further two years. She was accepted by the authority. In the meantime her husband had accepted a full-time post in another area. Ms Horsey applied for a secondment to another course so she could be near her husband. The authority rejected her application on the basis that she would be unlikely to return to work for the authority, since her husband had obtained full-time employment elsewhere. The Employment Appeal Tribunal held that in refusing her application for secondment, the authority had discriminated against her on grounds of marital status. While it could have refused the application on grounds of an intention to refuse to fulfil contractual obligations, it had simply assumed that she would so refuse because of a general assumption that married women gave up employment to join their husbands. *Horsey v Dyfed CC* (1982)

Race

It is unlawful to discriminate against any person on the ground of race, colour, ethnic origin or nationality (see Chap. 3).

Disability

It is unlawful to discriminate against any disabled person on the ground of his or her disability, if (and only if) that particular disability is defined by the DDA (see Chap. 4).

Recruitment

It is unlawful for employers to discriminate in the selection of employees. The aim of the legislation is to ensure that from recruitment right through to dismissal, all employees are treated equally. Selection and recruitment are the most obvious indicators of discrimination. Direct discrimination in recruitment occurs when someone is treated less favourably because of his or her race or sex (e.g. an employer only recruits white employees, or recruits women and ethnic minorities only to lower paid jobs). Indirect discrimination occurs when an employer imposes a condition or requirement which places some candidates (because of their race or colour) at a disadvantage in applying for the job.

> ### Examples
>
> To require all applicants for a job as a gardener on local authority land to speak fluent English would be to indirectly discriminate against all immigrants who cannot or do not choose to speak English as their first language.
>
> A social landlord advertises a vacancy in schools or colleges which are attended solely, or mainly, by white pupils. The landlord has thereby chosen to select from a limited pool of candidates which indirectly discriminates against candidates from ethnic minorities.

Advertising vacancies

'Advertising' includes not just adverts in newspapers or job centres, but notices in shop windows and other informal advertising (e.g. through a school). An advertisement is discriminatory if a reasonable person would understand, either owing to the words or illustration, that the advertisement is discriminatory. If it is discriminatory it remains discriminatory despite an anti-discrimination statement attached to it.

Accordingly, it is essential that all advertisements are composed with care and a good deal of thought. The use of gender specific job titles is also discouraged (e.g. 'tea lady'). Included in the advertisement should be a statement of commitment to equal opportunities. A frequently used phrase is: 'Applications are welcome from both sexes and persons of all races, national and ethnic origins. We are an equal opportunities employer.'

If an advertisement is discriminatory, only the EOC or the CRE can take action (SDA, s. 38; RRA, s. 29). If, however, a person applies for a job and feels he or she was discriminated against in the recruitment process, he or she may institute proceedings based on the discriminatory advertisement.

Targeting of advertisements

Advertisements may be targeted at a particular racial or sexual group if that group is under-represented. 'Under-representation' is defined differently in the RRA and the SDA. Such advertisements must, however, clearly indicate that there is no intention to discriminate against members of other groups. While one group may be targeted to encourage them to apply, for the purpose of actually selecting for the job it is unlawful to discriminate in favour of that group. Therefore, imbalances and under-representation can only be addressed by *encouraging* applications.

> **Example**
>
> A housing organisation is conscious that Asian people are under-represented in their housing department and wish to encourage more Asian people to apply. Advertisements may be placed in Asian newspapers and displayed in shops and schools where Asian people will see them.

Interviewing

It is possible unlawfully to discriminate in an interview by asking inappropriate questions. A question is inappropriate if it puts some candidates at an unfair disadvantage or would not be asked of someone from another sex or racial group. A common question still asked of single mothers is what they will do about child care arrangements. This is an unlawful question and exposes an employer to action for sexual discrimination.

When interviewing, questions should be confined to matters directly relevant to the job.

Positive action

As a general rule positive discrimination is unlawful. Positive discrimination is not permissible simply to increase the numbers of people from a certain group within the workplace. There are, however, notable exceptions.

Genuine occupational qualification

Section 5(2)(d) of RRA provides that being of a particular racial group is only a genuine occupational qualification if:
1. the job holder provides persons of that racial group with personal services promoting their welfare; and
2. those services can most effectively be provided by a person of that racial group.

In other words, if membership of a particular group is a genuine requirement because that person will be providing a personal service which promotes the welfare of members of that particular race, it is lawful to discriminate in favour of a member of that group. The services must be such that they can *best be provided* by a member of that group. This must be considered *objectively* and the employer must show a precise cultural, linguistic or ethical link between the employee and the customer or user of the service.

> **Example**
>
> A housing organisation caters specifically for West Indian people. Within the area there has been much

interracial tension between West Indians and the police and local authority. It is believed that only a West Indian housing officer would be welcomed into people's homes and be able to offer more assistance.

Section 7 of SDA provides that being of a particular sex can only be a genuine occupational qualification if:
1. the essential nature of the job calls for a person of a particular sex for reasons of physiology (excluding physical strength or stamina); or
2. to preserve decency or privacy; or
3. the nature of location of the establishment is such that it is impracticable for the worker to live elsewhere than in premises provided by the employer, and the only premises available are lived in by persons of the same sex with shared sleeping or sanitary facilities, and it is not reasonable to expect the employer to equip the premises with facilities to cater for the opposite sex; or
4. the nature of the establishment, or the part of it within which the person will work, requires the job to be done by a person of a particular sex because it is an establishment for persons requiring special care, supervision or attention, and those persons are all of the same sex; or
5. the job needs to be held by a person of a particular sex because it provides individuals with personal services promoting their welfare, or education, or similar personal services and those services can most effectively be provided by a person of that sex.

Example

An employer looking for a live-in warden at a Pakistani womens' refuge may confine the selection and recruitment procedure to Pakistani women.

It is not unlawful to discriminate in favour of a disabled person because of his or her disability (see Chap. 4).

Special needs

An employer cannot discriminate in favour of particular groups when recruiting, but he or she can take steps to ensure that people from those groups compete on an equal footing. This may include the provision of special training to members of a particular group.

Positive Action Training in Housing

Section 37 of RRA provides that it shall not be unlawful to afford only persons of a particular racial group access to facilities for training which would help them to carry out particular work where the proportion of persons doing that work in (or in a specific area of) Britain is small in comparison with the proportion of persons of that group among the population (or among the population of that area).

The Federation of Black Housing Organisations (FBHO), pursuant to section 37, has promoted Positive Action Training in Housing (PATH). The scheme is aimed at redressing the imbalance of black people employed in housing. Initially the idea was to provide opportunities for black people who had been let down by the educational establishments. As time went on the scheme became increasingly successful and has been added to with more ambitious targets. PATH (National) is an organisation committed to training black people for senior management and directorships of housing associations. There is also PATH (Local Authorities), which trains black people for middle management in local authorities.

Harassment

Harassment is not expressly recognised in the principal Acts. Employers, however, cannot avoid responsibility if it arises. The link between harassment and discrimination has already been considered in Chapter 1. It can be difficult to distinguish between harassment which amounts to discrimination under the Acts where it is as a result of prejudice, and harassment which arises independently of such prejudice.

Sexual harassment

Sexual harassment is not defined in the SDA, but the courts have held that harassment can amount to 'less favourable treatment' (see e.g. *Wileman v Minilec Engineering* (1988)). To come within this definition it is necessary to show that the person is disadvantaged because of his or her sex in a way in which a person of the opposite sex would not be so vulnerable.

Physical contact or verbal abuse which is of a sexual nature comes within the definition of 'unfavourable treatment'. Injury to feelings is a sufficient detriment for the purposes of the Act (see Chap. 3).

Racial harassment

Racial harassment can be compared to sexual harassment in that it arises where a person is subjected to a detriment, being abuse and offensive behaviour, which places him or her under a disadvantage because of his or her race, colour or ethnic origin. An omission to act in response to racial harassment does not of itself amount to harassment, but note that it can amount to 'victimisation' within the Act (see Chap. 3).

Subjective/objective test

It is essential when considering whether a person has been harassed contrary to the law that account is taken of how the *victim* views the harassment. A racial motive can often be hidden from the impassive observer which can only be divined on

It must be determined at the very start that there is a racial or sexual motive to the harassment.

> **Example**
>
> A housing manager harasses a member of his staff because he spoke critically of his management skills at a general meeting. The manager is not harassing his employee because of his race or sex but because he criticised him in public.

Act or ommission?

A 'deliberate omission' can amount to an act of discrimination (see Chaps 3 and 4). Accordingly, a complaint may be made against an employer who deliberately fails to take action on a complaint of harassment because of the complainant's sex or race.

> **Example**
>
> A housing manager receives a complaint that one female housing officer is being sexually harassed by her colleague. If the manager fails to take any action because of shared prejudice or fear of upsetting the officer who is guilty of the harassment, he or she is acting unlawfully.

Dealing with complaints

The *way* in which a housing organisation deals with complaints may be discriminatory.

> **Example**
>
> A manager reacts to the complaint in the above example by moving the victim against her will to a different neighbourhood office, leaving the perpetrator where he is. This could form the basis of a complaint being made that the manager had treated the officers differently, on grounds of sex, in the way in which he or she sought to resolve the harassment.

How to manage and eliminate incidents of harassment

To avoid formal complaints being made by staff, employers are well advised to develop and make avaliable to all staff members a written policy on dealing with harassment. It is suggested that such a policy should cover:
- the definition of harassment
- a commitment of support for those experiencing harassment
- an effective strategy for dealing with perpetrators
- liaison with other agencies and groups
- preventative action
- monitoring.

Information

Many victims of harassment do not make complaints. This can be for a number of reasons. The person may believe he or she must accept such behaviour as an everyday fact of life, may not appreciate that there is a complaints procedure or may not be well versed in utilising that procedure, or may be frightened that to complain will simply inflame the situation with little prospect of those in authority protecting him or her.

The first measure therefore must be to inform all members of staff of the policy on harassment. They must be made to feel that a complaint will be sensitively received and taken seriously.

Support

Anyone who does make a complaint must be given support, reassurance and kept informed of progress and whatever subsequent steps the employer or manager proposes to take. A victim of harassment may feel ostracised and isolated. It is the employer's duty to include him or her in the decision-making process and keep him or her updated.

Investigation

Every complaint, however reported, must be thoroughly investigated. It is good practice to follow the same procedure regardless of the source of the information. There should be a common starting point with all complaints channelled through an appropriate named officer. That officer must decide, after an initial investigation, whether using the harassment policy is the appropriate course. To assist officers in this determination, examples of harassment should be included in the policy document and, ideally, members of staff would receive training in identifying harassment.

The victim should be interviewed as soon as possible to build up a picture of the harassment as he or she sees it. At this stage it is important that the victim is assumed to be telling the truth.

The person investigating should then compile a report for consideration by senior officers or managers who may then make a recommendation. Throughout the procedure, monitoring must continue. It may be worth approaching the perpetrator direct as this can be sufficient to put an end to the harassment.

Proceedings by individuals

If a person believes he or she has been discriminated against by another contrary to Part III of the Acts, he or she may bring proceedings in a county court specially designated for the purpose by the Secretary of State or an employment tribunal (previously, until 31 July 1998, known as an industrial tribunal). For a detailed discussion of this subject, see Chapter 2.

Index